D1670264

Linguistics in the Netherlands 2004

Edited by

Leonie Cornips
Meertens Institute

Jenny Doetjes
University of Leiden & Utrecht University

John Benjamins Publishing Company
Amsterdam / Philadelphia

AVT Publications

AVT Publications is a series sponsored by the Algemene Vereniging
voor Taalwetenschap (Linguistic Society of the Netherlands).
In addition to the annual publication of *Linguistics in the Netherlands*
further publications, resulting from other activities promoted by the
Society, may appear in this series.

Algemene
Vereniging voor
Taalwetenschap

Volume 21

Linguistics in the Netherlands 2004
Edited by Leonie Cornips and Jenny Doetjes

Table of contents

Preface

The thirty-fifth annual meeting of the Linguistic Society of the Netherlands took place in Utrecht on February 7th, 2004. The aim of the annual meetings is to provide members with the opportunity to report on their research. At this year's meeting 85 papers were presented of which 42 were submitted. This volume contains a selection of these papers. The 20 articles in Linguistics of the Netherlands 2004 present an overview of research in different fields of linguistics. We wish to thank a large number of colleagues for their help in refereeing the papers submitted to this volume.

We are pleased to report that this year's winner of the AVT-Anéla dissertation award 2003, Dirk-Bart den Ouden, contributed a paper to this volume.

May 2004

Leonie Cornips
Jenny Doetjes

Linguistics in the Netherlands 2004 21 (2004), v.
ISSN 0929–7332 / E-ISSN 1569–9919 © Algemene Vereniging voor Taalwetenschap

Contributors

Enoch O. Aboh
University of Amsterdam
ACLC
Spuistraat 134
1012 VB Amsterdam
enoch.aboh@hum.uva.nl

Harald Baayen
University of Nijmegen & Max Planck Institute
Wundtlaan 1
6525 XD Nijmegen
harald.baayen@mpi.nl

Janneke ter Beek
University of Groningen
Department of Linguistics
P. O. Box 716
9700 AS Groningen
j.ter.beek@let.rug.nl

Ronny Boogaart
Free University
Department of Dutch Language and Culture
De Boelelaan 1105
1081 HV Amsterdam
rju.boogaart@let.vu.nl

Anne Breitbarth
University of Tilburg
Models of Grammar
P. O. Box 90153
5000 LE Tilburg
a.breitbarth@uvt.nl

Suzanne van der Feest
University of Nijmegen
Dutch Department
Erasmusplein 1
P. O. Box 9103
6500 HD Nijmegen
s.v.d.feest@let.kun.nl

Paula Fikkert
University of Nijmegen
Dutch Department
Erasmusplein 1
P. O. Box 9103
6500 HD Nijmegen
p.fikkert@let.kun.nl

Maria João Freitas
University of Lisboa
Departament de Linguística
1600–214 Lisboa, Portugal
joaofreitas@mail.doc.fl.ul.pt

Rik van Gijn
University of Nijmegen
Department of General Linguistics
Erasmusplein 1
P. O. Box 9103
6500 HD Nijmegen
r.v.gijn@let.kun.nl

Katharina Haude
University of Nijmegen
Department of General Linguistics
Erasmusplein 1
P. O. Box 9103
6500 HD Nijmegen
k.haude@let.kun.nl

Willemijn Heeren
Utrecht University
UiL OTS
Trans 10
3512 JK Utrecht
willemijn.heeren@let.uu.nl

Vincent J. van Heuven
University of Leiden
ULCL
P. O. Box 9515
2300 RA Leiden
v.j.j.p.van.heuven@let.leidenuniv.nl

Frans Hinskens
Meertens Instituut
Joan Muyskenweg 25
1096 CJ Amsterdam
frans.hinskens@meertens.knaw.nl

Jarich Hoekstra
Christian-Albrechts-Universität
Fach Friesische Philologie
Olshauenstrasse 40
D-24098 Kiel
j.hoekstra@nord-inst.uni-kiel.de

Frank Jansen
Utrecht University
UiL OTS
Trans 10
3512 JK Utrecht
frank.jansen@let.uu.nl

Robert S. Kirsner
University of California Los Angeles
Department of Germanic Languages
310 Royce Hall, PO Box 951539
Los Angeles CA 90095–1539 USA
kirsner@humnet.ucla.edu

Anneke Neijt
University of Nijmegen
Dutch Department
Erasmusplein 1
P. O. Box 9103
6500 HD Nijmegen
a.neijt@let.kun.nl

Dirk-Bart den Ouden
University of Groningen
Dutch Department
P. O. Box 716
9700 AS Groningen
denouden@let.rug.nl

Rob Schreuder
University of Nijmegen
Erasmusplein 1
P. O. Box 9103
6500 HD Nijmegen
r.schreuder@let.kun.nl

Petra Sleeman
University of Amsterdam
Department of French
Spuistraat 134
1012 VB Amsterdam
a.p.sleeman@uva.nl

Mark de Vos
University of Leiden
ULCL
P. O. Box 9515
2300 RA Leiden
m.a.de.vos@let.leidenuniv.nl

Rint Sybesma
University of Leiden
Department of Chinese Studies
P. O. Box 9515
2300 RA Leiden
r.p.e.sybesma@let.leidenuniv.nl

Radoslava Trnavac
University of Leiden
ULCL
P. O. Box 9515
2300 RA Leiden
r.trnavac@let.leidenuniv.nl

Mark de Vries
University of Groningen
Department of Linguistics
P. O. Box 716
9700 AS Groningen
mark.de.vries@let.rug.nl

Hongyan Wang
University of Leiden and Jilin University
ULCL
P. O. Box 9515
2300 RA Leiden
h.wang@let.leidenuniv.nl

Jeroen van de Weijer
University of Leiden
ULCL
P. O. Box 9515
2300 RA Leiden
j.m.van.de.weijer@let.leidenuniv.nl

Topic and focus within D[*]

Enoch O. Aboh
University of Amsterdam

1. Introduction

This paper proposes that, even though topic and focus are often considered to be clausal properties, these specifications may be encoded within the nominal structure as well. It is argued that the noun system involves an articulated left periphery, comparable to the clausal complementizer system, which involves discrete topic and focus projections, whose specifiers contain the fronted nominal topic and focus constituents. In some languages, the heads of these designated projections are morphologically realized as elements that are commonly known as determiners or articles. Section 2 sets the stage for the discussion, Section 3 discusses the topic-focus articulation within D, and Section 4 concludes the paper.

2. Setting the stage

The literature on topic and focus constructions often refers to situations where an element of discourse is seen as old information or important, and is marked as such syntactically or prosodically. In the Gungbe example (1), both the topicalized subject *Sétù* and the focused object *Màrí* appear within the left periphery where they are marked by the topic and focus markers, respectively. Note that the topic and focus constituents are sandwiched between the complementizer *ḍɔ̀* 'that' and the IP-internal third person subject pronoun *é*.

(1) Ùn nywèn ḍɔ̀ [Sétù] yà [Màrí] wὲ é dà
    1SG know that Setu TOP Mary FOC 3SG marry
    'I know that, as for Setu, he married MARY'

Linguistics in the Netherlands 2004 21 (2004), 1–12.
ISSN 0929–7332 / E-ISSN 1569–9919 ©Algemene Vereniging voor Taalwetenschap

Granted that topic and focus may target different constituents (e.g., arguments, adjuncts, adverbs, adjectives, verbs, or propositions, see Aboh 2004), one can conclude that topicalization and focalization are crucially clausal properties of which noun sequences only happen to be a target. There are, however, both empirical and theoretical reasons to suggest that the topic-focus articulation projects within the nominal domain as well. The following data provide partial evidence for such an approach.

Gungbe distinguishes between non-specific (i.e., non-discourse anaphoric) and specific (i.e., discourse anaphoric) noun phrases. Non-specific noun phrases surface as bare noun phrases, as in (2a). In this example, the noun phrase *lɛ̀sì gúkɔ́mɛ̀ tɔ̀n* is interpreted as definite, but not specific, because it is not pre-established in discourse. The example (2b), on the other hand, indicates that specific noun phrases must occur to the left of the specificity marker *lɔ́*. Here, the sequence *lɛ̀sì gúkɔ́mɛ̀ tɔ̀n lɔ́* is definite specific because it refers back to some particular rice that is pre-established in discourse or is known to the participants. This reminds us the notion of *assumed familiarity* as discussed in Prince (1981), or that of specificity as described in Enç (1991).

(2) a.   Sétù nɔ̀   xɔ̀   [lɛ̀sì Gúkɔ́mɛ̀ tɔ̀n]
          Setu HAB buy rice Gukome POSS
          'Setu habitually buys the rice from Gukome'
     b.   Sétù nɔ̀   xɔ̀   [lɛ̀sì Gúkɔ́mɛ̀ tɔ̀n   lɔ́]
          Setu HAB buy rice Gukome POSS DET[+spec;+def]
          'Setu habitually buys the aforementioned rice from Gukome'

If specificity (or *assumed familiarity*) and topicality are related in some sense, then the contrast in (2) suggests that the noun sequence in (2b) is marked for topicality. Yet, that sequence can be subsequently topicalized in the clause alongside with (2a), as shown in (3a) and (3b), respectively.

(3) a.   [Lɛ̀sì Gúkɔ́mɛ̀ tɔ̀n   lɔ́]   yà é   nɔ̀ víví gbáú
          rice Gukome POSS DET[+spec;+def] TOP 3SG HAB sweet very
          'As for the aforementioned rice from Gukome, it is very sweet'
     b.   [Lɛ̀sì Gúkɔ́mɛ̀ tɔ̀n] yà é   nɔ̀ víví gbáú
          rice Gukome POSS TOP 3SG HAB sweet very
          'As for the rice from Gukome, it is very sweet'

The reading in (3a) is that of a specific topic noun phrase (that is, a known/given referent), which is the topic of discussion. In (3b), however, the topic of discussion is expressed by a bare noun phrase that may be interpreted as (±definite) or (±generic) depending on the context. In this regard, the contrast between (2b) and (3b) is that the former represents a nominal topic, while the latter is a clausal topic. These facts lead me to suggest that there is topic specification both within the nominal left periphery and the clausal left periphery. Under this approach, the question arises how does nominal topicalization relate to clausal topicalization? I return to this issue in Section 3.2 where I propose that nominal topic may license clausal topic.

With regard to focusing within the noun phrase, Bernstein (2001) suggests that the Romance sentences in (4) differ in that the pre-nominal demonstrative in (4a) manifests a more basic word order and triggers an unmarked or neutral interpretation. On the other hand, the post-nominal demonstrative bears main stress and yields a focus reading (4b).

(4)　a.　Este libro interesante　　　　　　　　　　　　　　[Spanish]
　　　　　this book interesting
　　　　　'This interesting book'
　　b.　El libro interesante **este**
　　　　　the book interesting this
　　　　　'This interesting book' [Bernstein 2001:2]

This suggests that focus may be determined within the nominal domain. Yet, as the French examples under (5) show, a nominal that involves focus specification (i.e., *ci* is the French counterpart of Spanish *este*) can be attracted to the focus field within the clause just as any other nominal constituent.

(5)　a.　C'est ce livre que Jean a lu qui le rend triste
　　　　　it.is the book that John has read that him make sad
　　　　　'It is this book that John read, which makes him sad'
　　b.　C'est ce livre-**ci** que Jean a lu avant de partir
　　　　　it.is this book-here that John has read before Prep leave
　　　　　'It is this book here that John read before he left'

In the cleft sentence (5a), the definite noun phrase *ce livre* may be interpreted as contrastive, new information, or presentational focus depending on the context. In example (5b), however, the clefted noun phrase *ce livre-ci* is necessarily interpreted as contrastive focus because the noun phrase includes the demonstrative reinforcer *ci*. We therefore reach a situation that is similar to that of the topic whereby the clausal focus attracts a noun phrase that has been assigned focus within D. These facts lead me to conclude that the noun system allows the expression of topic and focus. Granted that topic and focus are the properties of distinct projections within the left periphery, I further propose that the nominal system involves a left peripheral topic-focus articulation.

2.1　The split-D hypothesis

This paper proposes that the facts described in (2) through (5) reflect properties of the nominal left periphery, that is, the D(eterminer)-system. Under this view, the D-system is comparable to the clausal left periphery: the C(omplementizer)-system. Like the C-system, the D-system involves topic and focus projections (TopP and FocP) whose specifiers host topic and focused constituents. TopP and FocP project between DP, the highest projection of the system, which expresses the interface between the discourse and the nominal expression, and NumP, the lowest projection, which links the D-system to the nominal I(nflectional)-system. As such, NumP encodes the agreement features and certain referential features (e.g., number, deixis) that parallel those of the nominal I-system (Aboh 2004). Following Campbell (1996), I also assume that noun phrases involve covert predication whereby the noun head functions as a predicate of the referent of the noun phrase. This would mean that the nominal I-system (i.e., FP in the representation 6) includes a subject position that may host the possessor in possessive constructions. Several empirical facts support the split-D analysis.

(6) $[_{DP}... [_{D}...$ topic... focus $[_{NumP} ...[_{Num}... [_{FP}...N...]]]]]$

2.1.1 *D is the nominal equivalent of Force*

Szabolcsi (1994) reports the following contrast in Hungarian.

(7) a.   (a) Mari   kalap-ja
           the Mari(-NOM) hat-POSS-3SG
           'Mary's hat'

    b.   Mari-nak a   kalap-ja
          Mari-DAT the hat-POSS-3SG   [pp. 186–7]
          'Mari's hat'

    c.   [Péter-nek] mindenki csak [a   kalap-já-t]   látta
          Peter-DAT everyone only the hat-POSS-3SG-ACC saw
          'As for Peter, everyone saw only his hat (e.g., no one saw his coat)' [p. 205]

The data under (7) indicate that the Hungarian nominative possessor always follows the determiner, as in (7a), while the dative possessor always precedes, as in (7b). Example (7c) further shows that the dative possessor may be wh-extracted out of the noun sequence, hence the so-called possessor extraction construction. According to Szabolcsi the paradigm in (7b–c) is comparable to subject extraction in the clause, via [SpecForceP]. Under this approach, the possessor moves to [SpecDP] where it enters a Spec–Head configuration with the subordinator *a*, the nominal counterpart of the clausal complementizer, e.g., *that* in English (7b). In the possessor extraction construction, however, the possessor subsequently extracts from [SpecDP] giving rise to example (7c). This would mean that the contrast in (7a–b) could be represented as in (8a–b), where DP is the nominal equivalent of CP and IP represents the nominal inflectional domain (see Knittel 1998, and Haegeman 2004 for alternative approaches).

(8) a. $[_{DP} [_{D^0}$ a $[_{IP}$ Mari$[_{nom}] [_{I^0}$ **minden** $[_{FP}$ kalap-ja$]]]]]$
    b. $[_{DP}$ Mari-nak$[_{acc}]_i [_{D^0}$ a $[_{IP}$ t$_i [_{I^0} [_{FP}$ kalap-ja$]]]]]$

In terms of this analysis, the determiner *a* in D is a subordinator, that is, a C-type element. On the other hand, the article *minden* is an I-type element, which merges under I and encodes nominal inflectional features such as definiteness. This analysis leads to two main conclusions: (i) [SpecDP] is a non-thematic operator position, as indicated by the dative extraction constructions under (7b–c), and (ii) the expression of definiteness is primarily determined within the nominal I-system, but may be reflected in the nominal left periphery (i.e., the D-system) due to definiteness concord (Aboh 2004).

2.1.2 *Num⁰ as the expression of [number] and [definiteness]*

I propose that NumP, which delimits the D-system downward, represents the juncture where definiteness concord is achieved. Put differently, NumP encodes the INFL features (e.g., deixis) that match those expressed in the I-system. Under this approach, Num^0 is comparable to the clausal Fin^0, which has also be shown to express inflection or agreement features that match those of the embedded IP (see Haegeman 1992, Rizzi 1997, Paoli 2001).

The following Gungbe facts on the number marker *lɛ́*, which realizes Num^0, support this view. In (9a), the sequence *àkwékwè àtɔ́n* 'five bananas' is indefinite, and may refer to any five bananas (e.g., out of a heap of ten). In (9b), however, the sequence *àkwékwè àtɔ́n lɛ́* is definite and denotes a pre-identified set of five bananas (e.g., each heap is made of five bananas). This contrast indicates that a sequence NP-*lɛ́* is necessarily interpreted as [+definite, +plural]. I (2004) propose that *lɛ́* encodes a bundle of features including [definite, number].

(9) a. Mì sà   àkwékwè àtɔ́n ná mì
         2PL sell banana   five for 1SG
         'Sell me five bananas'

     b. Mì sà   àkwékwè àtɔ́n lɛ́   ná mì
         2PL sell banana   five NUMB for 1SG
         'Sell me the five bananas'

Similarly, the number marker encodes agreement features because expressing numerals inside a specific definite noun phrase requires the presence of number *lɛ́*. Recall from previous discussion that the number and specificity markers need not co-occur.

(10) Mì sà   àkwékwè (lɔ́)   (lɛ́)   ná mì
      2PL sell banana   DET[+spec;+def] NUMB   for 1SG
      'Sell me (the aforementioned) banana(s)'

However, the complex noun-numeral *àkwékwè àtɔ́n* 'five bananas' cannot be marked as specific if number is absent. Contrast the grammatical example (11a), where the noun phrase includes *lɔ́-lɛ́*, and refers to a pre-established set of five bananas, to the ungrammatical noun phrase (11b), which lacks number *lɛ́*.

(11) a. Mì sà àkwékwè àtɔ́n lɔ́   lɛ́   ná mì
          2PL sell banana five DET[+spec,+def] NUMB for 1SG
          'Sell me the aforementioned five bananas'
      b. *Mì sà àkwékwè àtɔ́n lɔ́   — ná mì
          2PL sell banana five DET[+spec,+def]   for 1SG
          'Sell me the aforementioned five bananas'

These examples suggest that Num^0, realized as *lɛ́*, establishes a concord between the definiteness and plurality expressed in the nominal I-system and the D-system. In addition, the ungrammatical example (11b) indicates that DP dominates NumP, since *lɛ́* must merge before *lɔ́*.

3.   The topic-focus articulation

The previous discussion suggests that D and Num are the nominal counterparts of the clausal Force and Fin, respectively. In what follows, I argue that the topic-focus articulation projects within these two borderlines. Recall that Gungbe manifests bare NPs. These sequences are interpreted as (in)definite or generic depending on the context. They surface without the specificity or plural markers, but may include nominal modifiers (e.g., demonstratives, adjectives, numerals). In (12a), for instance, the bare NP *távò* 'table' is interpreted as indefinite. In (12b), however, the sequence *távò títán* 'first table' is interpreted as definite.

(12) a. Kɔ̀kú hèn **távò** wá   xwégbè
          Koku hold table come house
          'Koku brought a table home'
      b. Kɔ̀kú wè hèn **távò títán** wá   xwégbè
          Koku Foc hold table first come house
          'It is Koku who brought the first table home'

This contrasts with example (13a), where the sequence *távò cè* 'my table' is understood as definite non-specific, unlike the sequence *távò lɔ́*, which is interpreted as definite specific because it is pre-established in discourse. A similar contrast arises in example (13b) where the sequence *távò ɖé* is interpreted as indefinite specific as opposed to the sequence *távò cè*. The ungrammatical example (13c) suggests that the specificity *lɔ́* and *ɖé* exclude each other because they express complementary sets of features [+specific; ±definite].

(13) a. Kɔ̀kú mɔ̀n **távò** cè   bò ɖɔ̀ émì ná xɔ̀ **távò** lɔ́
          Koku see   table 1SG-POSS and say 3SG FUT buy table DET[+spec;+def]
          'Koku saw my table and said that he would buy that table'
      b. Kɔ̀kú mɔ̀n **távò** cè   bò ɖɔ̀ émì ná xɔ̀ **távò** ɖé
          Koku see   table 1SG-POSS and say 3SG FUT buy table DET[+spec;−def]
          'Koku saw my table and said that he would buy a certain table'

c. *Kòkú mɔ̀n távò lɔ́   ɖé
    Koku see table DET[+spec;+def] DET[+spec;−def]

The descriptive generalization is that a specific noun phrase requires the markers *lɔ́* or *ɖé* as the morphological realizations of the features [+specific, +definite], and [+specific, −definite], respectively. This would mean that bare NPs are necessarily specified as [−specific, +definite] or [−specific, −definite]. In previous work, I (2004) proposed that the specificity feature on the Gungbe head noun must be checked against D, which also bears the feature [+specific] encoded by the marker *lɔ́*. This requirement is achieved by nominal predicate fronting in Gungbe, because the language lacks N-to-D raising. Accordingly, the nominal predicate (i.e., FP in 14) is pied-piped to [SpecDP] (via [SpecNumP]).

(14) [$_{DP}$ [$_{FP}$ távò] [$_D$ lɔ́ [$_{NumP}$ t$_{távò}$ [$_{Num}$ lɛ́ [$_{FP}$ t$_{távò}$]]]]]

But there are good reasons for refining this analysis along the lines of (15a) for the Gungbe-type languages, which involve predicate fronting to [SpecTopP]. Under this approach, the predicate is attracted to [SpecTopP] to check the features [specific] under Top, which hosts the specificity marker. In the English-type languages, however, one may propose along the lines of Campbell (1996) that [SpecTopP] is filled by a null operator that binds the subject of predicate headed by the noun. Campbell (1996: 162) further assumes that "the specificity operator is a kind of DP-internal topic, which links the internal subject position (and hence the DP itself) to a referent identified previously in the discourse."[1]

(15) a. [$_{DP}$ [$_D$ [$_{TopP}$ [$_{FP}$ távò] [$_{Top^0}$ lɔ́ [$_{NumP}$ t$_{távò}$ [$_{Num}$ lɛ́ [$_{FP}$ t$_{távò}$]]]]]]]
      b. [$_{DP}$ [$_{TopP}$ Op$_i$ [$_{Top^0}$ the [$_{FP}$ [ec]$_i$ thief $_i$]]]]

3.1 Question marking and the topic-focus articulation within D

Pieces of evidence for refining the representation (14) as in (15a) come from nominal question marking in Gungbe. This language displays complex question words that consist of a noun phrase and a question marker as indicated by the forms *nú-té* 'what' and *fí-té* 'where' in (16a–b).

(16) a. [Nú-té] wὲ Kòfí xɔ̀?   b. [Fí-té] wὲ Kòfí yì?
          thing-Q FOC Kofi buy   place-Q FOC Kofi go
          'What (thing) did Kofi buy?'   'Where did Kofi go?'

The sentences in (17) further show that the questioned noun can be separated from the question word by intervening modifiers.

(17) a. [Távò xɔ́xɔ́ té] wὲ Kòfí xɔ̀?
          table old Q FOC Kofi buy
          'Which old table did Kofi buy?'

b. [Fí   jɔ̀-fí   té] wè Kòfí jéyí bò sàn mɔ́n?
    place well-known Q FOC Kofi go and dress so
    'To what important place is Kofi going to dress like that?'

These data indicate that the complex forms in (16) cannot be analyzed as [X-Y] adjunction structures where the questioned noun (X) and the question particle (Y) are two (lexical) heads. Instead, the bracketed sequences in (16–17) seem to involve structures where the element to the left of the question particle Q represents a phrase that is in the specifier of a Q-phrase, as schematized in (18).

(18) $[_{DP} ... [_{Q\text{-phrase}} XP [_Q té]]]$

The question now arises what is the nature of this Q-phrase? A parallel between the clausal and nominal question formation and focus constructions may help answer this question. The Gungbe focus and wh-questions require fronting of the focused constituent or wh-phrase to the left of the focus marker, as in (19a–b). The ungrammatical example (19c) indicates that wh-phrases and focused constituents are in complementary distribution.

(19) a. [[àkwékwè] wè] Kòfí xɔ̀   b. [[é-té] wè] Kòfí xɔ̀?
           banana   FOC Kofi buy   3SG-Q FOC Kofi buy
           'Kofi bought BANANA(s)'   'What did Kofi buy?'
      c. *é-té   Kòfí wè xɔ̀?
           3SG-Q Kofi FOC buy
           'What KOFI bought?'

These facts suggest that focused constituents and wh-phrases target the same position within the C-system. Accordingly, the focus head *wè* realises the feature [F] that is checked by focused- or wh-phrases as shown in (20a). By extending this analysis to the nominal domain, I reformulate (18) as in (20b), where the Q-phrase is a focus phrase whose head is realized by the element *té*. The latter encodes the feature [F] that is checked by the questioned or focused nominal elements in its specifier (Aboh 2004).

(20) a. $[_{FocP} XP[_F] [_{Foc} wè [_{FinP} ... t_{XP} ...]]]$
      b. $[_{FocP} XP[_F] [_{Foc} té [_{NumP} ... t_{XP} ...]]]$

This would mean that the D-system involves both a topic phrase (TopP) and a focus phrase (FocP), whose heads are realized as *lɔ́* and *té*, respectively. An apparent counter-argument to this analysis, though, is the incompatibility between the nominal question marker and the specificity markers.

(22) *[Távò xɔ́xɔ́ lɔ́/ɖé   té] wè Kòfí xɔ̀?
       table old   DET$[_{\pm spec;\pm def}]$ Q FOC Kofi buy
       'Which old aforementioned table did Kofi buy?'

In previous work, I (2004) concluded that these facts are expected if we assume that both the nominal question marker and the specificity marker encode D. In that system, the features [specific] and [interrogative] were amalgamated under D. But this seems counter-intuitive because interrogative features express some kind of force (Cheng 1991), while specificity relates to discourse-linked properties, such as known or shared information. In addition, a fine structure of the clausal C-system suggests that the functional head that hosts the feature interrogative (e.g., in Gungbe and Italian) is different from Force, which encodes clausal-type (Aboh 2004). If we maintain the parallelism between the clausal and nominal left peripheries, we are led to conclude that the nominal topic and interrogative features do not fall under the same head D. Put differently, the specificity and the focus markers *lɔ́* and *té* do not compete for the same position.

This conclusion is supported by the fact that, in Gungbe, sentence (17a), repeated here as (23a), has a second variant that is given in (23b), where the element *ɖě* intervenes between the fronted phrase and the question word *té*. It appears that speakers choose the strategy in (23b) in order to single out a particular (or specific) referent. Example (23c) further indicates that the question word and the particle *ɖě* may co-occur with the number marker.

(23) a. [Távò xɔ́xɔ́ té] wè Kòfí xɔ̀?
          table old   Q FOC Kofi buy
          'Which old table did Kofi buy?'
     b. [Távò xɔ́xɔ́ ɖě   té] wè Kòfí xɔ̀?
          table old PART Q FOC Kofi buy
          'Which one of the old table(s) did Kofi buy?'
     c. [Távò xɔ́xɔ́ ɖě   té lé]   wè Kòfí xɔ̀?
          table old PART Q NUMB FOC Kofi buy
          'Which one of the old tables did Kofi buy?'

It is not clear to me what is the origin of the particle *ɖě*, which may arguably derive from the relative marker *ɖě(xè)* 'that/who' or the numeral *(ò)ɖě* 'one'. Whichever the case, it seems reasonable to assume that this particle is a head that encodes the feature [ONE], which can be thought of as being discourse-anaphoric, just as specificity. Granted this, I further argue that, in situations such as (23b–c), the fronted element occurs in [SpecTopP] and binds an empty category in [SpecFocP]. Top and Foc are realized as *ɖě* and *té*, respectively (24).

(24) $[_D[_D[_{TopP}$ távò xɔ́xɔ́ $[_{Top^0}$ ɖě $[_{FocP}$ ec$[_{távò xɔ́xɔ́}]$ $[_{Foc}$ té $[_{NumP}$ t$[_{távò xɔ́xɔ́}]$ $[_{Num}$ lé $[_{FP}$ t$[_{távò xɔ́xɔ́}]]]]]]]]]]]$

Keeping the parallel with the clause, such nominal sequences are reminiscent of topic sentences in which the focused constituent is subsequently topicalized as the example (25) indicates. In this case, the topic constituent has been extracted from the focus position, which now contains the third person strong pronoun *úɔ̀*.

(25)   [$_{\text{ForceP}}$ [$_{\text{Force}}$ [$_{\text{TopP}}$ Kòfí$_i$ [$_{\text{Top0}}$ yà   [$_{\text{FocP}}$ úɔ̀$_i$ [$_{\text{Foc}}$ wè [$_{\text{FinP}}$ Àsíbá dà   t$_{[\text{Kòfi}]}$]]]]]]]]
               Kofi   TOP   3SG   FOC   Asiba marry
        'As for Kofi, Asiba married HIM'

Building on the discussed facts, I propose to represent the architecture of the nominal left periphery as in (26).

(26)   [$_\text{D}$ [$_\text{D}$ [$_{\text{TopP}}$ [$_{\text{Top0}}$ lɔ́/dě [$_{\text{FocP}}$ [$_{\text{Foc}}$ tέ [$_{\text{NumP}}$ [$_{\text{Num}}$ lέ [$_{\text{FP}}$ …N…]]]]]]]]]]

Under this approach, I conclude that the incompatibility in (22) is pragmatic/semantic, but I leave it to future research, what pragmatic/semantic properties are at work here.

3.2   The interaction between nominal and clausal topics

This section suggests that a nominal topic may license a clausal topic. Gungbe manifests argument versus adjunct asymmetry with regard to topicalization. Unlike arguments, not all adjuncts can function as topic in this language. Note the contrast between the time adjunct and the locative adjunct in (27).

(27)   a.   [Gbɔ̀jέ mὲ]   yà, Kòfí ná sá sὲn dó xɔ̀   lɔ́
           holiday POST[$_\text{inside}$] TOP Kofi FUT put paint PREP room DET[$_{+\text{spec};+\text{def}}$]
           'As for during the holidays, Kofi will paint the room'
     b.   *[Xɔ̀   kpá]   yà, Kòfí ná zà   flέn gbáú!
           room POST[$_\text{beside}$] TOP Kofi FUT sweep there indeed
           'As for beside the room, Kofi will sweep there!'

I (2004) proposed that the contrast in (27) can be explained, if we assume that the topic marker *yà* is referential in the sense that it expresses the fact that the element to its left refers to specific member(s) of a set in the mind of the speaker or pre-established in discourse. Under this interpretation, expressions like 'holiday' are referential because they express shared knowledge, and can therefore be topic. This is not the case with the bare sequence *xɔ̀ kpá*, 'room beside', where the speaker might be referring to any side of any room. In this regard it is interesting to notice that (27b) is grammatical if we insert the specificity marker, that is, if we make the room specific, as in (28).

(28)   [Xɔ̀   lɔ́   kpá]   yà, Kòfí ná zà   flέn gbáú!
      room DET POST[$_\text{beside}$] TOP Kofi FUT sweep there indeed
      'As for beside the aforementioned room, Kofi will sweep there!'

Under the proposed analysis, that *xɔ̀ lɔ́ kpá* 'beside the aforementioned room' is eligible for clausal topicalization is straightforward because it is itself a topic. This would mean that nominal topicalization may favor or license clausal topicalization because D and C interact at the interface level. But such conclusion need not be surprising though if we grant recent developments that C (and now D) is a strong phase. In addition, the proposed analysis makes strong predictions about the distribution or existence of pure bare nouns, but I hope to return to these issues in future work.

4. Conclusion

This paper argues that the D-system involves topic and focus projections, whose specifiers contain the fronted topic and focus constituents, and whose heads are morphologically realized by elements that are commonly known as determiners or articles. TopP and FocP project between DP, the highest projection of the D-system, which represents the interface between discourse and the nominal expression, and NumP, the lowest projection of the D-system that expresses the interface between the nominal left periphery and the nominal inflectional system.

Notes

* I thank L. Haegeman, H. Zeijlstra, the participants of the TIN-dag, and an anonymous reviewer for their valuable comments, which helped improve this paper significantly.

1. Alternatively, one could propose that the article moves to Top to encode the topic feature. The noun may remain in situ or move to some intermediate position within the I-system.

References

Aboh, E. O. (2004) *The morphosyntax of Complement-Head Sequences. Clause structure and word order patterns in Kwa.* Oxford University Press, New York.

Bernstein, J. (2001) 'Focusing the Right Way in Romance Determiner Phrases'. *Probus* 13–1: 1–29.

Cheng, L. (1991) *On the Typology of Wh-questions.* Doctoral dissertation, MIT.

Chomsky, N. (1995) *The minimalist Program.* MIT Press, Cambridge, Mass.

Enç, M. (1991) 'The Semantics of Specificity.' *Linguistic Inquiry* 22: 1–26.

Haegeman, L. (1992) *Theory and Description in Generative Syntax.* Cambridge University Press, Cambridge.

Haegeman, L. (2004) 'DP-Periphery and Clausal Periphery: Possessor Doubling in West Flemish.' In D. Adger, C. de Cat & G. Tsoulas eds, *Peripheries.* Studies in Natural Language and Linguistic Theory 59: 211–240.

Knittel, M.-L. (1998) 'La structure morphosyntaxique des syntagmes nominaux possessivés du Hongrois.' In Jacqueline Guéron, & Anne Zribi-Hertz, eds., *La grammaire de la possession.* Pulidix, Paris, Nanterre.

Paoli, S. (2001) 'Mapping the Left Periphery of the Clause. Evidence from North Western Italian Varieties'. In J. Quer [et al.] eds., *Romance Languages and Linguistic Theory.* Benjamins, Amsterdam, 263–277.

Prince, F. E. (1981) 'Toward a Taxonomy of Given-New Information.' In P. Cole, ed., *Radical Pragmatics*. Academic Press, New York, 223–255.

Rizzi, L. (1997) 'The Fine Structure of the Left Periphery.' In L. Haegeman, ed., *Elements of Grammar*. Kluwer, Dordrecht, 281–337.

Szabolcsi, A (1994) 'The Noun Phrase.' In F., Kiefer & Katalin E. Kiss, eds., *Syntax and Semantics. The Syntactic Structure of Hungarian* 27: 179–274. Academic Press, New York.

Is Dutch a multiple fronting language?[*]

Janneke ter Beek
University of Groningen

1. Introduction

If movement is driven by the need to eliminate a strong feature on a functional head, then wh-movement of one wh-phrase suffices to check the strong feature on interrogative C (Chomsky 1995). Hence, in English, only one wh-phrase is fronted. This leaves the fate of *what* in (1) uncertain:

(1)   Who bought what?

If the [+wh] feature of *what* is interpretable, then apparently it has no reason to move, and in fact, movement is prohibited by Greed. However, to be interpreted as a wh-phrase, it needs to takes scope over the sentence. Therefore, some authors have claimed that *in-situ* wh-phrases in multiple questions undergo LF-movement (e.g. Rizzi 1990). Others have proposed that *in-situ* wh-phrases may indeed be licensed *in-situ* (e.g. Reinhart 1993).

In this paper I discuss Pesetsky's (2000) approach to multiple questions, which connects several properties of multiple questions. I demonstrate how two parameters account for the patterns seen in Bulgarian, English and German. If tenable, a model like this may be preferred over models in which wh-phrases are licensed through movement in some cases and *in-situ* in others, in that the same two factors are responsible for the range of options observed across and within languages. However, I demonstrate that nothing else said, the pattern of Dutch does not show the predicted interaction of parameter settings. Furthermore, patterns seen in certain Slavic languages are not captured by the model. Some very brief suggestions are made to accommodate these observations.

Linguistics in the Netherlands 2004 21 (2004), 13–24.
ISSN 0929–7332 / E-ISSN 1569–9919 © Algemene Vereniging voor Taalwetenschap

2.   Basic assumptions

Pesetsky (2000) assumes that in principle the [+wh] feature of every wh-phrase must move to interrogative CP. Two parameters may blur our perception of this. The first is phonological: PF may spell out the higher or the lower copy of a wh-phrase (cf. 2.1). The second is syntactic: C is parameterised with respect to the number of specifiers it can host (cf. 2.2). Depending on the setting of the parameter, C may require or prohibit that one or more wh-phrases are displaced.

To describe the full range of options, two additional assumptions are needed. First, C attracts the closest [+wh] feature first. This is the condition Attract Closest (AC). In combination with the second parameter, AC accounts for the so-called Superiority effect.

Second, we distinguish two kinds of movement. Phrasal movement is movement of the relevant feature, pied-piping the phrase to which it belongs. This kind of movement is always overt; however, if the lower copy is spelled out, phrasal movement is not reflected in the surface word order. Feature movement is movement of the relevant feature, stranding the phrase to which it belongs. In principle, both types of movement are available in every language, pace Chomsky (2001). Which movement actually takes place depends on the setting of the second parameter. Since phrasal movement creates a specifier, contexts in which C requires multiple specifiers will typically force phrasal movement.

2.1 The position of Spell Out

The first parameter is formalised as a pronunciation rule. In some languages, PF spells out the highest copy of every wh-phrase; in others, it spells out the highest copy of only the first wh-phrase that undergoes phrasal movement, and in still other languages, PF spells out the lower copy of every wh-phrase. Bulgarian exemplifies the first setting:[1]

(2)   a.   *Koj$_1$ kakvo$_3$ na kago$_2$ dade ~~na kogo kakvo~~?*[2]   [Bulgarian]
           who what   to whom gave
      b.   **Koj$_1$ ~~na kogo kakvo~~ dade na kogo$_2$ kakvo$_3$?*
           who   gave to whom what
           'Who gave what to whom?'

In (2a), all three wh-phrases are fronted. The word order in (2b), with only one wh-phrase pronounced in CP, is not grammatical. The second setting is found in English:

(3)   Who$_1$ ~~what to whom~~ gave what$_2$ to whom$_3$?

In (3), only one wh-phrase pronounced in sentence initial position. It could be that this is in fact the only wh-phrase that undergoes movement; if so, the representation (3) is incorrect. Evidence for it discussed in 3.2.1.

2.2 The specifier potential of interrogative C

The second parameter concerns the specifier potential of C. In multiple questions, interrogative C may prohibit specifiers ($C_{0\text{-SPEC}}$). Alternatively, C may require exactly one specifier ($C_{1\text{-SPEC}}$), or more than one specifier ($C_{M\text{-SPEC}}$).

Since phrasal movement creates a specifier, languages in which C prohibits specifiers must show feature movement. Languages in which C can host only one specifier display wh-movement of one wh-phrase. Additional wh-phrases check their [+wh] feature through feature movement. It is argued in 3.2.2 that German represents this type:

(4) Wer [+wh]$_i$ ~~wer~~ sah [t$_i$ [was]]?[3]   [German]
     who   saw   what
     'Who saw what?'

C first attracts the higher wh-phrase *wer*, conform AC, but as German C tolerates only one specifier, secondary instances of wh-movement must be feature movement. Hence, *was* does not move, but only its [+wh] feature does.

Bulgarian and English complementisers are argued to require more than one specifier:

(5) a. *Kakvo$_2$ koj$_1$ na kago$_3$ ~~koj~~ dade ~~kakvo na kago~~?   [Bulgarian]
     b. Koj$_1$ kakvo$_3$ na kago$_2$ dade ~~na kogo kakvo~~?   (= (2a))
         'Who gave what to whom?'

C attracts the wh-phrases one by one, but it is crucial that the highest wh-phrase is attracted first; movement of any other wh-phrase violates Attract Closest (AC), as seen in (5a). A remark is in order here. As can be seen from the order in (5b), AC apparently needs to be satisfied only once; secondary instances of attraction need not target the closest the wh-phrase. Also, additional wh-phrases tuck in below the specifier created by movement of the first wh-phrase.

Pesetsky (2000) claims that the LF-representation of the English equivalent of (5) is as in (3) above. As in Bulgarian, all wh-movements are phrasal. Unlike in Bulgarian, the phonological component spells out the higher copy of only the highest specifier of C; additional wh-phrases are spelled out *in-situ*.

3. Predictions

The pronunciation parameter differentiates wh-*in-situ* languages from languages in which (some) wh-phrases are fronted. But it is well known that languages that have similar pronunciation patterns do not necessarily share other characteristics, for instance with regard to the Superiority effect. The parameter on the specifier potential of C is designed to capture such syntactic properties. The guiding hypothesis is that $C_{M\text{-SPEC}}$ languages share properties, which are not shared by $C_{1\text{-SPEC}}$ languages or $C_{0\text{-SPEC}}$ languages. In this sense, English is more like Bulgarian than like German.

We predict the following properties for multiple questions in $C_{M\text{-SPEC}}$ languages:

1. At least two wh-phrases undergo phrasal movement;
2. Double questions display Superiority effects;
3. Triple questions do not display Superiority effects;
4. Intervention effects are only found for the highest wh-phrase.[4]

For multiple questions in $C_{1\text{-SPEC}}$ languages we predict:

5. Only one wh-phrase is pronounced in CP;
6. There are no Superiority effects;
7. Every *in-situ* wh-phrase is sensitive to intervention effects.

In order to test these predictions, we need ways to distinguish feature movement from phrasal movement. These are discussed in the next subsections.

3.1 Phrasal movement licenses antecedent contained deletion

Antecedent contained deletion (ACD) sentences contain an empty VP, to be interpreted like an antecedent VP (6a). However, merely copying the antecedent into the elided VP results in infinite regress (6b). Therefore, the elided VP can only be interpreted felicitously if the object of the antecedent VP has moved out. In (6b) this is established by covert movement (6c):

(6) a.   Mary invited everyone that I did
     b.   Mary invited everyone that I invited everyone that I invited....
     c.   [everyone that I invited] Mary [invited t]

In (6c), movement is independently motivated as a case of QR. In contrast, relative clauses which lack an independent motivation for movement, do not license ACD:

(7) *Mary invited John, whom I did

Arguably, (7) is ungrammatical because infinite regress cannot be avoided.[5] Now, if phrasal movement licenses ACD, then on the assumption that *in-situ* wh-phrases undergo phrasal movement, *wh-in-situ* is expected to license ACD. The prediction is borne out:[6]

(8) Which girl$_1$ invited [which student$_2$ that John did]?

Therefore, the possibility of ACD can be taken as a diagnostic for phrasal movement. As an extra test, we can show that a wh-phrase *in-situ* that licenses ACD is not sensitive to the presence of a scopal element between it and interrogative C (see 3.2):

(9) Which girl$_1$ didn't invite [which student$_2$ that John did]?

3.2 [+wh] feature movement is sensitive to intervention by scopal elements

Let us look at a triple question:

(10)   What$_2$ ~~to whom~~ [+wh$_1$]$_i$ did [t$_i$ [who$_1$]] give ~~what~~ to whom$_3$?

Seemingly, AC is violated: the highest wh-phrase is spelled out *in-situ*. Alternatively, it could be that wh-phrase$_1$ has undergone feature movement, conform AC, as represented in (10). This is possible, as there are two other wh-phrases to create specifiers of CP. We can show this by adding a scopal element, like negation, between C and wh-phrase$_1$:

(11)   a.   *What$_2$ ~~to whom~~ [+wh$_1$]$_i$ **didn't** [t$_i$ [who] give ~~what~~ to whom$_3$?
     b.   What$_2$ ~~to whom~~ [+wh$_1$]$_i$ did [t$_i$ [who] **not** give ~~what~~ to whom$_3$?

If the scopal element intervenes between the [+wh] feature and its source, the sentence is ungrammatical (11a), but when it intervenes between C and the copy of wh$_3$, which has moved as a phrase, there is no such effect (11b). As an extra test, we can demonstrate that the *in-situ* wh-phrase that satisfies AC (i.e. wh$_1$) does not license ACD:

(12)   a.   *I need to know which girl$_2$ [+wh$_1$]$_i$ Sue ordered [t$_i$ [which boy$_1$]] that Mary (also) did] to congratulate ~~which girl~~
     b.   I need to know which girl$_1$ ~~which boy which girl~~ ordered [which boy$_2$ that Mary (also) did] to congratulate Sarah.

3.3 Testing the predictions

With these diagnostics, we can support the claim that English has C$_{M\text{-SPEC}}$, but German has C$_{1\text{-SPEC}}$.

3.3.1   *English*

This subsection focuses on English, but the same results should hold for other C$_{M\text{-SPEC}}$ languages. Dutch is discussed in Section 4.

Recall the first prediction: at least two wh-phrases undergo phrasal movement. This was shown in 3.1. The wh-phrase that is spelled out *in-situ* in (8) licenses ACD and can therefore be assumed to undergo phrasal movement.

The second prediction is that double questions display Superiority effects. Superiority effects arise if the higher of two wh-phrases is spelled out *in-situ*, as in (13). I refer to this order as the reverse order. The reverse order is ungrammatical in C$_{M\text{-SPEC}}$ contexts:

(13)   *What$_2$ [+wh$_1$]$_i$ did [t$_i$ [who$_1$]] buy ~~what~~?

As AC cannot be violated, the *in-situ* pronunciation of wh-phrase$_1$ in (13) must reflect feature movement.[7] It was shown in (12a) that wh$_1$ indeed fails to license

ACD. I therefore assume that the representation (13) is correct: *who* checks its [+wh] feature through feature movement, satisfying AC. The ungrammaticality results from the fact that C now has too few specifiers.

If so, we predict that the addition of a third wh-phrase in (14) improves the reverse order. The prediction is borne out: triple questions do not display the Superiority effect:

(14)   What$_2$ ~~where~~ [+wh$_1$]$_i$ did [t$_i$ [who$_1$]] buy ~~what~~ where?

The fourth prediction is that intervention effects are restricted to wh$_1$, as this is the only wh-phrase that undergoes feature movement. This was shown in (11) in 3.2. The result follows if it is assumed that only wh$_1$ undergoes feature movement. Section 4 discusses intervention effects in English in more detail.

3.3.2 *German*

This subsection offers support for the claim that German has C$_{1\text{-SPEC}}$. Recall the first prediction from Section 3: only one wh-phrase is pronounced in CP. This was shown in (4) above. Second, we predict that German does not have the Superiority effect. If German C tolerates only one specifier, then there should be no Superiority effect in the reverse order, since we assumed that the Superiority effect reflects a violation of C$_{M\text{-SPEC}}$. The prediction is borne out:

(15)   a.   *Wer$_1$* [+wh$_2$]$_i$ *sah* ~~wer~~ [t$_i$ [was$_2$]]?   (= (4))
      b.   *Was$_2$* [+wh$_1$]$_i$ *sah* [t$_i$ [wer$_1$]] ~~was~~?   [German]
           what   saw   who
           "Who saw what?"

It remains to be shown that *in-situ* wh-phrases in multiple questions have undergone feature movement. This seems to be the case:

(16) $^{??}$*Welche Kinder$_1$* [+wh$_2$]$_i$ *haben* ~~welche Kinder~~ *niemandem*
      which children   have   nobody
      [t$_i$ [welche Bilder$_2$]] *zeigen*   *wollen?*   [German]
        which pictures show.INF want.INF
      'Which children wanted to show nobody which pictures?'

If German has C$_{1\text{-SPEC}}$, we expect that the second instance of wh-movement in (16) will be feature movement. If so, then the presence of the scopal element *niemandem* "nobody" should cause deviance.[8] The reason for this is that a scopal element blocks the relation between a [+wh] feature and the stranded wh-phrase, but not that between a wh-phrase and its copy. We see that (16) is indeed degraded. The nature of the deviance is discussed in more detail in Section 4.

4.　Dutch

Dutch is like English and German in that one wh-phrase in a multiple question is pronounced in CP (17a). Suppose the *in-situ* wh-phrase checks its feature through phrasal movement. Then we expect a Superiority effect in the reverse order, like in English. The data seem to confirm this:[9]

(17)　a.　Wie$_1$ heeft wat$_2$ gekocht?　　　　　　　　　　　[Dutch]
　　　　　　who　has　what bought
　　　b.　$^{??}$Wat$_2$ heeft wie$_1$ gekocht?
　　　　　　who　has　what bought
　　　　　'Who bought what?'

The example in (17b) may not be fully ungrammatical; however, it is judged less acceptable than the order in (17a), and also less acceptable than a triple question in the reverse order (18) or an example with D-linked wh-phrases (19):

(18)　$^?$*Wat$_2$ heeft wie$_1$　waar$_3$　verstopt?*　　　　　　　　[Dutch]
　　　　what has　who where hidden
　　　　'What did who hide where?'

(19)　*Welke boeken$_2$ heeft welk　meisje$_1$ gelezen?*　　　　　　[Dutch]
　　　which books　has　which girl　　read
　　　'Which books did which girl read?'

The contrast between (17b) and (19) is important in what follows. It can also be observed in English:

(20)　a.　*What$_2$ did who$_1$ buy?
　　　b.　Which book$_2$ did which student$_1$ buy?

So far, the Dutch data suggest that interrogative C requires multiple specifiers, as in English. If so, then the *in-situ* wh-phrase in (17b) checks its feature by phrasal movement to CP. We can demonstrate this only indirectly, by investigating the interaction between wh-phrases and scopal elements. As it is difficult to construct an example with three wh-phrases in which we can manipulate the position of a scopal element, as in (11), I use an example with D-linked wh-phrases. Pesetsky (2000) proposes that such sentences are exceptional in that they allow for a violation of $C_{M\text{-}SPEC}$, that is, they allow [+wh] feature movement, but only in the reverse order:

(21)　a.　Which kid$_1$ ~~which dog which kid~~ hit which dog$_2$?
　　　b.　Which dog$_2$ [+wh$_1$]$_i$ did [t$_i$ [which kid$_1$]] hit ~~which dog~~?
　　　c.　Ann hit the poodle, Joe the sheepdog, and Pat the terrier.

Both (21a) and (21b) allow the pair-list answer in (21c).[10] If a scopal element intervenes between C and the *in-situ* wh-phrase, the pair-list reading is possible for the standard order (22a), but is lost in the reverse order (22b):

(22) a. Which kid$_1$ ~~which dog which kid~~ did **not** hit which dog$_2$?
b. $^{??}$Which dog$_2$ [+wh$_1$]$_i$ didn't [t$_i$ [which kid$_1$]] hit ~~which dog~~?
c. Ann didn't hit the poodle.

Pesetsky (2000) argues that a pair-list answer is only possible if the [+wh] feature of every wh-phrase that is paired in the answer has moved to interrogative CP. If one of the [+wh] features fails to move to CP, then the question anticipates a single pair answer at best. Thus, the interpretation (22c) for (22b) is exactly what is expected if scopal elements block [+wh] feature movement, and feature movement is required in this word order.

The contrast between (21b) and (22b) follows if C requires multiple specifiers where possible. In (22a), nothing prevents phrasal movement, so phrasal movement is preferred over feature movement. This is true despite the fact that feature movement is in principle possible, as evidenced by (21b). In (22b), however, the only possible derivation involves feature movement of wh-phrase$_1$, which is blocked by the scopal element. The result is degraded.

Now let us look at the Dutch examples (23) and (24). Both the standard order and the reverse order are in principle compatible with the pair-list answer (23c):

(23) a. Welke jongen$_1$ denkt Jan dat welk cadeau$_2$ heeft gekocht?
which guy thinks Jan that which present has bought
'Which guy does Jan think bought which present?'[11] [Dutch]
b. Welk cadeau$_2$ denkt Jan dat welke jongen$_1$ heeft gekocht?
which present thinks Jan that which guy has bought
'Which present does Jan think which guy bought?'
c. Jan thinks Don bought the book, Joe the TV, and Bob the DVD.

In order to determine how the *in-situ* wh-phrases in (23) check their [+wh] feature, I add a scopal element between interrogative C and the *in-situ* wh-phrase. Based on the Superiority effect in (17b), we expect phrasal movement in (24a) but not in (24b), as in the English (22). Thus, we expect that the scopal element induces an intervention effect in the reverse order, but not in the standard order. However, the data show an intervention effect both in the standard order and the reverse order: (24a) and (24b) are incompatible with a pair-list answer; the examples anticipate a single pair answer like (24c) at best:

(24) a. $^{?}$*Welke jongen$_1$ denkt* **bijna iedereen** *dat welk cadeau$_2$ heeft*
which guy thinks almost everyone that which present has
gekocht? [Dutch]
bought
b. $^{?}$*Welk cadeau$_2$ denkt* **bijna iedereen** *dat welke jongen$_1$ heeft*
'Which present does almost everyone think bought which present?'
c. $^{?}$Almost everyone thinks that Don bought the book.

The data in (24) are reminiscent of the German example in (16): the normal order is degraded. This follows if C tolerates only one specifier, forcing feature movement if there is more than one wh-phrase.

If the observations in this section are accurate, then at the present state of our knowledge, multiple questions in Dutch form a counterexample to the model proposed in Pesetsky (2000).

5. Discussion

Testing the predictions from Section 3, Dutch comes out Janus-faced, showing properties of complementary parameter settings. It might be possible to capture these results by allowing greater language internal variation of complementiser choice, but this would undermine the explanatory power of the model, since we do not understand why we observe such freedom in Dutch but not in English or German. An unfortunate conclusion presents itself: Dutch is a counter-example to the typology proposed in Pesetsky (2000).

Note that the $C_{M\text{-}SPEC}$ setting is primarily based on the Superiority test. Now, English is the prototypical example of a language that is sensitive to Superiority, while German is well known to lack such effects. Based on just these languages, it is legitimate to describe Superiority as a syntactic phenomenon. However, it is unexpected that there are languages like Dutch, in which Superiority effects can be observed which do not cause full ungrammaticality. Possibly, Superiority is not a purely syntactic phenomenon. Bošković (1998) observes that there are actually three kinds of Superiority. Syntactic Superiority is found in multiple questions in which the reverse order is ungrammatical with non-D-linked wh-phrases. Apparent Superiority holds when the reverse order is grammatical. If it is only grammatical in the single pair reading, however, Bošković speaks of interpretive Superiority. Perhaps a thorough investigation into the properties of interpretive Superiority, which is not in the scope of Pesetsky's model, could shed light on the unexpected results for Dutch.[12]

Much work has to be done to describe the precise properties of interpretive Superiority in the present framework, but it seems that this notion is independently needed to account for the patterns seen in certain Slavic languages. Pesetsky (2000) does not mention languages of the Serbo-Croatian and Polish type. As it stands, the model cannot account for the properties of these languages. In Serbo-Croatian, the reverse order does not show Superiority effects in monoclausal questions, suggesting $C_{1\text{-}SPEC}$. However, the reverse order, although fully grammatical even with non-D-linked wh-phrases, only allows a single pair answer, which is understood as an intervention effect in the present framework. But word order argues against an intervention effect, as all wh-phrases are fronted, strongly suggesting $C_{M\text{-}SPEC}$.

The fact that all wh-phrases are fronted, but may appear in the reverse order, has been taken as evidence that wh-phrases in Serbo-Croatian do not all target CP. Bošković (1998), among others, suggests that at most one wh-phrase moves to CP, while others undergo focus movement to the lower FocP. The contradictory results might be accounted for in Pesetsky's model if the specifier potential parameter is defined just for CP. Then Serbo-Croatian would be a $C_{1\text{-SPEC}}$ language, with the predicted Superiority properties.

Future research should determine the extent to which this adaptation is feasible. Problems may arise if more complex sentence types are taken into account. These may require variation of complementiser type, since the selection of C in Serbo-Croatian seems to depend in part on sentence structure. Moreover, the function of the specifier potential parameter has to be distributed over (at least) two independent projections, as $C_{M\text{-SPEC}}$ does not govern the licensing of features attracted by Foc^0 (but see Grohmann 2003). This complicates the model to the extent that our two parameters are no longer sufficient to describe the cross-linguistic fronting patterns.

But an adaptation along these lines may not only be profitable in the domain of Slavic languages. If the framework can be adapted to differentiate multiple wh-fronting languages according to the positions wh-phrases target, we may expect that each subtype of multiple wh-fronting language has a counterpart among the languages in which a lower copy of wh-movement is spelled out. Grohmann (2003) proposes an analysis for German in which the wh-phrases in multiple questions target different positions in a fine-grained CP-layer. Future research may determine whether Dutch still forms a counterexample in such an analysis.

6.   Concluding remarks

This paper discusses Pesetsky's (2000) model of multiple questions. Since the model is primarily based on data from a limited number of languages, the question arises whether the connection between Superiority effects and intervention effects is real. It is vital that the model is tested on more languages. The present paper is an attempt to do this for Dutch. It seems that the model as it is cannot account for the patterns observed. Perhaps the model can be modified to cover the larger CP-layer, which might also bring the movement patterns of a number of Slavic languages into its scope.

Notes

* I would like to thank my colleagues in Groningen, the audience of the TINdag, and an anonymous reviewer for helpful comments. All remaining errors are mine.

1. See Pesetsky (2000) for a discussion on D-linked wh-phrases.

2. Here and below, the numbers in subscript indicate the distance of the wh-phrase to interrogative C, prior to wh-movement. Wh_1 is the wh-phrase that is closest to C, wh_2 is second closest, and so on. Struck out wh-phrases represent copies.

3. Here and below, the copy left behind by verb movement is not represented.

4. Actually, this does not follow from the framework. As long as two wh-phrases create specifiers, nothing prevents a third wh-phrase from checking its [+wh] feature through feature movement. But for English, it turns out that only the highest wh-phrase does (cf. Section 4). If it does not conflict with the specifier potential of C, phrasal movement seems to be preferred.

5. Note that in the copy theory of movement, as Chomsky (2001) observes, QR does not empty the object position of the antecedent VP, because movement leaves a copy. The Dutch examples in (i) and (ii) also argue against an explanation in terms of infinite regress:

(i)   *Mary heeft iedereen die ik wilde uitgenodigd* "Mary invited everyone that I wished"

(ii) **Mary heeft John, die ik wilde uitgenodigd* "*Mary invited John, whom I wished"

The contrast cannot be caused by infinite regress in (ii), since the object has moved out of VP in both examples. Furthermore, the interpretation of the elided part is not that of the antecedent VP. The meaning of the relative clauses is "that I wished that she would invite" rather than "that I wished to invite". The English translations allow both interpretations, and according to Baltin and Fodor (2000), both interpretations represent cases of ACD. If the Dutch (ii) and its English translation are ungrammatical for the same reason, the "antecedent" VP cannot be responsible for the interpretation. Therefore, it is unclear whether ACD is resolved by copying the content of an antecedent VP into the elided part. If the examples in the main text are to receive the same account as (i) and (ii), the cause of the ungrammaticality of those is unclear too. Nevertheless, I follow Pesetsky (2000) in using ACD as a test for phrasal movement.

6. Note that Stroik (1992) presents examples of configurations that are predicted to license ACD in the present framework, but are nevertheless ungrammatical.

7. Alternatively, (13) could be derived by phrasal movement of both wh-phrases. In this case, either AC is violated, or the pronunciation rule is. Neither alternative can explain the contrast between (13) and (14).

8. We would like to demonstrate that the *in-situ* wh-phrase does not undergo phrasal movement. However, neither German nor Dutch has ACD structures. Constructions like those in footnote 5 seem to be impossible with wh-phrases. This cannot be taken as evidence that wh-phrases do not undergo phrasal movement, since English disallows such constructions as well: * *Which students will read which books that you wish to?*

9. There is little literature on multiple questions in Dutch, and some authors only report examples of the reverse order in embedded clauses, which are judged fully ungrammatical. Koster (1987) remarks that (17b) is definitely less acceptable than (17a).

10. These judgements are controversial. Although Hornstein (1995) agrees with Pesetsky, Grohmann (2003) claims that the reverse order does not allow a pair-list answer.

11. (23a) and (24a) may be slightly degraded due to the that-t effect. Most speakers I consulted do not judge it ungrammatical, though.

12. Note that this characterisation of interpretive Superiority does not apply to Dutch. The point is that Superiority is quite puzzling in itself. Investigation of all aspects may uncover more detailed typologies, in which Dutch may not be exceptional.

References

Baltin, M and J. Fodor (2000) 'Selection for a Surface Anaphor'. In S. Chung, J. McCloskey and N. Sanders, eds., *Jorge Hankamer WebFest*. (On line)

Bošković, Ž. (1998) 'On the Interpretation of Multiple Questions'. In J. Fodor, S.J. Keyser and A. Brand, eds., *A Celebration: Essays for Noam Chomsky's 70th Birthday*. MIT Press, Cambridge, Mass. (On line)

Chomsky, N. (1995) *The Minimalist Program*. MIT Press, Cambridge, Mass.

Chomsky, N. (2001) 'Beyond Explanatory Adequacy'. *MIT Occasional Papers in Linguistics* 20, 1–28.

Grohmann, K. (2003) 'German Is a Multiple Fronting Language!'. In C. Boeckx and K. Grohmann, eds., *Multiple Wh-Fronting*. John Benjamins, Amsterdam, 99–130.

Hornstein, N. (1995) *Logical Form: From GB to Minimalism*. Blackwell, Cambridge/Oxford.

Koster, J. (1987) *Domains and Dynasties*. Foris, Dordrecht.

Pesetsky, D. *Phrasal Movement and its Kin*. MIT Press, Cambridge, Mass.

Rizzi, L. (1990) *Relativized Minimality*. MIT Press, Cambridge, Mass.

Reinhart, T. (1993) 'Interpreting Wh-in-situ'. Ms., University of Tel Aviv.

Stroik, T. (1992) 'English Wh-*in-situ* Constructions'. *Linguistic Analysis* 22, 133–153.

Conditional imperatives in Dutch and Russian

Ronny Boogaart and Radoslava Trnavac
Free University Amsterdam / University of Leiden

1. Introduction

In addition to being used to perform a directive speech act (command, request etc.), imperative forms in both Dutch and Russian may be used in a conditional-like construction. The Dutch and Russian 'conditional imperative' constructions (CIC) are exemplified in (1) (Proeme 1991:39) and (2) (Fortuin 2000:182), respectively. In both examples, the imperative in the first clause may be paraphrased by means of a conditional *if*-clause.

(1) Hang de was   buiten en het gaat regenen.
    hang the laundry outside and it   goes rain
    'If you hang the laundry outside, it starts raining.'

(2) Мне кажется, что выскажись   мы —
    I.DAT seems   that say.IMPER.PERF.2SG we
    и   все   пойдет   по-старому
    and everything goes.PRES.PERF as before
    'It seems to me that if we speak out, everything will become as before.'

The fact that different languages use one and the same form to present both directives and conditionals suggests that directive and conditional meaning constitute a *semantic map* in the sense of Haspelmath (2003; cf. Croft's 2001 *conceptual space*). In this paper, we will show that the notion of a semantic map may be used to elucidate, first, the multifunctionality of a language-particular construction and, second, the differences in use between 'similar' constructions across languages. In Section 2, we will present three such differences between the Dutch and the Russian conditional use of the imperative. After having introduced, in Section 3.1, the idea of a semantic map connecting directive and conditional meaning, we will show what 'chunks' of the directive-conditional continuum are covered by the Dutch (3.2) and the Russian (3.3) construction. In the final section, we will present some questions for further research.

2.   Language-specific constraints on CIC

2.1 Subject of the imperative part of CIC

The most conspicuous difference between the Dutch and the Russian CIC, as exemplified in (1) and (2), concerns the subject of the imperative part of the construction. There are two 'subject constraints' on the Dutch CIC, both of which are not operative for the Russian construction.

The subject of the imperative in Dutch (1) can be either the addressee (paraphrase: "if you hang the laundry outside now, it will start raining") or it can be generic (paraphrase: "every time one hangs the laundry outside, it starts raining") (Proeme 1991: 39). The Dutch imperative, both in its directive and its conditional use, does not allow for a 1st or 3rd person implicit subject. Thus, the sentence in (3), despite the 1st person subject in the second part of the CIC, can only be interpreted as "if *you* miss this train, we'll definitely be late", and not as "if *we* miss this train, we'll definitely be late". (The latter, according to Clark 1993: 116, is a possible reading of its English equivalent.)

> (3)   Mis die trein en we komen zeker te laat.
> 'Miss that train and we'll definitely be late.'

In Russian, the subject of the imperative in the CIC can be any person in both numbers. The subject in (2) is 1st person plural, the one in (4) is 1st person singular.

> (4)   Свари   я эту картошку во время,
> boil.IMPER.PERF.2SG I this potatoes in time
> мы бы   не опоздали.
> we PART not late
> 'If I had boiled the potatoes in time, we would not have been late.'

In addition to being restricted to 2nd person subjects, the imperative part of the Dutch CIC does not allow for the subject to be explicit. Unlike the first constraint, this one can not be regarded as inherited from the directive use of the imperative since in the directive use, the subject of the imperative can be explicit, at least in the presence of (untranslatable) particles such as *maar*, *eens*, and *maar eens*. The sentence in (5a), for instance, is fine, but the one in (5b) is incoherent.[1]

> (5)   a.   Hang jij de was   maar eens buiten.
> hang you the laundry PARTICLES outside
> 'Hang the laundry outside.'

b. *Hang jij de was   buiten en het gaat regenen
   hang you the laundry outside and it   goes rain

In Russian, the subject of the imperative, at least when used in the CIC, is always explicit, as was demonstrated in examples (2) and (4); in the directive use, the subject need not be explicit. In addition, impersonal verbs may occur in the conditional part of the Russian CIC, as in (6), whereas these are ungrammatical in the Dutch construction, as can be seen in (7).

(6) Темней   вчера   пораньше, мы бы
     be dark.IMPER.IMPERF.2SG yesterday earlier   we PART
     не пошли   в парк.
     not go.PAST PARTICIPLE to park
     'If it had been dark earlier yesterday, we would not have gone to the park.'

(7) *Was eerder donker geweest en we waren niet naar het park gegaan.
     Lit. Had been dark earlier en we would not have gone to the park

In sum, there are no constraints at all on the possible subject of the imperative in the Russian CIC, but the Dutch construction is restricted to 2nd person and generic (but not impersonal) subjects, that, moreover, can not be explicit.

2.2 Kind of conditional relation compatible with CIC

A common constraint of the Dutch and the Russian CIC is that neither is compatible with a pragmatic conditional relation. 'If-constructions' may be used to express such relations, in which the two events are not temporally — let alone causally — related, as is demonstrated for English in (8) (Athanasiadou & Dirven 1997).

(8) If you're thirsty, there's beer in the fridge.

Pragmatic conditional relations are to be distinguished from content conditional relations, that suggest a definite temporal and, very often, causal relation between the events presented in the protasis and apodosis. If we present the two events of (8) by means of a CIC, as in (9), a content relation seems to be the only possible reading.

(9) Heb dorst en er is bier in de koelkast
     'Be thirsty and there is beer in the fridge.'

The sentence may be used, for instance, to suggest that the beer somehow appears in the fridge at the very moment you're being thirsty. Thus, the CIC in (9) imposes a 'content conditional reading', i.e. a sequence reading, in which the second event comes after, and may in fact be caused by, the first event.

Within the domain of content conditional relations, there is an important difference between the Dutch and the Russian CIC. The Russian construction allows for hypothetical and counterfactual content readings equally well; the Dutch construction usually resists a counterfactual reading. In Russian, the counterfactual reading of the CIC can be distinguished from the hypothetical reading on formal grounds, since, on the counterfactual reading, the verb in the apodosis appears in the subjunctive form, while on the hypothetical reading, the apodosis usually contains perfective present (see examples (4) and (2), respectively). In the protasis, there seems to be a subtle difference as well (Trnavac 2003): on the hypothetical reading, the imperative form has perfective aspect (see example (2)), whereas in the counterfactual reading it may have either perfective aspect, as in (4), or imperfective aspect, as in (6) and (10).

(10)   Открывай   я окно   постоянно,
        open.IMPER-IMPERF.2SG I window regularly
        он бы   простудился.
        he PART get flu.PAST PARTICIPLE
        'If I opened the window regularly, he would get the flu.'

Dutch may use tense to distinguish between hypothetical and counterfactual readings of the CIC.[2] More specifically, a past perfect imperative in the protasis of the construction indicates 'counterfactuality to the past' (Duinhoven 1995); the apodosis in these cases may contain either a simple past form, or a 'future in the past' (consisting of the past tense of the auxiliary *zullen* ('will') and an infinitive).

(11)   Had het gisteren afgemaakt en je hoefde vandaag niet te werken.
        Lit. Had finished it yesterday and you would not have to work today.
        'If you had finished it yesterday, you would not have to work today.'

However, unlike in Russian, the counterfactual reading of the Dutch CIC is marginal at best. While it is possible to express 'counterfactuality to the past', as in (11), it is difficult to trigger 'counterfactuality to the present'. In principle, one could use a simple past, rather than past perfect, imperative in the protasis of the CIC to get this reading, as in (12), but such cases seem to be rare.

(12)   ?Stopte met roken en je voelde je veel fitter.
        Lit. Quit smoking and you would feel much better.

Moreover, instances of the Dutch CIC containing a past imperative in the protasis such as (12) prefer a habitual past reading (see Section 3.2). In fact, all of the Dutch examples given so far allow for a habitual reading, whereas the Russian CIC is incompatible with such an interpretation.

2.3 Order of protasis and apodosis

In accordance with our claim that the CIC typically expresses content relations of sequence and causality, the order of protasis and apodosis in the CIC is relatively fixed: the events are presesented iconically, i.e. in the order in which they happened, or would happen in a hypothetical or counterfactual world. For the Dutch CIC, this is the only possible order; for Russian, however, counter-examples, such as (13), can be found.

(13) Лично   мне все едино,   будь   вы хоть зеленого цвета.
      personally I.DAT all the same be.IMPER you even green   skin
      'Personally, it's all the same to me, even if you had green skin.'
      (Fortuin 2000: 180)

2.4 Summary

The different constraints on the Dutch and the Russian CIC can be summarized as follows.

	Subject	Order	Relation
Dutch CIC	– 2nd person (hearer or generic) – not explicit	Fixed	– Hypothetical – Counterfactual? – Habitual
Russian CIC	– 1st/2nd/3rd – impersonal verbs – explicit	Free	– Hypothetical – Counterfactual

3.   Towards a semantic map for directives and conditionals

3.1 From directive to conditional

While constructions, are, by definition, language-specific (Croft 2001), one would obviously not want to claim that it is just a coincidence that in different languages one grammatical category is used to perform both a directive and a conditional function. To show how directive and conditional meaning are related, and how the Dutch and the Russian CIC are related, we will use the notion of a *semantic map* (Haspelmath 2003; cf. Croft's 2001 *conceptual space*). According to Haspelmath, "the leading idea of the semantic map method is that multifunctionality of a gram occurs only when the various functions of the gram are similar." (2003:215). So in what sense are directive and conditional readings 'similar'?

As pointed out by De Haan (1986), the common semantic denominator of directives and conditionals is that both refer not to an actual event but to an event that may be realized in some 'possible world', in a 'mental space' that is not the 'base space', but rather a generic, a hypothetical, or a counterfactual space (Fauconnier 1985). It is part of the meaning of directives that the event presented is not realized (yet); directives, in addition, have as part of their meaning that the speaker wants the addressee to make sure that the event does get realized. The latter part of the meaning of directives — the fact that they are 'hearer directed' — is absent when an imperative is interpreted exclusively as a conditional.

The conceptual link between directive and conditional meaning is captured by assuming that they constitute parts of one semantic map, which is supposed to be universal.[3] When relating language-specific constructions to the map, this should happen in accordance with the Semantic Map Connectivity Hypothesis: "Language-specific and construction-specific grammatical categories should map onto connected regions of conceptual space" (Croft 2001:105). The boundaries of the semantic domain covered by a specific construction may be fuzzy. In the following section we will try to put the Dutch and the Russian CIC 'on the map'. We will show that there is ample evidence for the existence of an intermediate category of directive/conditional meaning, which, especially in Russian, corresponds to a specific construction distinct from the CIC, namely the CDIC (Conditional Directive Imperative Construction). Thus, the semantic map for directives and conditionals is arguably as follows.

DIRECTIVE – DIRECTIVE/CONDITIONAL – CONDITIONAL

3.2 Putting the Dutch CIC on the map

Which part of the semantic map given in 3.1 is covered by the imperative as used in the Dutch CIC? Starting at the left hand side of the directive-conditional continuum, it should first be noted that an imperative occurring in the Dutch grammatical pattern "IMPERATIVE + *en* + DECLARATIVE" may still be a pure directive. This is at least one of the readings of (14).

> (14)   Zet dat boek daar neer en je mag naar huis.
>   'Put the book there and you can go home.'

In the first clause, the speaker directs the addressee to put the book at the appointed place; the imperative is interpreted no differently than when occurring in an independent clause. Such examples, then, allow for a strictly compositional analysis: they can be treated as the coordination of two different constructions — a Directive Imperative Construction (DIC) and a Declarative Construction — rather than as instances of one complex CIC. In (14), the conditional element may be the result of a pragmatic inference, more specifically a 'bridging inference' needed to arrive at a 'maximally relevant' interpretation (Clark 1993).

Let us now turn to the conditional part of the continuum. There are four types of contexts in which the imperative in the CIC necessarily gets a conditional rather than a directive reading. The first type is constituted by contexts in which it is clear that the speaker does not want the addressee to execute the action of the imperative. Thus, in (15), the imperative can not be strictly directive. (Unless, of course, the addressee is looking for a place to put a book that he'd rather never see again in his life.)

(15) Zet dat boek daar neer en je vindt het nooit meer terug.
      'Put the book there and you will never find it again.'

A directive reading is also ruled out in the generic cases mentioned earlier; in order for an imperative to be interpreted as a directive, the agent of the imperative clause has to be the addressee. Thus, on the generic reading of (14), the sentence constitutes an unambiguous instance of the CIC. Yet another 'felicity condition' of a directive speech act is that the hearer is able to execute the action requested. Therefore, situations that are beyond the control of the addressee cannot occur in the Directive Imperative Construction, as demonstrated in (16).

(16) ?Heb blond haar!
      'Have blond hair'

However, they can be used in the CIC, as in (17), which is then necessarily interpreted as strictly conditional.

(17) Heb blond haar en ze denken dat je dom bent.
      Lit. Have blond hair and they think you are stupid.
      'If you are a blond, people automatically assume you are stupid.'

Finally, the Dutch CIC allows for past tensed imperatives, as in (18).

(18) Vergat je fiets op slot te zetten en hij werd gestolen.
      Lit. Forgot (past imperative) to lock your bike and it got stolen.

The past tense is incompatible with a directive reading of the imperative as well, since when using a directive, the speaker is trying to get the addressee to realize an action in the (near) future.

Thus, the examples in (15), (17) and (18) clearly belong in the conditional part of the semantic map outlined in Section 3.1. Many other occurrences of the Dutch grammatical pattern "IMPERATIVE + *en* + DECLARATIVE" are more difficult to 'put on the map', since, as discussed with respect to example (14), the Directive Imperative Construction (DIC) is not incompatible with an inference of conditionality either and it is impossible to determine at precisely which point such an inference becomes part of the conventionalized meaning of the construction.

3.3 Putting the Russian CIC and CDIC on the map

Since, as seen in Section 2, the Russian CIC does not have any of the constraints of the Dutch CIC, we assume that it covers the entire conditional domain of the semantic map outlined in 3.1. The left side of the map in Russian, like in Dutch, is occupied by the directive use of the imperative (DIC). In addition, Russian has a construction that corresponds rather neatly to the intermediate domain of the semantic map, namely the Conditional Directive Imperative Construction. The CDIC is exemplified in (19).

(19) Скажи   кому-нибудь хоть слово и   я никогда тебя
      tell.IMPER-PERF.2SG anybody   even word and I never   you
      не прощу!
      not forgive.PRES-PERF
      'Tell anyone about this and I will never forgive you.' (Internet)

The CDIC is a construction in its own right, since it has formal and semantic characteristics that make it different from the CIC (see also Fortuin 2000). For instance, the aspect of the imperative in the CDIC can be both perfective and imperfective whereas in the hypothetical CIC, the imperative can only be perfective (see Section 2.2). Since Dutch does not have overt, grammatical aspect (Boogaart 1999), it is difficult to compare this feature of the Russian CDIC with the Dutch construction. However, it turns out that other defining characteristics of the Russian CDIC are shared by the Dutch construction. Most notably:

— The CDIC is possible with implicitly or explicitly expressed 2nd person singular or plural subjects (cf. Section 2.1).
— When the subject is implicit, the sentence gets a generic reading (cf. Section 2.1).
— The order of protasis and apodosis is fixed (cf. Section 2.3).
— Non-controllable events are not always possible in the CDIC, whereas in the CIC they are always possible.[4] This is evidenced in (20) and (21).

(20) *Очутись   в Москве и   все будет хорошо!
      happen to be.IMPER.PERF.2SG in Moscow and all is   fine
      Lit. Happen to be in Moscow and all is fine.

(21) Очутись   он в Москве, он бы   ее навестил.
      happen to be.IMPER-PERF.2SG he in Moscow he PART her visit
      'If he had happened to be in Moscow at that time, he would have visited her.'

— The CDIC is incompatible with counterfactual readings. In this respect, the Russian construction differs from the Dutch one, which does allow for counterfactual readings, albeit only marginally so (cf. Section 2.2)

3.4 Summary

Since, in many respects, the Dutch construction is much more like the Russian CDIC than like the Russian CIC, it makes sense to refer to the Dutch construction as a CDIC as well. We will still assume that the Dutch construction covers part of the strictly 'conditional' domain of the map, because of its compatibility with uncontrollable events, counterfactual readings, and past tense. The different semantic domains covered by the directive and conditional imperative constructions of Dutch and Russian can now be represented in the following way.[5]

	Directive	Directive/conditional Hypothetical	Conditional Hypothetical/counterfactual
Dutch	DIC		
		CDIC	
Russian	DIC		
		CDIC	
			CIC

4. Conclusion

In this paper, we tried to provide insight into the differences and similarities between the Dutch and the Russian 'Conditional Imperative' by relating both of them to different regions of a semantic map we hypothesize to exist for directive and conditional meaning. Among the questions that remain for future research are the following. Why is the habitual reading so prominent for the Dutch construction, while it is not compatible with the Russian CIC, nor with the Russian CDIC? Why is the counterfactual reading so common for the Russian CIC, but hardly possible for the Dutch construction? Furthermore, as Haspelmath (2003: 233) notes, semantic maps can be an important tool for the study of grammaticalization, since they may predict the different stages of diachronic change. For the development from directives to conditionals, our research on the Dutch and Russian conditional imperative suggests that the following 'grammaticalization chains' are relevant.

1. Directive → Conditional Directive → Conditional
2. Hypothetical → Counterfactual (→ Pragmatic?)
3. Subject: Addressee → Generic → All persons

Differences between similar constructions across languages may then be regarded as resulting from the different degree to which such language-specific constructions have grammaticalized.[6] In order to substantiate our semantic map, we obviously need to look at more languages and at actual diachronic developments. An important question will be if the relation between directive and conditional meaning is unidirectional, as is suggested by the diachronic version of our semantic map. Examples such as (22), where a conditional sentence is used as a directive, suggest that the conceptual link between these notions may, in fact, be more flexible than is suggested by the grammaticalization approach.[7]

(22)   Als jij nou eens je mond hield.
       Lit. If you kept your mouth shut
       'You just keep your mouth shut'.

Notes

1. Independent of the subject being explicit or not, the particles are themselves also incompatible with a strictly conditional reading of the imperative. An exception is constituted by the '*maar eens*-construction', as in *Verlies maar eens je paspoort* ('Imagine loosing your passport') (Proeme 1991), which may also occur as the first part of the Dutch conditional imperative construction.

2. In Russian, the imperative does not have tense; whether the counterfactuality involved is 'to the present' or 'to the past' has to be derived from temporal adverbials or context.

3. An anonymous reviewer suggested that, in addition, the semantic map may provide a useful tool to describe the directive use of declaratives (*You will report to the dean tomorrow!*) and interrogatives (*Why don't you leave me alone?!*) .

4. In Section 3.2, we showed that uncontrollable events may occur in the imperative part of the Dutch construction (see example (17)), but this possibility seems to be as restricted as it is in the Russian CDIC.

5. To graphically represent the notion of a semantic map, we use the format of the 'synchronic grammaticalization tables' from Boogaart (1999), whose description of the perfect in English and Dutch may serve as a further illustration of the semantic map method.

6. Moreover, each language-specific construction constitutes a 'node' in a taxonomic network of closely related constructions (Croft & Cruse 2004: 262 ff.), so differences between languages are partly determined by the availability of alternative means of expression within the language, and the functional range of those other constructions.

7. We want to thank Theo Janssen for bringing this example to our attention.

References

Athanasiadou, A. & R. Dirven (1997) "Conditionality, hypotheticality, counterfactuality". In: Athanasiadou & Dirven (eds.) *On Conditionals Again.* Amsterdam/Philadelphia: John Benjamins, pp. 61–97.

Boogaart, R. (1999) *Aspect and temporal ordering: A contrastive analysis of Dutch and English.* Den Haag: Holland Academic Graphics.

Clark, B. (1993) "Relevance and 'pseudo-imperatives'". In: *Linguistics and Philosophy* 16, 79–121.

Croft, William (2001) *Radical Construction Grammar.* Oxford: Oxford University Press.

Croft, William & D. Alan Cruse (2004) *Cognitive Linguistics.* Cambridge: Cambridge University Press.

Duinhoven, A.M. (1995) "Had gebeld! De irreële imperatief". In: *TNTL* 111, pp. 346–364.

Fauconnier, G. (1985) *Mental Spaces*. Cambridge/London: MIT press.

Fortuin, Egbert (2000) *Polysemy or monosemy: Interpretation of the imperative and the dative-infinitive construction in Russian*. ILLC Dissertation Series.

Haan, S. de (1986) "Gebruiksmogelijkheden van de Nederlandse imperatief". In: C. Hoppenbrouwers et al. (red.), *Proeven van Taalwetenschap. Ter gelegenheid van het emeritaat van Albert Sassen*, pp. 250–260.

Haspelmath, Martin (2003) "The Geometry of Grammatical Meaning: Semantic Maps and Cross-linguistic Comparison." In: Michael Tomasello (ed.) *The New Psychology of Language: Cognitive and Functional Approaches to Language Structure*. Mahwah, New Jersey & London: Lawrence Erlbaum, pp. 211–242.

Proeme, H. (1991) *Studies over het Poolse, Nederlandse en Russische werkwoord*. Dissertation, Rijksuniversiteit Leiden.

Russkaja Grammatika (1980) Shvedova, N. Ju. (ed.) Vols 1–2. Moskva: Izdatel'stvo Nauka.

Trnavac, R. (2003) *Aspect and subjectivity: conditional imperatives in Russian*. Paper presented at the Tabu-dag Groningen, June 20th, 2003.

Auxiliary drop in Early Modern German[*]

Anne Breitbarth
University of Tilburg

1. Introduction

The so-called 'afinite construction' (Ebert 1986; 132ff, Ebert et al. 1993; 440ff) in Early Modern German (EMG) (ca. 1350–1650) is an ellipsis of finite auxiliaries (especially) in embedded clauses. It emerges towards the end of the 15th century (Biener 1925), spreads widely throughout the 16th and 17th centuries, but disappears again before ever taking over completely. Especially the latter fact makes it an interesting topic for studies on syntactic change and its principles. As modern Swedish shows a similar phenomenon of optionally dropping a finite perfect auxiliary in embedded clauses (Den Besten 1989,[1] Julien 2000), the afinite construction and especially its licensing conditions are also interesting from a more 'universal' perspective. Both topics — the driving motives behind the syntactic change as well as the the licensing conditions on such an ellipsis of a finite auxiliary — will be addressed in this paper.

2. The afinite construction

The hallmark of the 'afinite' construction is that the finite auxiliary is omitted from a periphrastic verb form. When the construction emerges in EMG, it first affects the perfect auxiliaries (*haben/sein* 'have/be' + past participle) and then spreads to passive (*sein/werden* 'be/become' + passive participle) and constructions with *haben/sein* 'have/be' + *zu* 'to'-infinitive. Furthermore, copulae (cf. (2)) and, rarely, future auxiliaries (*werden* 'be(come)' + infinitive) and modal verbs can be dropped.

In the analysis of a corpus of about 150,000 words, I found that 82% of these auxiliary ellipses occur in dependent clauses,[2] especially in relative and adjunct clauses, cf. (1a) and (1b).

Linguistics in the Netherlands 2004 21 (2004), 36–46.
ISSN 0929–7332 / E-ISSN 1569–9919 ©Algemene Vereniging voor Taalwetenschap

(1) a. (Schorer (1660; 5,01–02)

die grosse Noth / welche sie in dem Schmalkaldischen
the big   misery which they in the   Schmalkaldian
Krieg außgestanden [_]
war   suffered   [have]
'the big misery they suffered in the war of Schmalkalden'

b. (Aviso (1609; 3/6,1–2))

da er nun schuᵉldig [_] / wird gewißlich ein ernstlich
if he now guilty   [is] will certainly a   serious
Exempel an jhme statuirt werden.
example of him   made   become
'If found guilty, he will certainly be punished rigorously.'

As the afinite construction spreads, ellipses in coordinations distinct from regular conjunction reductions such as Gapping become possible (cf. Section 2.2 below). An example for what Schröder (1985) calls 'ungrammatical' coordination ellipsis because the overt auxiliary in one conjunct is different from the covert one in the other in subject agreement, tense, lexical item, etc. can be seen in (2), where overt *ist* 'is' is opposed to covert *hat* 'has'. There are also examples where all auxiliaries are covert.

(2) (Lavater (1578;17v,02–04))

So ist gmein   wenn der wyn im   kopff
such is common when the wine in.the head
überhandgenommen [_]   vnnd meister worden ist /
taken.over   [has] and   master become is
'This is typical when the wine takes possession of the head and becomes its master.'

In literary style, afinite constructions survive until well into the 20th century, however restricted to perfect and passive auxiliaries, and disallowing 'ungrammatical' ellipsis in coordinations. This literary use of uncoordinated afinite constructions is still felt familiar as 'archaic/poetic' style.

3.   The emergence of the afinite construction

The afinite construction only emerges in the end of the 15th century,[3] but spreads rapidly during the following two centuries. In some texts between 1650 and 1700, overt auxiliaries in embedded clauses are even exceptional, ellipsis being the default case (cf. Admoni 1980).

There are four questions suggesting themselves in this respect. First, why does the afinite construction emerge? Second, why does it emerge exactly at this time? Third, how is the ellipsis of the finite auxiliary licensed? And last, why does it never take over completely and even disappear again later, apart from very peripheral stylistic usages? The last question may consitute a certain challenge to current theories of language change as proposed by Kroch (1994) or Lightfoot (1999), but will be dealt with in a separate publication.

Concerning the first question, it has been claimed that the afinite construction was never more than a stylistic variant and as such a legitimate option within the grammatical system.[4] This is however where the second question becomes relevant: if that was indeed the case, why do we not find afinite constructions in Old or Middle High German? At least the perfect periphrases had developed a longer time before the emergence of the afinite construction (Ebert 1978;59). Nevertheless, perfect auxiliaries are only beginning to be dropped around 1500. Table (3) gives the percentages of dropped present perfect auxiliaries as opposed to non-elliptic forms.

(3)		1450–1500	1500–1550	1550–1600	1600–1650	1650+
ratio present perfect		3.6%	28.3%	70.3%	85.6%	90.1%

We therefore have to wonder whether there are conditioning factors related to this emergence. And indeed, there are.

As indicated above, EMG auxiliary ellipses are especially frequent in embedded clauses. Stronger in fact, they are especially frequent in embedded clauses with overt complementizers (there are no auxiliary ellipses in asyndetic embedded clauses in my corpus) and right sentential bracket. Here is the connection to the second question, that is, why they only emerge at the end of the 15th century: First, the possibilities for the formation of hypotactical constructions extend strongly in EMG, accompanied by an extension and refinement of the complementizer system as compared to MHG. The complementizer system is grammaticalizing in its present day form right in the period in question (Gelhaus 1972, Ebert et al. 1993). Second, the sentence-final positioning of the finite verb as a formal mark of embedded clauses is becoming fixed (Ebert 1980, Demske-Neumann 1990). Thus, the formal distinction of main and embedded clauses becomes explicit in this period. The increase in auxiliary ellipses in relative and adjunct clauses can be seen in the table in (4).

(4)		1450–1500	1500–1550	1550–1600	1600–1650	1650+
ratio relative & adjunct clauses		2.7%	14.6%	55.1%	65.3%	70.7%

It could therefore be claimed that due to these changes located in the T- and C-domains of EMG clause structure, the information coded in the finite auxiliary became redundant and could be dropped. This is what the third question is about and will be addressed in more detail in the following section.

4.   Traditional assumptions about licensing conditions

In the traditional literature, three assumptions can be found. First, for the cases of total ellipsis it is argued that they may not even be ellipses, but rather constructions in which the participle alone can function as a full-fledged predicate *instead* of a finite verb (e.g. Biener 1925, Schröder 1985). Second, it is assumed that the auxiliary ellipses in coordinations are conjunction reductions under parallelism (e.g. Grimm 1898[1967];202). Third, it has been proposed (Behaghel 1928;491) that omitting an auxiliary can be a strategy of avoiding the contact positioning of two eponymous auxiliaries at a clause boundary, thus a form of haplology. Neither of these assumptions is entirely plausible.

4.1   Total auxiliary ellipsis is no ellipsis

Schröder (1985), argues that if if there is no overt auxiliary (coordinated or uncoordinated sentences), there is no ellipsis at all, but the past participle (he is only talking about constructions with past participle, that is, perfect tenses and passives) is used as a full predicate *instead* of a finite verb. In the same vein, it is proposed by Behaghel (1928) that the old function of the participial prefix *ge-* as a perfective aspect marker, which as such could also combine with finite verbs, possibly caused the omission of the auxiliary to remain unnoticed. According to Ebert et al. (1993;386), however, resultative *ge-* + finite verb becomes very rare in the 15th century and disappears entirely in the early 16th century. As this is exactly the time when the afinite construction emerges, this correlation is doubtful. Furthermore, verbs with non-separable prefixes (5) which do not go with *ge-* and the existence of afinite constructions with copulae, or *haben/sein* with *zu*-infinitives, cf. (6), are evidence against this hypothesis.

(5)   (Lavater (1578; 12r,25–12v,01))

    eins teils darum-   / dz   jnen der   dingen jr   laᵉbē
    one   part because.of   that them these things   their life
    lang nichts   sonders begaᵉgnet   [_]
    long nothing special   encountered   [is]
    'For one part, it is because no such thing has ever happened to them in their whole life'

(6)   a.   (Herberstein (1557; 3v,23))

        wo   dein Haubt [_]   / daselbsten werden auch vnsere Heubter sein
        where your head   [is]   there.self   will   also   our   heads   be
        'where there is your head, our heads will be as well'

    b.   (Rauwolf (1587; 12,27–29))

        das also nichts   sonders inn der Jnsel   / dieweil sie nit
        that thus nothing special   in   the island   while   it   not
        bewohnet wirt / zufinden [_]   / dann allein die wilde Capparen
        inhabited is   to.find   [is]   than alone the wild   capers

'that thus on this island, which is not inhabited, nothing special is to be found apart from wild capers'

Last, there are no obvious syntactic differences between sentences with and without auxiliary ellipsis, nor any context restrictions as there are with freely used participles in Modern German like the imperative use in (7).[5]

(7)   Aufgepasst!
      attention.paid
      'Attention please'

4.2   Auxiliary ellipses in coordinations are conjunction reductions

While there are of course regular coordination ellipses like Right Node Raising (RNR) or Gapping[6] of finite auxiliaries in EMG as there have been in all historical stages of the language, many auxiliary ellipses in coordinations are rather similar to the uncoordinated afinite constructions as they do not have the properties known from Gapping or RNR. These cases include backward Gapping,[7] forward RNR, cases where no finite auxiliary is present in any conjunct, and Schröder's (1985) 'ungrammatical' coordination ellipses (cf. (2) above), contradicting a licensing under parallelism. Furthermore, there are apparent cases of elliptic auxiliaries in coordination with finite main verbs:

(8)   (Schorer (1660; 6,11–12))
      weil   aber   die Leuth vngleich [_]   / einer gern   dß /
      because however the people different [are] one   preferably this
      ein anderer was   anders **liset** /
      an other   something else   reads
      'but because people are different [and] one prefers to read this, another one something else'

All these cases suggest that it is perhaps only necessary that the abstract representatives of finiteness have to be parallel, not the actual identity of the auxiliaries.

4.3   Haplology?

Last, some researchers have suggested that cases like (9), which are rather frequent, are a form of haplology (Behaghel 1928;491, cf. also Ebert et al. 1993:442).

(9)   (Herberstein (1557; 2v,07))
      Wer erstlichen der   Reissen   Herr   gwest [_]   / ist zweiffelich /
      *who as.the.first the.*GEN *Russian's master been   [is]   is doubtful*
      'who was the first leader of the Russians is unknown'

This is not very plausible in the light of the many cases without such an adjacency at the clause boundary or those cases where the verb following the gap is a different auxiliary or even a main verb.

(10)   (Herberstein (1557; 3v,08–10))

Als   Swatoslaw seine Khinder versehen   [_] /
when Swatoslaw his   children taken.care.of [*had*]
ist er in BVLGERN gezogen /
is he in Bulgaria   drawn
'when Swatoslaw had taken care of his children he invaded Bulgaria'

5. The licensing conditions formalized

In this section, I will present a more formally grounded analysis of the licensing conditions on EMG auxiliary ellipsis. Two things we have discussed above will be crucial for the proposal. First, afinite constructions are overproportionally frequent in embedded clauses and second, coordination ellipsis does not seem to require full parallelism of the finite auxiliaries in the different conjuncts, but finiteness alone seems to be enough.

Generally, we can say that what an auxiliary itself spells out is finiteness information, that is, agreement with the subject and temporal information. The (semantic) function of finiteness can be seen as the anchoring of the verbal event in space and time (Svenonius 1996). It is generally seen as an operator mediating between the tense and agreement systems on the one hand (clause-internally relevant functional structure, the T/I-domain), and the higher, discourse/clause-externally relevant functional structure (the C-domain). According to Rizzi (1997), finiteness is a formal feature represented in syntax as the lowest functional head of the C-domain, thus establishing this link.

The question is, How can finiteness information be recovered in case its carrier, the finite auxiliary, is not spelt out?

According to Julien (2000), finiteness must be overtly realized for a clause to count as finite (Julien 2000;47). Besides the temporal dependency of the embedded clause from the embedding clause, Julien argues that the presence of an overt subject is a crucial factor in the licensing of the Swedish *ha*-deletion in embedded clauses. Nominative case has often been argued to be related to finiteness,[8] which is why she relates it to Rizzi's Fin-head. Julien assumes the presence of an overt subject to be sufficient to license the agreement part of the missing auxiliary.

As hinted at in Section 3, the presence of an overt complementizer is a crucial condition on EMG auxiliary ellipsis. We can assume that an overt complementizer or relative pronoun is a finiteness marker itself. Before we formalize this idea, we can also relate the obligatory presence of an overt complementizer in EMG afinite constructions to the recovery of temporal information.

For this, we can make use of an idea provided by Klein (1994; Section 11.2), namely that some complementizers can provide temporal information of their own (such as *before*) while others are transparent for this information to be passed down from the embedding clause (such as *that* or relative pronouns).

These intuitive ideas can be formalized as follows.

Using an idea from Chomsky (2001), we would like to draw a link between finiteness and the presence of a complex of C- and T-head in the derivation. Chomsky assumes that T is a defective head, because by itself it is φ-*incomplete*, that is, it does not by itself have a complete set of φ-features (person, number and gender). As a consequence, it cannot assign nominative case to a subject on its own as can be seen in infinitives. For C on the other hand, Chomsky argues that it is *always* φ-complete. T is φ-complete only if selected by C (Chomsky 2001;8). As argued for by Julien, the presence of an overt nominative subject is an indication for the finiteness of a clause, so this correlation is crucial.

We will now combine the observations and assumptions made so far. If C is always φ-complete and always entails a φ-complete T, it follows that as soon as there is a C head present in the derivation, the respective clause is finite and has an overt subject. The finiteness of a sentence is therefore given by the presence of a complete C+T-complex. Furthermore, as the functional information regarding finiteness is already given by the presence of an overt C-head (filled with a complementizer/relative pronoun), it is not necessary (for EMG) to make it visible by a finite auxiliary in T. This fits in nicely with our discussion of the diachronic factors in Section 3.

A φ-complete T allows the finite verb to agree with the subject. Julien's (2000) proposal, according to which the [+FINITE] feature of the clause is identified by the overt nominative subject can now be reformulated as follows: the φ-features in T are uninterpretable at LF, that is, they have to be 'neutralized' in syntax (*checking*) (Chomsky 1995, 2001). This is done by agreement with the subject, whose φ-features are always interpretable.[9] An overt subject should therefore be sufficient to license non-overt agreement morphology in T. Because of the close connection of T and C, built into the theory anyway, no extra [+FINITE] feature has to be assumed.

Thus, the connection of obligatorily overt complementizers and subjects in EMG auxiliary drop is accounted for — C indicates that the clause is finite and the subject recovers the φ-features of T.

A further assumption I would like to make is that part of the temporal information on T is or can be shared by C as well, cf. the possible temporal contributions of complementizers as discussed above (Klein 1994). I would like to claim that C contains temporal information not only in case of complementizers like German *nachdem, bevor* 'after, before' or *als* 'when', but *always*. In the general case, this will a sort of *default*-tense. In case of the complementizers just mentioned, it will be a specified variant. My proposal is that there is a feature [±PAST] in C by default, and that it can be specified as [+PAST] by a certain lexical selection (complementizers like *nachdem* 'after') or by the embedding clause. In all other cases, it will surface as [−PAST].[10]

(11)

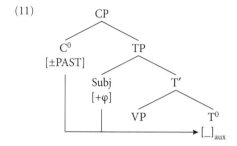

As for the 'ungrammatical' auxiliary ellipses in coordinations as well as those coordination ellipses which cannot be explained in terms of Gapping or RNR, we suggested in Section 4.2 that the licensing parallelism of the conjuncts is not formulated in terms of superficial identity but must be defined on a more abstract level. We now understand that it is the the C+T-complexes of the two conjuncts that have to be parallel.

(12)

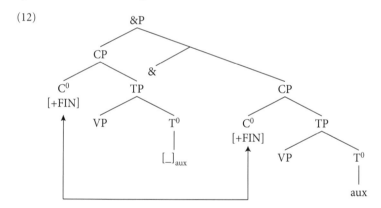

6. Concluding Remarks

The present paper tried to elucidate two facets of the auxiliary drop phenomenon known as the afinite construction in EMG. First, we discussed the conditions on the emergence of the afinite construction in EMG, identified as the refinement of the complementizer system and the development of the right sentential bracket. Second, a formal account of the licensing conditions to be assumed behind EMG auxiliary ellipsis was proposed. The crucial factor here was argued to be the spellout of finiteness information on C^0 (together with overt subjects), rendering further spellout on an auxiliary unnecessary.

Notes

* I would like to thank the audiences of the various talks I gave on this topic (at the Grammatical Models Group Staff Seminar in Tilburg, at ConSOLE 2003 in Patras/Greece, in the PhD-student's course on language change of the Graduiertenkolleg *Komplexität und Ökonomie in der Sprache* at the Humboldt University Berlin and the TiN-dag 2004) for giving me their feedback on different versions of the material presented in this paper. Special thanks to professor Karin Donhauser at the Humboldt University for the many fruitful discussions during my visit as a guest of the Graduiertenkolleg in the fall term 2003/2004. I am furthermore grateful to professor Ulrike Demske (Saarland University) and to the anonymous reviewer for the LiN-bundle for their very helpful comments.

1. Den Besten (1989) is the first to discuss the auxiliary drop phenomena of Swedish and archaic German in a formal framework, namely transformational grammar. His approach assumes that these ellipses are the effect of a domain-restricted deletion rule, with VP as its applicational domain, which is why it is bled by V2. As this approach is incompatible with the licensing approach taken in Section 5, which links EMG auxiliary drop to the overt expression of finiteness, it will not be pursued in this paper.

2. Reasons of space do not permit me to discuss my corpus analysis in detail. I have so far considered 16 texts partly from printed editions, but mainly from the Bonn IKP online corpus of EMG (http://www.ikp.uni-bonn.de/dt/forsch/fnhd/).

3. Cf. Biener (1925), Schröder (1985) and the research on the evolution of complex sentences in EMG by Admoni (1980).

4. Cf. e.g. Grimm (1898[1967]; 202f).

5. For extensive discussion of the syntactic, semantic and pragmatic restrictions on such constructions, cf. Fries (1983).

6. Gapping is a forward ellipsis including at least the finite verb, i.e. the shared part is overt in the first, but not in the second conjunct. RNR is the sharing of right-peripheral material, not necessarily a constituent. Cf. Hartmann (2000).

7. Argued not to exist by Maling (1972) (contra Ross (1970)), now the generally accepted view.

8. Cf. e.g. Branigan (1996), Platzack & Rosengren (1998).

9. φ-features on D are always [+int], cf. Chomsky (1995, 2001).

10. There can be more temporal information encoded in the syntax of a sentence that may help recover functional information on dropped auxiliaries. In my corpus, 76% (average) of the auxiliary ellipses occur in perfect tenses. Assuming that participial morphology is provided by a special Asp head (cf. e.g. Demirdache & Uribe-Etxebarria (2000)), we get two temporal-aspectual heads in the clause structure. Even if one does not want to go as far as Julien (2000) as to assume a biclausal analysis of the perfect tenses in which the participial morphology is the reflex of a non-finite past, it seems reasonable to assume that the Asp-head expresses temporal boundedness of the verbal event. Furthermore, the form of the main verb (past participle, infinitive, *zu*-infinitive, …) will delimit the choice among possible auxiliaries.

References

Admoni, Wladimir G. (1980). *Zur Ausbildung der Norm der deutschen Literatursprache im Bereich des neuhochdeutschen Satzgefüges (1470–1730)*. Berlin: Akademie-Verlag.

Behaghel, Otto (1928). *Deutsche Syntax*. Vol.III: *Die Satzgebilde*. Heidelberg: Winter.

Besten, Hans den (1989). "On the Interaction of Root Transformations and Lexical Deletive Rules". In *Studies in West Germanic Syntax*. PhD Diss., University of Tilburg; 14–100.

Biener, Clemens (1925). "Von der sog. Auslassung der Kopula in eingeleiteten Nebensätzen". *Die neueren Sprachen* 33; 291–297.

Branigan, Phil (1996). "Verb-second and the A-bar syntax of subjects". *Studia Linguistica* 50; 50–79.

Chomsky, Noam (1995). *The Minimalist Program*. Cambridge/Mass.: The MIT Press.

Chomsky, Noam (2001). "Derivation by Phase". In: Kenstowicz, Michael (ed.): *Ken Hale. A Life in Language*. Cambridge/Mass.: The MIT Press; 1–52.

Demirdache, Hamida & Myriam Uribe-Etxebarria (2000). "The Primitives of Temporal Relations". In Roger Martin, David Michaels & Juan Uriagereka (eds.), *Step by Step: Essays on Minimalist Syntax in Honor of Howard Lasnik*. Cambridge: MIT Press; 157–187.

Demske-Neumann, Ulrike (1990). "Charakteristische Strukturen von Satzgefügen in den Zeitungen des 17. Jhs". In: Anne Betten (ed.): *Neuere Forschungen zur historischen Syntax des Deutschen*. Tübingen: Niemeyer; 239–252.

Ebert, Robert P. (1978). *Historische Syntax des Deutschen*. Stuttgart: Metzler.

Ebert, Robert P. (1980). "Social and Stylistc Variation in Early New High German Word Order: The Sentence Frame ('Satzrahmen')". *PBB (= Beiträge zur Geschichte der deutschen Sprache und Literatur)* 102; 357–398.

Ebert, Robert P. (1986). *Historische Syntax des Deutschen* II: *1300–1750*. Bern/Frankfurt/M./ New York: Peter Lang.

Ebert, Robert P., Oskar Reichmann, Hans-Joachim Solms & Klaus-Peter Wegera (1993). *Frühneuhochdeutsche Grammatik*. Tübingen: Niemeyer.

Fries, Norbert (1983). *Syntaktische und semantische Sudien zum frei verwendeten Infinitiv und zu verwandten Erscheinungen im Deutschen*. Tübingen: Narr.

Gelhaus, Hermann (1972). *Synchronie und Diachronie. Zwei Vorträge über Probleme der nebensatzeinleitenden Konjunktionen und der Consecutio temporum*. Bern/Frankfurt/M.

Grimm, Jakob. (1898[1967]). *Deutsche Grammatik*. IV: *Syntax*. Ed. by Gustav Roethe & Edward Schröder.

Hartmann, Katharina (2000). *Right Node Raising and Gapping — Interface Conditions on Prosodic Deletion*. Amsterdam: Benjamins.

Julien, Marit (2000). "Optional *ha* in Swedish and Norwegian". *Working Papers in Scandinavian Syntax* 66; 33–74.

Klein, Wolfgang (1994). *Time in Language*. London/New York: Blackwell.

Kroch, Anthony (1994). "Morphosyntactic Variation". www.ling.upenn.edu/~kroch/online.html.

Lightfoot, David (1999). *The Development of Language. Acquisition, Change, and Evolution*. Oxford: Blackwell.

Maling, Joan M. (1972). "On 'Gapping and the Order of Constituents'". *Linguistic Inquiry* 3; 101–108.

Platzack, Christer & Inger Rosengren (1998). "On the subject of imperatives: A minimalist accout of the imperative clause". *The Journal of Comparative Germanic Linguistics* 1; 177–224.

Rizzi, Luigi (1997). "The Fine Structure of the Left Periphery". In: Haegeman, Liane (ed.): *Elements of Grammar*, Dordrecht: Kluwer; 281–337.

Ross, John R. (1970). "Gapping and the Order of Constituents". In: Bierwisch, Manfred & Karl Erich Heidolph (eds.), *Progress in Linguistics*. The Hague: Mouton.

Schröder, Werner (1985). *Auxiliar-Ellipsen bei Geiler von Keyserberg und bei Luther.* Akademie der Wissenschaften und der Literatur Mainz. Abhandlungen der geistes- und sozialwissenschaftl. Kl., Jg. 1985, Nr. 5. Stuttgart: Franz Steiner Verlag.

Svenonius, Peter (1996). "Predication and functional heads". In: José Camacho, Lina Choueri & Maki Watanabe (eds.), Proceedings of the 14th West Coast Conference on Formal Linguistics. Stanford/CA: CSLI Publications; 493–507.

Acquiring voicing in Dutch

The role of function words[*]

Suzanne van der Feest
University of Nijmegen

1. Introduction

In order to build up a representation of the Dutch voicing contrast in the lexical representations of words, the learner must first identify the relevant phonological contrast in the language. In Dutch, the main acoustic cue for voicing in initial position is Voice Onset Time (VOT): Voiced stops (e.g. /b/, /d/) have a negative VOT value of around − 4 ms., while voiceless stops (e.g. /p/, /t/) have a VOT value between 0 and 25 ms. (Lisker & Abramson 1964, among others). Thus, children acquiring Dutch need to learn to perceive and produce this VOT contrast. This paper will discuss early production data from Dutch children aged 1;0–2;8. The production of word-initial voicing will be discussed in Section 2 and 3. In Section 4, we will explore the hypothesis that the acquisition of the word-initial /d/–/t/ contrast is influenced by variation in voicing of /d/-initial function words. We argue that in the early stages of acquisition, this variation is what leads to an apparent delay of the development of the voicing contrast in coronals as compared to labials, and to more variation in productions within /d/-initial word-types. The conclusions are summarized in Section 5.

2. Production of plosives in initial position

To investigate the production of voicing in initial position, longitudinal data from 11 Dutch children were examined. The data were taken from the CLPF database from CHILDES (Fikkert 1994, Levelt 1994). This database contains ~20,000 utterances of monolingual Dutch children between the ages of 1;0–2;8. All word-initial /b/, /d/, /p/ and /t/ target segments that children produced with

ISSN 0929–7332 / E-ISSN 1569–9919 © Algemene Vereniging voor Taalwetenschap

correct place of articulation were coded for how voicing was realized. For instance, initial /b/'s were coded for whether the child produced them as /b/ (correct, e.g. *bus* (bus) (Tom, 1;5) or as /p/ (incorrect, e.g. *pus*, Noortje, 2;1). Similarly, voiceless segments such as /p/ were coded as /p/ (correct, *papa* (Catootje, 1;11) or as /b/ (incorrect, *bapa*, Robin, 1;8). Note that /k/ was not coded, because Dutch lacks a voicing contrast in velar stops. Also, fricatives were not examined because the voicing contrast in fricatives is disappearing in large areas of the Netherlands (Ernestus 2000, a.o.).

Figure 1 shows the error pattern collapsed across all children. The errors in initial /b/, /d/, /p/ and /t/ were collapsed, thus showing the mean error percentages in the production of voicing in labial and coronal stops. The main conclusion that can be drawn from these data is that children acquiring Dutch have not yet completely mastered the voicing contrast by the age of 2;6. This has also been shown by Beers (1995) and Kuijpers (1993).

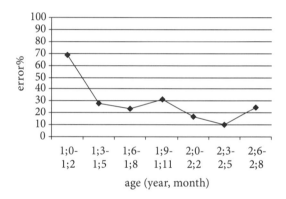

Figure 1. Overall error % in initial /b/, /p/, /d/ and /t/

In Figure 2, the errors have been split up according to place of articulation: this figure shows the errors made in coronal stops versus the errors made in labial stops. When we look at the group results, there is no main effect for place of articulation. While coronals appear to be produced less faithfully, there was no significant difference (*t-test*, $p=0.15$, two-tailed) between the errors in the productions of coronals (M = 24.3, SD = 9.04) as compared to labials (M = 21.5, SD = 6.3). Voiced and voiceless stops are not produced more or less faithful in labials than in coronals.

However, when the errors are split into voiced targets (/b/ and /d/) versus voiceless targets (/p/ and /t/), a clear effect is visible. In Figure 3 voiced targets produced incorrectly are coded as devoicing errors (e.g., /b/ and /d/ become /p/ and /t/, respectively) and voiceless targets produced incorrectly are coded as voicing errors (e.g., /p/ and /t/ become /b/ and /d/, respectively). We can now see that there were more devoicing errors (M = 32, SD = 11.6) than voicing

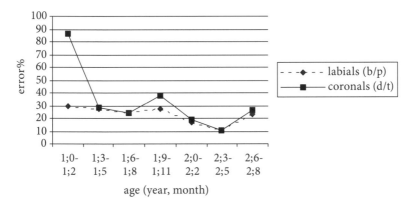

Figure 2. Direction of errors — place of articulation

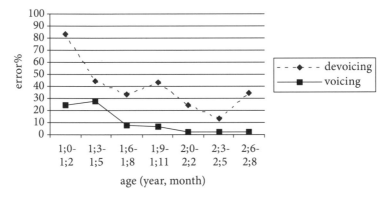

Figure 3. Direction of errors — voicing

errors (M = 8.17, SD = 10.08). This difference was significant (*t-test*, p ≤ 0.01, two-tailed).

Interestingly, when we look at the distribution of voicing in initial position for the target-words that children attempt, it turns out that there are more voiced than voiceless initial targets overall (4871 voiced targets versus 2244 voiceless targets words). However, even though more target words have initial voiced stops, children are more accurate in producing voiceless stops (see Figure 3). This shows that the frequency of voicing in the targets that children attempt to produce does not reflect the order of acquisition. Therefore, frequency cannot account for the difference in acquisition between voiced and voiceless stops in Dutch.

On the basis of these Dutch data and based on acquisition data from German and English, Kager et al. (forthcoming) argue that the privative feature [voice] is the active and marked feature in Dutch. This means that voiceless segments are unmarked for voice. If children have not yet specified the voicing feature in the lexical representation of a word, they will tend to produce the unmarked feature value, resulting in voiceless productions of voiced stops. In

Section 4.2, it will be argued that this is what happens in productions of Dutch /d/-initial function words, which remain unspecified longer due to the variation children encounter in the input.

3.   Acquisition of /d/ versus /b/

When the data were collapsed across children, no significant effect was found for how voicing was realized in different places of articulation. However, a significant effect is found when we look at the data from individual children. When comparing errors in the realization of voicing per segment, the patterns of four of the eleven children show more errors in coronal- than in labial-initial words. The data from these four children are shown in Figure 4. This figure shows the error percentages for /b/ versus /d/-initial words.

The children that show this pattern are the youngest children in the CLPF database (Tom 1;0–2;3, Eva 1;4–1;11, Jarmo 1;4–2;4 and Leonie, who was monitored for a short period between 1;9–1;11). The age difference with the other children in the database is minimal, but the other children appear to be in a later stage of the acquisition of the voicing contrast.[1]

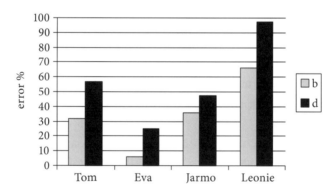

Figure 4. Graph with four children, /b/ versus /d/

The difference between the errors in /b/ versus /d/-initial words in this group of four children was significant ($\chi^2 = 23.49$, $p \leq 0.001$, 980 tokens), as was the difference between coronals (/d/ plus /t/) and labials (/b/ plus /p/) ($\chi^2 = 24.85$, $p \leq 0.001$, 1552 tokens). We also conducted χ^2 for individual children — the pattern held for each child. Thus, the youngest children show an effect for place of articulation, which was not shown for the group of children as a whole across all stages. We next examined whether the older children showed an effect for place of articulation when only the initial-voiced targets (i.e. /b/ and /d/ targets) were taken into account. We found that there was no difference between the number of errors made in /d/ as opposed to /b/-initial words

($\chi^2 = 1.20$, n.s., 3903 tokens). Moreover, the opposite pattern is never shown: no children in the database make significantly more errors in /b/-initial words.

This suggests that the /d/–/t/ contrast is acquired slightly later than the /b/–/p/ contrast. An explanation for this could be given by an articulatory account — because the closure of the mouth is complete when producing labials, it is easier to produce voicing in a labial (/b/) than in a coronal stop (/d/) (e.g. Van Alphen, 2004). However, a closer examination of the difference between content words and function words suggests that this explanation cannot account for the acquisition patterns discussed in this paper. Instead, we hypothesize that the difference between the error rates in labials versus coronals can be explained by a possible influence from the variation that children encounter in the input. This variation comes from the voicing in /d/-initial function words. We will now turn to a discussion of the role of function words in Dutch.

4. Function words

4.1 Content versus Function words

Many function words in Dutch are /d/-initial, such as *die* (that), *deze* (this), *dit* (this), *dat* (that), *daar* (there) and *de* (the). These function words are very frequent in Dutch, and function words comprise a large proportion of the /d/-initial target words children attempt — 23.9% of all examined target words were function words and 39% (1701 tokens) of all /d/-initial target words consisted of function words. Dutch has a few /t/, /b/ and /p/-initial function words (for example *bij* (with) and *te* (particle 'to'), but these words were not or very rarely produced by the children in the database. The majority of the produced function words (99%) were /d/-initial. In general, function words are phonologically less salient than content words (function words tend to have for example shorter vowel duration, weaker amplitude and simplified syllable structure compared to content words) (Shi et al. 1999).

In utterance-medial position there is a lot of variation in how voicing is realized in these Dutch function words (Ernestus 2000, among others). For example, '*Wat is dat?*' ('What is that') is often produced as '*Wat is tat*', with a devoiced /d/ in the function word '*dat*'.[2] This variation is allowed in utterance-medial position in standard Dutch. However, 66% of all plosive initial words in the database were produced in utterance-initial position (4699 out of 7115 tokens). In this position, variation in the voicing of the initial segment is not allowed in standard Dutch. This means that the children in the database were not merely devoicing segments where this is optional in Dutch, but also in utterance-initial position where this does not occur in adult speech. Also, the data of the four children who made more voicing errors in /d/-initial than in

/b/-initial words cannot be explained by a higher percentage of voiced stops occurring in utterance-medial position. On the contrary, these children produced 82% of their target words in utterance-initial position: thus, they devoice even more often in a position where this is not allowed.

Our next step was to determine whether the errors children made in the voicing of word initial /d/ came primarily from function words. In order to do this, we looked at children's production of voicing in content words only. When we look at the error percentages of just /d/-initial content words, the patterns of Tom, Eva, Jarmo and Leonie, match up more with the patterns of the other seven children's production of /d/-initial words (collapsed across function words and content words, as well as in content words only)

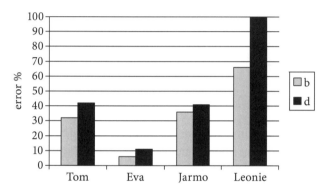

Figure 5. /b/ versus /d/, content words only

There is no longer a significant difference between their errors in /b/ and /d/-words collapsed across these four children ($\chi^2 = 5.08$, n.s., 624 tokens). At the level of individual children, only Leonie still made significantly more errors in /d/-initial content words than in /b/-initial content words ($\chi^2 = 9.42$, $p \leq 0.01$, 78 tokens). Thus, only for Leonie the claim could hold that voicing in coronals is harder to produce than voicing in labials. Note that Leonie was monitored for a short period of time, therefore providing less data than the other children. The productions of all other children in the database do not seem to be in line with an articulatory account.

These data show that the delay of the /d/–/t/ contrast versus the /b/–/p/ contrast in the children's earliest productions can be attributed to the errors in /d/-initial function words. In the next section we will explore the hypothesis that children leave the voicing specification in function words underspecified in the earliest stages of acquisition. These representations remain underspecified longer because children have not yet learned in which positions the variation in voicing is allowed: /d/-initial function words are thus produced mainly voiceless (the unmarked value). This is what results in the delay of the acquisition of /d/ versus /b/. If we assume that /d/ is underspecified in function words, the question is whether /d/ is only underspecified in function words or also in content words. This will be examined in the remainder of this paragraph. Section 4.2 will discuss previous research on the recognition of function words — in Section 4.3 we will examine the variation that occurs within the types that children produce. We will investigate whether the variation in /d/-initial function words also leads to more variation within the productions of /d/-initial content word-types.

4.2 The role of function words

The function versus content category difference is universally present in human languages. Previous research has shown that newborn infants (1 to 3 day-olds) are already able to discriminate lists of English function words from lists of English content words. (Shi et al. 1999) All tested infants were able to do this — even when the first language of their mother was not English. Thus, infants seem to have the ability to pick up on the typical prosodic features of content words versus those of function words. Six month-olds are still able to discriminate between the two categories, and even prefer to listen to lists of content words over lists of function words (Shi & Werker 2001). Further research has shown that 13 month-olds (but not 8 month-olds) can discriminate between real function words (e.g. *the*, *his*) and minimally different nonsense function words (e.g. *kuh*, *ris*) (Shi et al. 2003). These findings might suggest that 13 month-old children already have a detailed lexical representation of function words, and that infants from birth are already able to pick up on the differences between content and function words. This would not be in line with our hypothesis that children maintain an underspecified representation of voicing in function words. However, the following points should be considered.

First of all, studies on the recognition of function words have not tested recognition of real versus nonsense function words when only the laryngeal feature was changed in the non-word (e.g. the Dutch function word *daar* (there) changed into *taar*). It is thus still possible that children do not have a detailed stored representation of the voicing features of function words. Furthermore, Dutch children encounter variation in the realization of voicing in function words in the input. This variation is restricted to certain contexts, but these contexts do include positions where variation in content words is not allowed. As was mentioned in Section 4.1, '*Wat is dat*' (what is that) can be pronounced as '*Wat is tat*' with a devoiced /d/. This however is impossible in a phrase like: '*Wat is duiken?*' (what is diving): *'W*at is tuiken' is not allowed. Thus, our claim is that despite the fact that young infants are able to differentiate function words from content words and function words from nonsense function words, Dutch children at the earliest stages of production do not yet have a detailed stored representation of voicing features in function words.

Children need to acquire in which contexts the variation in voicing is allowed — only when they have learned that the variation is not random, can they specify the voicing value of the initial segment in their lexical representations of function words.

4.3 Variation within types

If children have underspecified voice representations in /d/-initial function words, what does this mean for the acquisition of the /d/–/t/ contrast in general? In Sections 2 and 3 we showed that children did not produce significantly more errors in /d/- than in /b/-initial content words. Our next question is whether the variation in /d/-initial function words only leads to more devoicing of these function words than is allowed, or whether there is also an effect on the productions of /d/-initial content words. If such an effect would occur, then children initially will allow for more variation in /d/-initial words than in /b/-initial words. In order to test this, we analyzed the variation within word-types. For each plosive-initial type (all /d/, /t/, /b/ and /p/ types), we checked whether the voicing in this word was produced consistently or with variation, i.e. produced either correct or incorrect by the same child at the same age. This would mean that for example the /p/ in *paard* (horse) was sometimes produced correctly (as *paard*) and sometimes incorrectly (as *baard*). Figure 6 shows the percentage of word-types that were produced with variation by the same child. The data of all eleven children have been collapsed in this graph. The error rates in /d/-initial word-types are split up into function words versus content words.

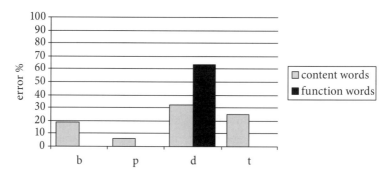

Figure 6. Variation within word-types — all eleven children

When looking at all types (function words and content words together), there was significantly more variation within coronal-initial types than within labial-initial types. This held for the four youngest children ($\chi^2 = 13.45$, $p \leq 0.001$, 648 types) as well as for the whole group ($\chi^2 = 48.26$, $p \leq 0.001$, 3005 types). This place effect can be ascribed to the fact that the variation within types is larger in function words than in content words. (The difference between the variation in content words versus function words in /d/ was significant ($\chi^2 = 90.6$, $p \leq 0.001$, 3021 types).) When looking at content words only, there was no longer a significant effect for place of articulation, neither for the group as a whole (($\chi^2 = 1.03$, n.s., 2686), nor for the youngest age group (($\chi^2 = 4.45$, n.s. on a $p \leq 0.01$ level, 742 types).

However, when we looked at /d/-initial words only, we did find a difference between the four youngest children and the seven older children in the database. For the older children, the variation within types of /d/-initial function words was significantly greater than in /d/-initial content words ($\chi^2 = 18.23$, $p \leq 0.001$, 674 types). This effect was also significant for the group of children as a whole ($\chi^2 = 16.72$, $p \leq 0.001$, 887 types). Thus, as would be expected on the basis of the input, children show more within-type variation in function words than in content words. This turned out not to be the case for the youngest children. In /d/-initial words, Tom, Jarmo, Eva and Leonie show just as much within-type variation in content words as in function words: the difference between them was not significant ($\chi^2 = 1.81$, n.s. 211 types). They show more variation in /d/-initial content words than the older children ($\chi^2 = 20.13$, $p \leq 0.001$ 894 types). This suggests that the variation in the /d/-initial function words carries over to the /d/-initial content words in the productions of these youngest children. An articulatory account predicting that voicing in /d/ is harder than voicing in /b/ would not account for these data: when voicing in /d/ is acquired later, we would expect more errors in /d/-initial words overall. However, the only effect we found was not for the overall errors in /d/, but for the variation within /d/-initial types compared to /b/-initial types. Thus, we claim that the variation in the function words in the input is taken into account when children are acquiring the /d/–/t/ contrast, resulting in more within-type variation in /d/-initial content words in the initial stages of acquisition.

5. Conclusions and discussion

Function words clearly do not facilitate the acquisition process of initial voiced coronal stops in Dutch. They form a highly frequent category in Dutch, and they are essential for syntactic bootstrapping in the early stages of acquisition. Therefore, infants' ability to distinguish content words from function words on the basis of their prosodic characteristics is crucial. The prosodic cues that make them different, such as the ones mentioned in Section 4.1, are therefore crucially present. But this does not mean that function words also provide clear evidence for the phonology of a language — in this case, for the voicing system of Dutch. In fact, assuming that children take all the acoustic input into account when acquiring phonological contrasts, /d/-initial Dutch function words make this process harder. The variation children encounter in these function words prevents them from specifying the voicing value in their early lexical representations of these words. This results in an apparent delay in the acquisition of the initial /d/–/t/ contrast compared to the initial /b/–/p/ contrast. We have tried to show that this cannot be explained by an articulatory account stating that voicing in /d/ is simply harder to produce. We argued that the difference can be ascribed to the influence of the function words. The laryngeal features in the representations of function words will remain unspecified longer than those in content words — where the child does not encounter variation. Thus, there is a carry-over effect to contexts (utterance-initial position) where this variation is not allowed. Initially, there is also a carry-over effect to /d/-initial content words, where the younger children allowed for more variation within types than the older children.

In conclusion, patterns in initial voicing in the productions of these Dutch children can give us an insight into what their early lexical representations may look like. Perception experiments with children in the same age ranges might provide further evidence for our claims on voicing in early lexical representations, and the role of the function words.

Notes

* The author would like to thank the members of the NWO project group 'Development of Phonological Representations for Perception and Production' (grant 360–70–100) and the audience at the TIN-dag 2004 for their comments.

1. This does not count for Noortje who was late in her overall phonological development (Fikkert 1994). She made more than 75% errors in both /b/ and /d/ (The difference between /b/ and /d/ was not significant ($\chi^2 = 0.0003$, n.s., 436 tokens).

2. Dutch is an interesting language, since both progressive and regressive voicing assimilation occur. Ernestus (2000) claims that the voicing of the /d/-initial function word in utterance position determines the voicing value of the preceding segment. Thus, when the function word is realized as voiced, this leads to regressive voicing assimilation and 'Wat is dat' will produced as 'Wat iz dat' with a voiced fricative. When the function word is produced voiceless, which is optional, the phrase will be produced as 'Wat is tat' with a voiceless fricative.

References

Alphen, P.M. van (2004). *Perceptual relevance of voicing in Dutch.* PhD dissertation, University of Nijmegen. MPI series in Psycholinguistics, Wageningen.

Beers, M. (1995). *The phonology of normally developing and language-impaired children.* PhD Dissertation, University of Amsterdam.

Ernestus, M. (2000). *Voice Assimilation and Segment Reduction in Casual Dutch. A Corpus-based study of the phonology-phonetics interface.* PhD Dissertation, Vrije Universiteit Amsterdam. LOT, Utrecht.

Fikkert, P. (1994). *On the acquisition of prosodic structure*. PhD dissertation, Leiden University. HIL dissertations, The Hague.

Kager, R., S.V.H. van der Feest, P. Fikkert, A. Kerkhoff & T.S. Zamuner (to appear). 'Representations of [voice]: Evidence from Acquisition.' In: J. van de Weijer & E.J. van der Torre (eds.) *Voicing in Dutch*.

Kuijpers, C. (1993). *Temporal coordination in speech development: a study of voicing contrast and assimilation in voicing*. PhD dissertation, University of Amsterdam.

Levelt, C.C. (1994). *On the acquisition of place*. PhD dissertation, Leiden University. HIL dissertations, The Hague.

Lisker, L. & A.S. Abramson (1964). 'A cross-language study of voicing in initial stops: acoustical measurements.' In: *Word* 20, 384–422.

Shi, R. & J. Werker (2001). 'Six-month-old infants' preference for lexical words.' In: *Psychological Science* 12, 70–75.

Shi, R., J. Werker & A. Cutler (2003). 'Function words in early speech perception.' In: *Proceedings of the 15th International Conference of Phonological Sciences*.

Shi, R., J. Werker & J. Morgan (1999). 'Newborn infants' sensitivity to perceptual cues to lexical and grammatical words.' In: *Cognition* 72, B11-B21.

Swingley, D. (2003). 'Phonetic Detail in the Developing Lexicon.' In: *Language & Speech* 46, 265–294.

Swingley, D. & R.N. Aslin (2000). 'Spoken word recognition and lexical representations in very young children.' In: *Cognition* 76, 147–166.

The role of language-specific phonotactics in the acquisition of onset clusters[*]

Paula Fikkert and Maria João Freitas
University of Nijmegen / University of Lisbon

1. Introduction

Recently, the acquisition of onset clusters has been much investigated (Goad & Rose 2004, Pater & Barlow 2003, Jongstra 2003, Ohala 1999, Barlow 1997, Freitas 1997, 2003, Fikkert 1994, among others). Most studies focus on onset clusters in isolation, and only seldom learning paths or development over time is discussed. Valuable as these studies are, this study shows that by considering cross-linguistic differences in the acquisition of onsets, development over time, and the language system as a whole, deeper insight is gained into the phonological system and the representations that children are constructing.

It is a well-known fact that children simplify onset clusters for quite some time before they start producing them correctly. Moreover, they do so in a very systematic fashion. A frequently attested simplification strategy is to select the least sonorous element of the target cluster for production. For onset clusters that obey the Sonority Sequencing Principle (Selkirk 1984, among others) — i.e. obstruent-sonorant clusters — the obstruent is realized. For clusters that do not obey this principle — usually, clusters consisting of a (palatal)-alveolar sibilant plus an obstruent — the obstruent is chosen as well. An account that relies on sonority-based onset selection is able to provide a uniform account for both types of clusters. Others have argued that the selection is only indirectly sonority-based: At first, children only realize the head of the onset constituent, but since the optimal head is the least sonorant consonant, both accounts converge for the initial stage.[1,2] Whether directly or indirectly, all accounts mention that an important role is assigned to sonority in onset selection. The data in (1) provide some examples from English (1a), Dutch (1b) and European Portuguese (1c). The patterns are highly similar in the three languages.

Linguistics in the Netherlands 2004 21 (2004), **58–68**.
ISSN 0929–7332 / E-ISSN 1569–9919 © Algemene Vereniging voor Taalwetenschap

(1) a.   English child language; data from Amahl (Smith 1973)

      [b̥eːt]   'plate'   [b̥aidə]   'spider'

      [d̥eːɪ]   'tray'   [d̥if]   'stiff'

      [g̥ɔt]   'cross'   [g̥ip]   'skipping'

    b.   Dutch child language; data from Robin (Fikkert 1994)

      [bat]   brand[3]   'fire'   [pije]   spelen   'to play'

      [tɪkə]   drinken   'to drink'   [tu]   stoel   'chair'

      [kɛin]   klein   'small'   [taːt]   straat   'street'

    c.   European Portuguese child language; data from João Pedro (Freitas 1997)

      [baʃu]   braço   'arm'   [ta]   está[4]   'it is'

      [te]   três   'three'   [paja]   Espanha 'Spain'

      [kawa]   Clara   *name*   [kaʃa]   escada   'stairs'

However, detailed investigation of longitudinal cross-linguistic data show that (a) there is considerable variation in the learning paths towards the adult target form, even for children acquiring the same language, and (b) children acquiring different languages that have the same surface clusters follow different learning paths. The first type of variation can be accounted for by looking at the child's whole system, as will be shown in Section 3.2 (see also Pater & Barlow 2003). If we consider, for example, *sn*-clusters, Eva first realizes the nasal, and at a later stage, the fricative (2a), whereas Robin has exactly the opposite pattern (2b):

(2) a.   Nasal > Fricative

      [nœyt]   snuit   'snout'   Eva   (1;6.1)

      [zuːpi]   Snoopy   *name*   Eva   (1;9.8)

    b.   Fricative > Nasal

      [fuːpi]   snoepje   'candy'   Robin   (1;10.21)

      [neːw]   sneeuw   'snow'   Robin   (2;1.7)

It turns out that Eva does not have initial fricatives yet, and therefore chooses the nasal first, whereas Robin produces initial nasals consistently correctly about six months later than initial fricatives. For him the fricative is the best option. In other words, the child's segmental phonological system determines the possible realizations of onset clusters.

The second type of variation is the main focus of this paper. We consider children's developmental patterns in Dutch and European Portuguese, two languages from different language families. On the surface they have fairly similar complex onsets. As we saw in (1bc) both Dutch and European Portuguese, henceforth EP, share two types of onset clusters: obstruent-liquid clusters (henceforth CL-clusters) and /s/-obstruent clusters (henceforth sC-clusters), as shown in (3) and (4) for Dutch and EP, respectively.

(3)   Word-initial surface clusters in Dutch

       CL: pr, br, tr, dr, kr, pl, bl, kl, fr, vr, χr, fl, vl, sl, χl

       sC: sp(r, l), st(r), sk(r), sχ(r)

(4)   Word-initial surface clusters in EP
CL: pr, br, tr, dr, kr, gr, pl, bl, tl, kl, gl, fr, vr, fl, ʒl
sC:[5]   ʃp(r, l), ʃt(r), ʃk(r), ʃf(r)

On the surface the onset clusters of Dutch and EP are very similar. There are a couple of minor differences, though. In the CL-cluster series, Dutch has velar fricatives, which EP lacks. Dutch lacks voiced velar stops, which are present in EP. EP allows 'tl' clusters, but Dutch does not. Dutch has 'vl' and 'sl', EP 'ʒl'. Both languages have 15 different CL-clusters. In the sC-cluster series, the place specification of the initial sibilant differs. However, if we consider the clusters that children attempt the set of clusters is comparable in both languages.

As children acquire lexical phonological representations on the basis of overt output forms, the null hypothesis is that children learning similar surface clusters will show a similar acquisition pattern. This hypothesis will be refuted in this paper, as children acquiring Dutch and EP clearly follow different strategies and acquire a different phonological system on the basis of similar overt input data. We argue that a number of differences in the phonological systems of the two languages give rise to different analyses of the same surface facts. Thus, whereas previous studies have focused on onset clusters in isolation, this paper argues that full insight into the matter can only be gained by considering the language system as a whole.

The paper is organized as follows. In Section 2, we describe the methodology of the study. Section 3 presents the acquisition data, of which a comparative analysis is presented in Section 4. Section 5 summarizes the conclusions.

2.   The methodology

The data come from two longitudinal corpora of spontaneous speech. The Dutch CLPF database (Fikkert 1994, Levelt 1994) contains data of 12 children acquiring Dutch as their first language. The children vary in age between 1;0 and 2;0 at the start of a one-year period of data collection. DAT-recordings were made every other week during play sessions at the child's home. The EP database contains data of 7 children acquiring the Lisbon dialect of EP as their first language. These children were videotaped during play sessions from between 0;10 and 2;0 at the start of a one-year period of data collection. One child was followed for two years (Freitas 1997).

From both sets of data all targets with word-initial clusters were taken and analyzed. We focus on the description of CL-clusters and sC-clusters here, as those are shared by the two languages. For each of the children the developmental patterns in the production of the two cluster types are described. We compared per child and per language which clusters are produced first and how different clusters are produced in the course of development. The main focus in this study lies on accounting for the similarities and differences in the developmental patterns.

3.   The acquisition data

3.1   Order of acquisition of different types of onset clusters

Comparing the acquisition of CL- and sC-clusters, the developmental patterns in (5) and (6) can be observed for Dutch and EP, respectively, where 'S' stands for sibilant, 'P' for plosive, 'L' for liquid, and 'F' for fricative. Most Dutch children acquire CL-clusters before sC-clusters, but a small subset of the children has the opposite order of acquisition.

(5)   Dutch children
    a.   SP   (Robin, Noortje)[6]
    b.   PL > FL >   SP   (Other Dutch children)

All EP children have sC-clusters long before CL-clusters, despite the fact that, as in Dutch, the latter type of clusters are much more frequent in the language than the former (Andrade & Viana 1993, Vigário & Falé 1993). About 10% of the intake, i.e. the words that children attempt to produce, contains words with CL-clusters, whereas only 3% contains an sC-cluster.

(6)   EP children
    SP >   PL >   FL   all children

Both the Dutch and the EP children acquire PL-clusters before FL-clusters, and similarly, SP is acquired before SF.

    There is a striking difference in the order of acquisition of cluster types: EP children acquire sC-clusters much earlier (around age two), than the Dutch children (around 2;6), whereas the opposite is true for CL-clusters. Dutch children start producing these clusters correctly around age two, which is three to six months earlier than EP children. The obvious question is: what leads to these different acquisition paths? Why do EP and most Dutch children differ in the order of acquisition of clusters? Another important question is why Robin and Noortje behave differently from the other Dutch children, even though their input is likely to be similar to that of the Dutch other children? Before we will turn to these questions in Section 4, let us first look at the two types of clusters in more detail.

3.2   CL-clusters

The first stage for both EP and Dutch children is the same: they realize the least sonorous element of the cluster. The final stage is the same as well. Intermediate stages show considerable variation for both languages. Four different strategies are attested in the Dutch data. Some children produce plosive-glide clusters, as shown in (7a) and (8a). Others produce clusters in which both members share place of articulation, as in (7b) and (8b). A third group produces just the sonorant (6c–7c). Finally, although not very frequent, vowel epenthesis is also attested (7d–8d).

(7)   Developmental pattern for plosive-liquid clusters (Dutch children)

	Stage 1	Stage 2	Stage 3
a.	P	[PG]	PL
b.		$[PA]_{PoA}$	
c.		[L]	
d.		[PvL]	

where [ ] indicates optional stage

(8)   Plosive-liquid clusters
   a.   Plosive > Plosive-Glide > PL

[kjant]	krant	/krant/	'newspaper'	Catootje	(1;11.9)
[tje:n]	trein	/trein/	'train'	Catootje	(1;11.9)

   b.   Plosive > (Plosive-Approximant)$_{PoA}$ > PL

| [tlatjəs] | blaadjes | /blat͡ʃəs/ | 'leaves' | Jarmo | (2;1.8) |
| [puuk] | broek | /bruk/ | 'trousers' | Jarmo | (2;3.9) |

   c.   Plosive > Liquid > PL

| [lok] | klok | /klɔk/ | 'clock' | Leonie | (1;10.29)|
| [liŋkə] | drinken | /drɪŋkə/ | 'to drink' | Leonie | (1;10.29)|

   d.

| [pəlaw] | blauw | /blauw/ | 'blue' | Tom | (1;6.25) |
| [kəlɔk] | klok | /klɔk/ | 'clock' | Tom | (1;6.25) |

Clearly, there is a lot of variation in the way children get to the end state. In part, the choice for PG or PL depends on whether a child has acquired liquids or glides first; in part, some children strive for a maximal sonority contrast in the onset (see Fikkert 1994 for more detail).

EP children, too, have an optional stage in which just the sonorant is realized, as shown in (9a) and (10a). This stage is followed by one in which the cluster is realized with an epenthetic vowel, as in stage 3 in (9a) and (10b).

(9)   Realization and development of initial plosive-liquid clusters (EP)

	Stage 1	Stage 2	Stage 3	Stage 4
a.	P	[L]	P(V)L	PL
b.		Complex segment		

(10) EP acquisition data
　　a.　[bɨsiletɐ]　bicicleta　/bisiklɛtɐ/　'bicycle'　　Luís　(2;2.27)
　　　　[lo]　　　flor　　　/floɾ/　　　'flower'　　Luís　(1;9.29)
　　b.　[tɨreʃ]　　três　　　/tɾeʃ/　　　'three'　　　Laura(2;2.30
　　c.　[pɾajɐ]　　praia　　　/pɾajɐ/　　'beach'　　　Luís　(2.2.0)
　　　　[flor]　　flor　　　/floɾ/　　　'flower'　　Laura(2;4.30)

The difference between stage 2 in (9b) and stage 4 in (9a) is not audible. In both
cases the cluster is realized. However, the data show a U-shaped development
for some children: an early stage in which the cluster is realized at the surface is
followed by a subsequent period with epenthesis between the two members of
the cluster, before the cluster surfaces correctly again. Laura's data in (11)
illustrate this:

(11) Laura's data
　　a.　[flor]　　　flor　　　/floɾ/　　　'flower'　　Laura　　(2;4.30)
　　b.　[fɨloɫ]　　idem　　　/floɾ/　　　idem　　　Laura　　(2;7.16)
　　c.　[florʃ]　　flores　　/floɾiʃ/　　idem pl.　　Laura　　(3;0.5)

Freitas (1997, 2003) argued that the first cluster is actually a complex segment,
and only the second time that onset cluster appear are they genuine onset
clusters. These clusters behave very similarly to the initial onsets in *quarto*
/kʷaɾtu/ 'room', etc., which are considered complex segments, not clusters
(Andrade & Viana 1993).

　　Overall, there appears to be a lot of variation: children show different
learning paths probably largely due to their different segmental phonologies.
No salient differences between the two languages can be discovered.

3.3 sC-clusters

At first, only the second member of sC-clusters is realized in both Dutch and
EP. Some Dutch children have an intermediate stage in which the sibilant is
realized, as in (13b), before realizing the cluster in an adult-like fashion.

(12) Realization and development of sC-clusters (Dutch)

Stage 1	Stage 2	Stage 3
C	[s]	sC

(13) Development of sC-clusters
　　a.　[tɛp]　　　step　　　/stɛp/　　　'scooter'　　Tirza　　(1;11.19)
　　b.　[su]　　　stoel　　　/stul/　　　'chair'　　　Tirza　　(2;0.5)
　　c.　[spokə]　　spoken　　/spokə/　　'ghosts'　　Tirza　　(2;5.5)

If we consider the EP data clear differences emerge. EP children do not use the
[s] only intermediate strategy. However, epenthesis is frequently attested, both

in front of the cluster and in front of the obstruent, as shown in (14) and (15bc). This is only reported marginally in the Dutch data (Fikkert 1994:112).

(14)   Realization and development of sC-clusters (EP)

Stage 1	Stage 2	Stage 3
C	VsC	sC
	VC	

(15)   EP acquisition data

a.	[kɛfɨ]	escreve	/ʃkrɛvɨ/	'write$_{imp}$'	Marta	(1;8.18)
b.	[iʃtɐɲɐ]	estranha	/ʃtrɐɲɐ/	'strange'	Marta	(1;10.4)
c.	[ɨkɛf]	escreve	/ʃkrɛvɨ/	'write$_{imp}$'	Marta	(1;11.10)
d.	[ʃtɛlɐ]	estrela	/ʃtrɛlɐ/	'star'	Marta	(2;1.19)

To conclude this section, whereas no clear differences could be found in the learning paths with regard to CL-clusters, those with respect to sC-clusters differ in important ways. EP children often utilize word-initial epenthesis, while this is rare in Dutch.

4.   A comparative analysis of acquisition of sC-clusters in Dutch and EP

There are two major questions that need to be addressed in this section. First, why do EP children acquire sC-clusters much earlier than CL-clusters, despite the fact that the latter type of clusters is far more frequent? Second, why do EP, but not Dutch children, employ the strategy of using epenthesis before sC-clusters? A final question concerns the Dutch data: why does a small subset of the children acquire sC- before CL-clusters?

In the developmental phonologies of EP children there is a striking coincidence: sC-clusters and fricative codas are faithfully realized at the same time, as (16) shows.

(16)   a.   Coda fricatives

[kaʃkɐ]	casca	/kaʃkɐ/	'skin'	Marta	(1;8.18)
[gɔʃtu]	gosto	/gɔʃtu/	'I like'	Marta	(1;11.10)

    b.   sC-clusters

[kɛfi]	escreve	/ʃkrɛvɨ/	'write'$_{imp}$	Marta	(1;8.18)
[ʃtɛlɐ]	estrela	/ʃtrɛlɐ/	'star'	Marta	(1;11.10)

This suggests that the initial sibilant in sC-clusters is a coda. The fact that a vowel is added to the beginning of the word, allowing the sibilant to surface in coda position points to a similar conclusion. Codas often are acquired earlier than complex onsets.

EP has a lot of external sandhi, giving rise to massive resyllabification in various contexts (Mateus & Andrade 2000). A special role is assigned to the very frequent verb *estar* 'to be', which surfaces as [tar], [ʃtar], [iʃtar] in the adult language and is targeted frequently by the EP children. This verb often forms one prosodic domain with a preceding word. As many words end in a vowel, the sibilant is often syllabified as the coda of the preceding word. These external sandhi phenomena provide ample evidence for the child that the sibilant in sC-clusters behaves as a coda. Dutch does not have comparable data.

In the acquisition of Dutch, the realization of coda fricatives is very early and precedes the correct realization of sC-clusters by many months. Therefore, there is no reason to assume the sibilant in sC-clusters to be codas. However, Dutch has a far more complex rhyme structure than EP (Fikkert & Freitas 1997). Whereas EP only allows one consonant — [l, ɾ, ʃ, ʒ] — in postvocalic position within the rhyme, Dutch vowels can be followed by two or more consonants, as in *lamp* 'lamp', *plaatst* 'places, 3P.SG.', etc. These words are often analyzed as consisting of a bipositional nucleus (long vowel) followed by a coda, which, in turn, can be followed by coronal obstruents, which form the appendix (Booij 1995). We therefore investigated whether the appearance of sC-clusters in Dutch child language correlates with the acquisition of complex rhyme structures. In (17) the different developmental paths of initial CL- and sC-clusters, and final sonorant-obstruent (-NC)[7] and obstruent-obstruent (-CC) clusters are represented.

(17)   Different developmental orders

a.	CL-	>	-CC					(Leonie, Tom)
b.	CL-	>	-CC	>	-NC			(Jarmo)
c.	CL-	>	-NC, sC-, -CC					(Elke)
d.	-NC	>	-CC	>	sC-			(Robin, Noortje)
e.	-NC	>	-CC	>	CL-	>	sC-	(Catootje, Tirza, Eva)

From inspecting (17) only one strong generalization can be made: if a child has sC-clusters, he or she also has clusters in final position. In other words, sC-clusters imply final clusters. What do final clusters and sC-clusters have in common? The answer seems to be that both have an extrasyllabic position: the /s/ in sC-clusters because it does not obey the SSP; the final C in final clusters falls outside the bipositional rhyme. The data do not show a different behavior for the two types of final clusters.

Recall that Robin and Noortje both had sC-clusters before CL-clusters. Both have postvocalic clusters before having any onset clusters. However, Elke, Eva, Catootje and Tirza also have final NC- and CC-clusters, yet they have acquired CL-clusters before sC-clusters. Frequency cannot account for the difference either: both Noortje and Robin attempt many more targets with initial clusters (particularly of the type CL) than final clusters. It seems therefore that the acquisition of CL-clusters is unrelated to that of sC-clusters. However, the presence of complex postvocalic consonant clusters in the child's system may provide the child evidence for special allowances at word-edges. Knowledge about the existence of extrasyllabic material at right word boundaries may helps the acquisition of an extrasyllabic position at the left word edge, and hence, sC- onset clusters in Dutch.

5. Conclusions

We have shown in this paper that it is important to consider the language system as a whole to interpret the data, both to explain differences between children acquiring the same language (i.e. the child's own phonological system determines what optimal realizations for clusters are), and between children acquiring different languages. Although EP and Dutch have similar onset clusters on the surface, children do not necessarily show the same learning paths. The phonological system of the language as a whole provides the child cues for analyzing the overt input forms. The analysis has shown that the initial sibilant in sC-clusters is analyzed as a coda in EP. To realize this coda children often produce an initial vowel in early stages of acquisition. This vowel does only surfaces in running speech due to external sandhi in adult EP. For Dutch, the appearance of sC-clusters requires knowledge of extrasyllabicity, and correlates with final clusters.

The differences between Dutch and EP child data can hardly be ascribed to ease of perception and/or articulation, nor to a universal order of development. It also seems that frequency is not playing a significant role either: In both EP and Dutch CL-clusters outrank sC-clusters by far. Yet, some Dutch and all EP children acquire the latter type of cluster earlier. Why some Dutch children acquire sC-clusters before CL-clusters remains a puzzling fact, which warrants further research.

Notes

* This research is supported by the NWO (project 016.024.009) granted to Paula Fikkert. We are thankful for comments from Janet Grijzenhout, Claartje Levelt, Tania Zamuner and an anonymous reviewer.

1. For /s/-sonorant clusters the two accounts make different predictions: a sonority-based account predicts the /s/, a head-based account the sonorant to surface. For an elaborate discussion the reader is referred to Jongstra (2003) or Goad & Rose (2004). Here, we focus on sC- and CL-clusters, as both languages share these.

2. Fikkert (1994) and Goad and Rose (2004) argue that because of differences in sonority profiles children are able to assign different syllabic structure to CL- and sC-clusters. In other words, the SSP is guiding the learning of prosodic structure.

3. Phonetic transcriptions of adult forms:
Dutch: blaadjes /blatɕəs/, blauw /blɑuw/, brand /brɑnt/, broek /bruk/, drinken /drɪŋkə/, klein /klɛin/, klok /klɔk/, krant /krɑnt/, spelen /spelə/, stoel /stul/, straat /strat/, trein /trɛin/.
Portuguese: braço /bɾasu/, três /tɾes/, clara /klaɾɐ/, está /(i)ʃta/, Espanha /ʃpɐɲɐ/, escada /ʃkadɐ/.

4. EP spelling suggests that these words start with a vowel, but this vowel is not produced in the Lisbon dialect of EP.

5. In addition to the clusters in (4) EP also has 3b(r), 3d(r), 3g(r), 3v. Thus, EP has voiced sC-clusters, which Dutch lacks. However, targets with voiced sC-clusters do not occur in the database.

6. Robin and Noortje did not produce any CL-clusters during the recording sessions.

7. Nasal-Obstruent clusters are acquired before Liquid-Obstruent clusters, but -NC stands for both.

References

Andrade, Ernesto & C. Viana (1993). 'Sinérese, diérese e estrutura silábica'. In *Actas do IX Encontro Nacional da Associação Portuguesa de Linguística*. Lisbon: APL. 31–42.

Barlow, Jessica (1997). *A constraint-based account of syllable onsets: Evidence from developing systems*. PhD Dissertation, Indiana University.

Booij, Geert (1995). *The phonology of Dutch*. Oxford: Oxford University Press.

Fikkert, Paula (1994). *On the acquisition of prosodic structure*. PhD Dissertation, HIL, Leiden University.

Fikkert, Paula & Maria João Freitas (1997). 'Acquisition of syllable structure constraints: Evidence from Dutch and Portuguese'. In *Language acquisition: Knowledge representation and processing. Proceedings of GALA '97*. Edinburgh: Edinburgh University Press. 217–222.

Freitas, Maria João (1997). *Aquisição da estrutura silábica do Português Europeu*. PhD Dissertation, University of Lisbon.

Freitas, Maria João (2003). 'The acquisition of Onset clusters in European Portuguese'. *Probus* 15: 27–46.

Goad, Heather & Yvan Rose (2004). 'Input elaboration, head faithfulness, and evidence for representation in the acquisition of left-edge clusters in West Germanic'. In Kager et al. 109–157.

Jongstra, Wenckje (2003). *Variation in reduction strategies in Dutch word-initial consonant clusters*. PhD Dissertation, University of Toronto.

Kager, Rene, Joe Pater & Wim Zonneveld (eds.) (2004), *Constraints in phonological acquisition*. Cambridge: Cambridge University Press.

Levelt, Clara (1994). *On the acquisition of place*. PhD Dissertation, HIL, Leiden University.

Mateus, Maria Helena & Ernesto d'Andreade (2000). *The phonology of Portuguese*. Oxford: OUP.

Ohala, Diane (1999). 'The influence of sonority on children's cluster reductions'. *Journal of Communication Disorders* 32: 397–422.

Pater, Joe & Jessica Barlow (2003). 'Constraint conflict in cluster reduction'. *Journal of Child Language* 30: 487–526.

Selkirk, Elizabeth (1984). 'On the major class features and syllable theory'. In Mark Aronoff & Richard Oehrle (eds.), *Language sound structure*. Cambridge: MIT.

Smith, Neil (1973). *The acquisition of phonology: A case study*. London: CUP.

Vigário, Marina & I. Falé (1993). 'A sílaba do Português fundamental: Uma descrição e algumas considerações de ordem teórica'. In *Actas do IX Encontro Nacional da Associação Portuguesa de Linguística*. Lisbon: APL. 465–478.

Number in the Yurakaré noun phrase[*]

Rik van Gijn
University of Nijmegen

1. Introduction

The category of number is often underestimated. In many languages, however, at closer inspection, it poses many difficulties. In Yurakaré — an unclassified language spoken in central Bolivia by approximately 2500 speakers — there is a basic opposition between a marked form =*w* and the absence of that marker. At first sight, it is not really clear what these two forms mean. They both seem to mean 'singular' in some contexts and 'plural' in others. In this paper I will try to come to an analysis with stable meanings for these two forms.

2. The problem

Consider the following data:

(1) a. shunñe -Ø[1] 'man'   shunñe =w[2] 'men'
     b. ewete   =w   'broom'   ewete   =w   'brooms'
     c. sibbë   -Ø   'house'   sibbë   -Ø   'houses'
     d. tomete =w   'arrow'   tomete -Ø   'arrows

In (1) we see all logical possibilities for the distribution patterns of -Ø and =*w*. Looking at these data, how can we establish the meaning of the enclitic =*w* versus its absence? The patterns of (1) are schematized in Table 1.

I will try to connect Table 1 with Table 2 below, which is Corbett's (2000: 80) summary of Jackendoff's (1991) classification of nominal semantic categories. I will argue for an analysis where the marker =*w* indicates [+internal structure], while its absence means [−internal structure] or 'unspecified'. Boundedness is indicated on modifiers, as will become clear.

In Table 1, nouns of type I form the largest group, this is the 'normal' case.

Linguistics in the Netherlands 2004 21 (2004), **69–79.**
ISSN 0929-7332 / E-ISSN 1569-9919 ©Algemene Vereniging voor Taalwetenschap

Table 1. Patterns of marking singular and plural[3]

Type number	Example	Singular	Plural	Section
I	shunñe	-Ø	=w	3
II	ewete	=w	=w	4
III	sibbë	-Ø	-Ø	5
IV	tomete	=w	-Ø/=w[4]	6

Table 2. Semantic categories of noun phrase (Jackendoff 1991)

Feature values	Category	Yurakaré-category
+bounded, −internal structure	individuals	singulars
+bounded, +internal structure	groups	inherently plurals
−bounded, −internal structure	substances	inherently singulars
−bounded, +internal structure	aggregates	plurals

I will refer to these nouns as count nouns (cf. Section 3). I call the nouns of type II 'inherently plural nouns' (cf. Section 4) and nouns of type III 'inherently singular nouns' (cf. Section 5). Section 6, finally, deals with 'hybrid' nouns, that have some characteristics of type II nouns, and some of type III nouns.

3. Count nouns

Count nouns, by far the largest group, are obligatorily marked for plural with the enclitic =w. In terms of Jackendoff (1991): individuals [+bounded, −internal structure] when singular, aggregates [−bounded, +internal structure] when plural. As can be seen in example (2), nouns of this class can denote humans, non-human animates (all animates are in this group), or inanimates:

(2) a. shunñe 'man'   shunñe   =w 'men'
     b. dyaya 'mosquito' dyaya   =w 'mosquitos'
     c. pojore 'canoe'   pojore   =w 'canoes'

Quantifying elements that imply a plurality obligatorily trigger the plural marker, as can be seen in the following examples:[5]

(3) a. lëshie shunñe   =w   (*lëshie shunñe)
         two   man   =PL   two   man
         'two men'
     b. bëmë   yee   =w   (*bëmë   yee)
         much/many woman   =PL   much/many woman
         'many women'

When a noun phrase is plural, elements modifying the head noun can be marked for distributive or collective. Understanding this will facilitate our understanding of some of the other phenomena that we will see. The collective marker *-ima* on a modifier indicates that the quality or quantity expressed by the modifier applies to the group as a bounded whole rather than to each member individually. The distributive marker *-uma* has exactly the opposite effect: it indicates that the quality or quantity expressed by the modifier applies to each member individually rather than to the group as a whole. These differences can be illustrated with the following examples:

(4)   a.   palanta matat -ima =w
           banana big   -COL =PL
           'a big bunch of bananas/*big bananas'
      b.   palanta matat -uma =w
           banana big   -DST =PL
           'big bananas/*a big bunch of bananas'

In example (4a), the marker *-ima* forces the interpretation of a bunch of bananas, while *-uma* in (4b) forces the interpretation where the bananas are viewed as separate entities. The marking of modifiers for collective or distributive is optional. In terms of the features of Jackendoff (1991), specified above, *-ima* adds boundedness to an aggregate, making it a group:

(5)   aggregate   >   group
      [−bounded, +internal structure]   >   [+bounded, +internal structure]

We might hypothesize that *=w* indicates [+internal structure], *-ima* then indicates [+bounded], and *-uma* is an overt marker for [−bounded]. I will come back to this hypothesis below in Section 5.

4.   Inherently plural nouns

There are a number of nouns that always carry the plural marker *=w*, even when they denote singular objects. I will argue that the entities that these nouns refer to are in fact seen as things that are composed of smaller parts, i.e. having internal structure. The group of inherently plural nouns includes body parts, some tools, ornaments and hair. Some examples are given in Table 3.

When these objects are modified, the modifier will in most cases carry the

Table 3. Examples of inherently plural nouns

Yurakaré	English	Yurakaré	English
bannaw	arm	puptaw	fan
tewwew	foot	meyetew	earring
wishwiw	tail	tenchew	necklace
ewetew	broom	simpatiw	braid

collective marker. Note that whether or not these nouns denote conceptually plural entities has no bearing on the number marking of the NP (-Ø vs. =*w*):

(6)   matat -ima ti-   bana =w[6]
      big   -COL 1SG- arm =PL
      'my big arm/my big arms'

These inherently plural nouns act like the bunch of bananas in example (4a) above. For instance, *ewetew* 'broom' consists of small twigs tied together around a stick; *puptaw* 'fan' are feathers tied together; earrings and necklaces are also composed of smaller parts such as pieces of wood, iron, beads, etc; and a braid is hair tied together. Less prototypically inherently plural are nouns like *bannaw* 'arm', and *wishwiw* 'tail'. An arm and a tail consist of several bones. Other body parts that are inherently plural, such as *pishishiw* 'lower leg' and *bolembolew* 'lower arm' also have more than one bone. A noun like *oteta* 'hip' consists of one bone and is a normal count noun rather than an inherently plural noun. On the other hand, *shishta* 'finger or toe', an entity which consists of several bones, is not seen as having internal structure, but as an individual entity lacking internal structure.

More generally speaking it is hard to find criteria where Yurakaré-speakers draw the line between individuals and groups on the one hand, and groups and aggregates on the other. The distinction between groups and substances can also be problematic. Examples of this are *shuppëw* 'urine' and *dyarru* 'maize or manioc beer', which are seen as inherently plural.[7] Psycholinguistic experiments should be carried out in order to shed some light on this issue. Nevertheless, there does seem to be a separate category of groups in Yurakaré.

5.   Inherently singular nouns

The nouns of this type are always grammatically singular. They never take the plural marker =*w* and they do not trigger plural verbal agreement either. Nouns that are in this class are among others typical mass nouns (i.e. substance-like things), scenery, some body parts, tools and utensils, crops, as well as other categories. Examples are in Table 4, Spanish loanwords are in italics.

These semantic types do not seem to have anything in common with each other. There are some semantic patterns that emerge, but we will see that we can not predict the nouns that fall into this class on purely semantic grounds. I will discuss each semantic type and we will see that almost every semantic pattern that can be observed has exceptions.

First of all, 'semantic' mass nouns generally fall into the class of inherently singular nouns (top left column in Table 4). With semantic mass nouns I mean nouns that refer to concepts that fit the canonical idea of what a mass is: an

Table 4. Inherently singular nouns according to semantic type

1. masses		2. scenery		3. body parts	
samma	water	püü	road	*perente*	forehead
asuja	sugar	puyni	sun	dyukku	buttocks
sëjsë	grease	lëtëmë	jungle	meyye	ear
awaryente	alcohol	mororo	hill	unti	nose

4. utensils, artifacts		5. crops		6. other	
kuchilu	knife	ñowwo	manioc	sibbë	house
werta	basket	winnu	pepper	ëshshë	stone
shoshto	comb	shilli	maize	bishmita	cigarette
martillu	hammer	korre	tobacco	*libru*	book

unbounded substance without internal structure (cf. the feature model of Jackendoff 1991 outlined above). There are, however, nouns denoting canonical masses that fall into the category of inherently plural nouns, like *dyarru* 'maize or manioc beer' and *shuppëw* 'urine' (cf. above).

When we look at nouns denoting scenery, it often concerns nouns that are uniquely referring, like *puyni* 'sun' or *lëtëmë* 'jungle'. Other nouns can be said to be canonically uniquely referring. For instance roads and hills are not uniquely existing entities, but they can be said to be unique to a village or a certain area. In Spanish conversation the Yurakaré generally do not speak about 'a road' or 'a hill', but '*the* road' and '*the* hill'.

As for the body-parts, the list includes concepts that prototypically come in pairs, like *meyye* 'ears', *dyukku* 'buttocks'. There are also concepts in this class that are prototypically singular, like, *perente* 'forehead', *unti* 'nose'. However, there are also body parts that prototypically come in pairs that belong to another class, like the inherently plural nouns *bannaw* 'arm', *tewwew* 'foot'. One might argue that feet and arms are not really symmetrical pairs and they perform separate functions, but there are also examples such as the following:

(7) a.   lëtta pullë   b.   lëshie pullë   =w
           one testicle   two   testicle =PL
           'one testicle'   'two testicles'

Testicles prototypically come in pairs, just as ears do. Still, speakers distinguish between singular and plural with testicles, and not with ears. This again shows that, although there seems to be some semantic transparency, it does not allow us to predict class membership.

There are many utensils or artifacts in this class. However, as we have seen, there are also tools in the inherently plural class, like *ewetew* 'broom' *puptaw* 'fan'. There seems to be no principal reason to classify *ewetew* 'broom' as an inherently plural noun, and *werta* as an inherently singular noun. This again shows that class membership is lexically determined.

The crops in this class are relatively small crops that grow inside a containing element (e.g. *shilli* 'maize', *winnu* 'chilipepper'). For instance bananas grow in bunches and they are in the count noun class. Corbett (2000: 80), following Jackendoff (1991), mentions that the size of the component parts may have something to do with whether nouns referring to them distinguish singular and plural forms. The larger the size of the component parts, the more likely it is they are treated as individual entities, the smaller the component part, the more likely it is that they are not individually distinguished. Although this is generally true for Yurakaré, a noun like *arush* 'rice' (from Spanish *arroz*) can nevertheless be pluralized.

A final remark that can be made is that there are many loanwords in this class, like *kuchilu* 'knife', *machitu* 'machete', *katcha* 'ax', *martillu* 'hammer', *libru* 'book'. Although certainly not all loanwords are in this class, it may be the case that more recent loanwords generally fall into this class. An in-depth study of the history of the Yurakaré and loanwords in the area is necessary to give a decisive answer on this matter.

In short, the general semantic tendencies mentioned here are neither necessary nor sufficient criteria for predicting whether a noun falls into the class of inherently singular nouns or not. It may be that there once existed meaning-related criteria to define nouns as belonging to the class of inherently singular nouns, but nowadays this choice is largely lexically determined, and should be learned. The fact that the system is gradually being lost — younger speakers tend to lose the class-distinctions, due to the influence of Spanish — may be a result of this.

Chierchia (1998: 55) mentions the non-availability of plural morphology as one of the defining characteristics of mass nouns. Furthermore, he claims that, although there are semantic aspects to mass nouns, it is eventually a lexically determined matter. This can be illustrated by the following English data (Chierchia 1998: 56):

(8) a.   shoes   vs.   footwear
     b.   clothes vs.   clothing
     c.   coins   vs.   change
     d.   carpets vs.   carpeting

In the mass examples (to the right) the atoms are backgrounded, made unimportant. This could also be the case with Yurakaré inherently singular nouns. Still, many nouns in the in this class can be counted without problems:

(9) a.   lëtta kabu
          one soap
          'one piece of soap'
     b.   liwi   biskotcho
          three bread

'three pieces of bread'

This is not problematic for the mass-analysis either. For English, Allan (1980) established that mass and count are lexically determined preferences that can be recategorized by syntactic environments, like in 'two coffee' in English, and that these countability preferences are gradual.

Within the group of inherently singular nouns in Yurakaré, there seems to be such a difference in countability preference. Nouns like *kabu* 'soap' in (9a) and *biskotcho* 'bread' in (9b) can apparently also mean 'piece of soap' and 'piece of bread', respectively. When modifiers of nouns like *kabu* or *biskotcho* are marked with -*ima*, the result is similar to that of plural NPs:

(10) a. lëtt -ima kabu
          one -COL soap
          'one package of soap (containing several pieces)'
      b. lëtt -ima biskotcho
          one -COL bread
          'one bag of bread'

Some nouns, particularly substances, are less countable. They need the collective marker -*ima* on an modifying element, which yields the interpretation of 'a bounded body of the mass X'. This confirms the analysis of -*ima* as a binder (cf. Table 5):

(11) a. lëtt -ima asuja
          one -COL sugar
          'one bag of sugar'
      b. lëtt -ima samma
          one -COL water
          'one lake or river'

Table 5. The meaning of -*ima*

category	features	+*ima*	category	features
aggregate	−bnd, +int'l. struct.	>	group	+bnd, +int'l struct.
substance	−bnd, −int'l. struct.	>	individual	+bnd, −int'l struct.

Modifiers of inherently singular artifacts also often carry the marker -*ima*.

(12) a. lëtt -ima werta
          one -COL basket
          'one basket'
      b. matat -ima kuchilu
          big   -COL knife
          'a big knife'

It is not very clear how the idea of boundedness should apply to these nouns. There are two possible analyses. One is that these artifacts are of the type *kabu*, in the sense that they consist of smaller atoms (e.g. several pieces of liana in the case of 'basket', a blade and a handle in the case of 'knife'). The other possible analysis is that the nouns in (12) are like *asuja* and *samma* in the sense that the literal translations of (12) would be 'one piece of basketry' and 'one piece of cutting material', respectively. Again, psycholinguistic experiments should be carried out in order to investigate the way these entities are conceptualized.

Taking the data of this section into consideration, we can conclude that the absence of the plural marker =w within this class does not precisely indicate lack of internal structure, since in plural environments (e.g. with a plural quantifier) the plural marker still does not appear. In those cases, the absence of the plural marker means 'unspecified for number'. The interpretation of the number of the complete NP then depends on the syntactic environment.

6. 'Hybrid' nouns

It is questionable whether we are dealing with a separate class of hybrid nouns, or whether these are simply inherently plural nouns with some deviant tendencies. Hybrid nouns act exactly like inherently plural nouns when referring to singular concepts. The difference becomes apparent in plural contexts, where hybrid nouns have a strong tendency to have zero marking for number on the NP and to trigger singular verb agreement. Examples are clothing items like *ossow* 'traditional shirt', *tarapu* (from Spanish *trapo* 'blanket, cloth'), and types of arrows like *tometew* and *turumaw*.

We can explore a similar line of reasoning to explain the appearance of the plural marker in singular contexts as we did with the inherently plural nouns of Section 4. Clothing items used to be made of several pieces of inner bark of a tree, thumped together at the rims. From this collection of pieces of inner bark, clothing items were made (cf. Richter 1930:391). Arrows are pieces of wood glued or tied together, and can therefore be analyzed as collectives. And indeed elements modifying these nouns are mostly marked with -*ima* for collective. Again, we do not have to adapt the meaning of the enclitic =w to be able to account for occurrences in singular environments. Now consider the following examples:

(13) a. tomete dula -Ø
          arrow   make -3
          'He made arrows.'
      b. së   =ja bëjta -y   kamisa bëmë
          1SG:PRN =s see   -1SG:s   shirt   much/many
          'I see many shirts.'

In (13) we see that the conceptually plural nouns are not only unmarked for plural, they trigger singular (zero) object agreement on the verb as well. This indicates that these nouns are grammatically singular.

There is no absolute grammatical rule that tells us when these nouns are and when they are not marked for plural, but there is a tendency that the higher the quantity, and the more unspecific the quantity, the more chance there is that these nouns are zero marked. This tendency is schematized in Table 6.

Table 6. Tendencies in plural marking of hybrid nouns

Quantifier	Number marking
lëtta (1)	=w
lëshie (2), liwi (3), lëpsha (4)	=w/-Ø
bëmë (many), no quantifier	-Ø/=w

I have not encountered singular encodings of the inherently plural nouns of Section 4, but it is quite possible that these nouns can in some circumstances be grammatically singular in plural contexts as well.[8] There is, however, a strong preference of hybrid nouns to be encoded as grammatically singular in indefinite plural contexts, which is absent in inherently plural nouns. Some speakers even disallow plural encoding of these nouns in these contexts.

Chierchia (1998:69) claims that the crucial difference between plural count nouns and mass nouns is that, "while atomic structure is foregrounded in a count noun (in that, by definition, it's extension singles out a set of atoms), such a structure, though present also in a mass noun, is present in it only implicitly in that the lexical entry is not directly associated with atoms."

Without going into the discussion about what exactly is the meaning of mass, this backgrounding of atoms may be the semantic effect of the absence of the plural marker in hybrid nouns as well, metaphorically extending the idea of mass to these nouns. The fact that a noun like *ewetew* 'broom' does not show the behavior of hybrid nouns is because, while people usually possess several arrows and shirts or trousers, people usually only have one broom, or maybe two. This makes it less natural to talk about 'brooming' than 'arrowing'.

7.   Conclusion

Let us go back to the initial question of the article. How can we explain the facts in example (1) above, here repeated as (14)?

(14) a.   shunñe   -Ø   'man'   shunñe   =w   'men'
      b.   ewete   =w   'broom'   ewete   =w   'brooms'
      c.   sibbë   -Ø   'house'   sibbë   -Ø   'houses'
      d.   tomete   =w   'arrow'   tomete   -Ø   'arrows

We have seen that we can explain all occurrences of the enclitic =w as a marker of [+internal structure]. When used in singular contexts, this marker is added to nouns that denote entities that consist of smaller, identifiable parts.

The interpretation of the absence of this enclitic depends on lexical features (some nouns simply cannot take the plural marker). Syntactic contexts can disambiguate, such as the presence of quantifiers. We can analyze nouns that never take the plural marker as mass nouns if we see mass as a lexically deter- mined category (albeit based on semantics).

Hybrid nouns often behave like mass nouns in plural contexts. The semantic effect of this is that the focus is on the collective class rather than the individual objects, much in the same way as English mass nouns 'furniture', 'basketry' and 'clothing'.

Notes

* I would like to thank Mily Crevels, Katharina Haude, Helen de Hoop, Pieter Muysken and an anonymous reviewer for comments on earlier drafts of this paper.

1. I do not assume the zero marker to be an actual morpheme. It is rather an opposition of the presence versus the absence of a morpheme. I use the symbol Ø for reasons of clarity only. The same holds for the Ø-markers in Table 1.

2. I consider the plural marker to be an enclitic because it usually appears on the final element of the noun phrase, independently of the order of elements within the NP:

shuyulë yee   =w vs. yee   shuyulë =w
beautiful woman =PL   woman beautiful =PL
'beautiful women'

The elements to the left of the final element are optionally marked for plural as well, but the minimally marked word is the rightmost element.

3. Whether nouns of the type numbers II, III, and to a lesser extent IV (cf. Section 6) are plural or singular, can only be indicated by context or quantificational elements.

4. Both forms occur; we are dealing with a tendency, not an absolute rule, cf. Section 6.

5. Abbreviations used: 1 first person; 3 third person; COL collective; DST distributive; PL plural; s subject; SG singular.

6. Some nouns lose their gemination when affixed.

7. The plural nature of *dyarru* may have something to do with the fact that there is visible internal structure: pieces of manioc root or maize. *Shuppëw* is harder to explain. It might have something to do with drops of urine, or it might be that urine is seen as the product of several actions of urinating. The verb 'to urinate' is a verbalization (*i-shupë*) which literally means to have urine.

8. Plural count nouns can in some circumstances behave like mass nouns, with the effect of backgrounding the atoms, e.g. decheche-Ø too [collect-3 bone] 'She was collecting bone', meaning several. The frequency of this construction, as well as the combinatory possibilities with quantifiers differs from these hybrid nouns. These constructions are probably related, however.

References

Allan, Keith (1980) 'Nouns and countability'. *Language* 56, 541–567.

Chierchia, Gennaro (1998) 'Plurality of mass nouns and the notion of 'semantic parameter'. In: Susan Rothstein, ed., *Events and grammar*. Dordrecht: Kluwer. Pp.53–103.

Corbett, Greville G (2000) *Number*. Cambridge: Cambridge University Press.

Jackendoff, Ray (1991) 'Parts and boundaries'. *Cognition* 41, 9–45.

Richter, Hans (1930) 'Kleidung, Schmuck, Bemahlung und Tatuierung der Yuracare-Indianer in Nordost-Bolivien. *Erdball* IV, 390–396.

Nominal tense marking in Movima

Nominal or clausal scope?*

Katharina Haude
University of Nijmegen

1. Introduction

In most languages, tense marking takes place on the verb or in the verb phrase. This is because tense marking usually serves to locate a situation in time, and situations are typically expressed by verbs. However, there are languages in which tense marking is not associated with the verb, but rather with the noun.

Movima, an unclassified language spoken in lowland Bolivia, is such a language. The opposition between past, the time span up to the morning of the day of speaking, and nonpast, the time from the morning of the day of speaking into the future, is not encoded on the verb, but by the article, which is an obligatory element of the noun phrase:

(1) a.   *aj wu'tu* 'the/a pot (nonpast)'   b.   *oj wu'tu* 'the/a pot (past)'

In a language that marks tense on the noun phrase, the question arises what exactly is temporally located. In contrast to verbs, nouns typically denote more time-stable concepts and have a referential function. Does this type of tense marking, then, have its scope only over the NP, like the English nominal prefix *ex-* in 'ex-husband'? Or does it have a clausal scope, comparable to verbal tense marking in other languages?

This question is discussed by Nordlinger & Sadler (2003), who label the first type "independent" and the second type "propositional" nominal tense marking. They find that languages with nominal tense marking can be divided into two typological groups. The first group consists of languages in which nominal tense marking serves to locate just the nominal concept in time (e.g. Guaraní). In the languages of the second group (e.g. the Arawakan language Chamicuro), nominal tense marking has its scope over the clause as a whole.

Linguistics in the Netherlands 2004 21 (2004), **80–90**.
ISSN 0929–7332 / E-ISSN 1569–9919 © Algemene Vereniging voor Taalwetenschap

Movima, however, is a language in which the same marker represents both types of nominal tense marking. On the one hand, the choice of the article mainly depends on temporal properties of the nominal referent. On the other hand, a past-tense NP usually implies that the predicate has to be understood as expressing a past situation as well. Hence, the distinction between propositional and independent nominal tense marking is blurred in Movima. The aim of this paper is to find out up to which degree tense marking has a strictly nominal scope and under which conditions it is applied for clausal tense marking.

This paper is organized as follows. Section 2 gives an overview of the forms and functions of the Movima article. In Section 3, I describe the circumstances under which nominal tense marking has a scope over the NP only. In Section 4, I discuss the cases in which nominal tense marking is used to mark clausal past tense. It will be shown that, although the scope of Movima past-tense marking is primarily over the NP, it is usually interpreted as clausal tense marking. Finally, Section 5 presents an idea on what may be the underlying reasons for the intricacies of Movima nominal tense marking.[1]

2.   The article: Forms and functions

The Movima article specifies the noun for semantic gender and number and indicates temporal and spatial properties of the referent.[2] The different forms are presented in Table 1.

Table 1. The Movima article[3]

	m	f	n	pl
unmarked	uj	i'nej	aj	ij
absentive	kuj	kinoj	koj	kij
past	uj	isnoj	oj	ij, (isoj)

The categories unmarked, absentive, and past indicate the spatial or temporal location of the referent with respect to the speaker and the speech situation. The unmarked article is used with nouns whose referents are located in the surroundings of the speaker at the time of speaking and with nouns denoting "absolute" concepts (cf. 3.1). The absentive article basically indicates that the nominal referent either exists somewhere outside the surroundings of the speaker or that it is within the speaker's surroundings, but inaccessible (e.g. when its exact location is not known).[4] With temporal and action nouns, it is employed to mark "immediate past", a subcategory of nonpast, which covers the time span from the morning up to the moment of speaking (cf. 3.2).

The function of the past-tense article will be specified in the remainder of this paper. Apart from this article, past tense can be specified by tense particles: *la'* 'before' and *kwil* or *kwilka* 'long ago'. However, the past-tense form of the article is usually sufficient for the encoding of past tense. In past-tense narratives, it is the only regular indicator of tense, comparable to past-tense verb forms in languages like English.

The masculine and plural past-tense articles are identical with the respective unmarked ones (the past-tense form of the plural article, *isoj*, is only used in remote-past contexts). I consider them different, homophonous morphemes, because their interpretation depends on the actual speech situation: when a masculine or plural NP contains the unmarked article and the referent is not present in the surroundings of the speaker, this usually implies past-tense reference.

3.   Nominal past-tense marking with scope over the NP only

In this section, I describe the cases in which the choice of the article is determined by properties of the referent, irrespective of the context. I will present the possibility of nominal past-tense marking in past-tense and in nonpast contexts.

3.1   Nouns denoting "absolute" concepts

One type of nouns always receives the unmarked article, independently of the referent's location relative to the speaker and of the temporal context. Nouns of this type denote "absolute" concepts, i.e. concepts which do not change location and which are conceived of as highly time-stable. Typical representatives of this type are nouns referring to specific places (as in (2)), institutions (3), and generic concepts (4). All examples contain overt past-tense reference, which shows that the marking of these nouns is not affected by contextual tense.

(2)   *kwilka   jo'yaj ij   dirinka n-aj   Aperema:to*
      long.ago arrive ART.PL gringa O-ART.N (place name)
      'Long ago, the *gringas* arrived at the Apere Mato (river fork).'

(3)   *isoj   ve'e:-piṅ   di' jelra=aj   ele:siya[5]*
      ART.PL.P fire-CL.long, thin REL light=ART.N church
      'the candles that illuminated the church'

(4)   *n-oł   dichi(ye:~)ye toł ma'nespa:na aj   tadoyni*
      O-ART.N.P.1SG child⟨PRD~⟩ INT like   ART.N sweet
      'When I was a child, oh dear how much I liked sweets.'

The fact that these nouns are not sensitive to the temporal context is an indication that the choice of the article depends on properties of the nominal referent: high time stability of the referent impedes the use of the past-tense article.

3.2 Temporal and action nouns

As opposed to nouns denoting absolute concepts, there are nouns which are always marked according to the temporal context, i.e. they receive the past-tense article in past-tense contexts. These are the temporal and action nouns, as represented by (5) and (6), respectively. Since these nouns denote concepts which are not time-stable, they are automatically marked for past tense when they refer to a time or event before the day of speaking:

(5) *jo'yaj=us   n-oj   la'   walaylo*
arrive=3M.A O-ART.N.P before afternoon
'He arrived yesterday afternoon.'

(6) *n-oj   ayloba-wa=y'łi   nosdé   n-aj   kole:giyo*
O-ART.N.P gather-NMZ=1EXCL over.there O-ART.N school
'when we gathered over there at the school'

With temporal and action nouns, another tense category can be encoded by the article: "immediate past", which is a subcategory of nonpast. It is marked by combining a temporal or action noun with the absentive article, which, of course, cannot serve as a marker of spatial location here. The time span covered is that from the morning up to the actual moment of speaking:[6]

(7) *che no-koj   ima:yoj jayna pó'mo=us   jayna*[7]
and O-ART.N.A morning then get.up=3M.A already
'And he got up (today) in the morning.'

In short, nouns denoting concepts which are not time-stable, such as times and events, are also marked according to the "existence" of their referents, i.e. they receive marking as soon as the time or event is over.

3.3 Nouns denoting present entities or humans

I will now turn to the intermediate types of nouns: those denoting concrete entities. As can be expected from the marking of the noun types described above, the condition for past-tense marking of NPs referring to concrete entities is basically that the referent has ceased to exist at the moment of speaking. This is shown by the following minimal pair, in which clausal past tense is indicated by the particle *la'* 'before', and the article is chosen according to the actual existence of the referent:

(8) a. *la'   iň jo'yaj n-aj   asna*
before 1SG.S arrive O-ART.N my.home
'Some time ago I arrived at home (where I am now).'

b. *la'   iň jo'yaj n-oj   asna*
before 1SG.S arrive O-ART.N.P my.home
'Some time ago I arrived at home (which doesn't exist anymore).'

However, there are more factors which influence the applicability of the past-tense article with concrete nouns, apart from the actual existence of the referent. These are the referent's presence or absence with respect to the speaker's surroundings, and its animacy (i.e., the distinction between human and non-human).

When the referent is present in the speaker's surroundings, it is encoded by an unmarked NP, independently of the contextual tense. (Accordingly, nouns referring to the speaker's body parts never receive past-tense marking — but see (22) below for an exception.)

(9) *n-oj   to⟨chi~⟩chik-a='nej   majni*
     O-ART.N.P little⟨PRD~⟩-LV=ART.F my.child
     'when my (present) daughter was little'

When the referent is absent from the speaker's surroundings, the choice of either the absentive or the past-tense article is primarily determined by the animacy of the referent: whereas non-human referents are automatically marked for past tense in past-tense contexts, irrespective of their actual existence (cf. 4.1), nouns referring to humans are marked according to the actual physical existence of the referent.

A living human referent who is absent from the speaker's surroundings is encoded by an absentive NP (cf. (10)). Also when the person has died recently, as is the case in (11), he/she is referred to in this way. When he/she has been dead for a long time, a human is referred to by a past-tense NP, as in (12a); absentive marking is ungrammatical in that case, as shown by (12b).

(10) *oj   ya:lowe-wa=kinoj kweya=us   ney=j   alkol*
     ART.N.P drink-NMZ=ART.F.A woman=3M.A DEF=ART alcohol
     '[He didn't like] that his wife drank that alcohol.'

(11) *kinoj   ney ay'ku   di' jayna   kayni*
     ART.F.A DEF my.aunt REL already be.dead
     'That (absent) aunt of mine who died [yesterday].'

(12) a. *la'   n-oj   soṅ-tino:na' kayni   isnoj   ay'ku*
          before O-ART.N other-IN:year be.dead ART.F.P my.aunt
          'Last year my aunt died.'
     b. *...kinoj   ay'ku*
          ART.F.A my.aunt

Thus, in the case of concrete referents which are present in the speaker's surroundings and with human referents, the possibility of past-tense marking depends on the physical existence of the referent at the time of speaking. Like the marking of absolute concepts and that of highly non-time-stable concepts discussed above, this shows that nominal tense marking in Movima basically has a nominal scope. The case of nouns referring to absent non-human entities, which are marked according to the temporal context, will be discussed in 4.1 below.

3.4 Past-tense marking in a nonpast context

In order to provide the final evidence that Movima nominal tense marking is basically of the independent type, I will now turn to the past-tense marking of NPs in nonpast contexts. As in past-tense contexts, this is determined by the actual existence of the referent.

In example (13), the present-tense context is provided by the personal pronoun *a'ko*. The past-tense NP refers to an entity that has completely ceased to exist (i.e., it is not the case that the dress is torn apart and therefore not recognizable):

(13) *a'ko*   *rey*   *łała⟨kwa~⟩-kwá=oj*   *do'we*
      PRO.N.PRS again seam⟨POSS~⟩-ABS=ART.N.P my.dress
      'This is the seam of my (former) dress.'

The following example shows that also in a future context, which can be indicated e.g. by the verbal inchoative aspect particle *loy*, it is possible to mark a NP for past tense if its referent has ceased to exist. This construction is common when the clausal head is an informative verb.

(14) *ajalo:maj loy oj*   *no:no di' pa:ko*
      tell:TR   INC ART.N.P pet   REL dog
      'I'll tell you about my (former, deceased) pet dog.'

However, it is important to point out that the past-tense article has this restricted nominal scope only when the clause contains another element which overtly indicates nonpast tense, as is the case in (13) and (14). When there is no such element, a clause with a past-tense NP is automatically interpreted as referring to a situation in the past. Consider the following example, which nearly forms a minimal pair with (14) above. In contrast to (14), there is no indicator of future tense, so that the entire clause is understood as past.

(15) *dokoy, kena:pa n-oj*   *joy-wa n-aj*   *Tirinra*
      good inform O-ART.N.P go-NMZ O-ART.N (place name)
      'Okay, I told you how I went (lit. of my (past) going) to Trinidad.'

This shows that, while Movima nominal past-tense marking is basically of the independent type, in its actual use its scope is often over the entire proposition. In the cases in which clausal and nominal tense diverge, this has to be explicitly marked, as in (13) and (14) above.

In any case, the situations in which a noun phrase can be marked for past-tense in a nonpast context are relatively rare. This is because entities which have simply lost their function or identity, of the type that can be referred to in English by the prefix *ex-*, are not automatically referred to by a past-tense NP in Movima. This could already be seen above with respect to the encoding of recently-died humans (cf. (11)). The loss of function or identity is expressed differently, e.g. by a past-tense particle, as in (16), or by the lexical aspect of the verb, as in (17).

(16)   *iso'*   *ij*   *wulna n-aj*   *kwil*   *asna*
       DEM.exist.P   ART.PL   plant O-ART.N   long.ago   my.home
       'I had plants at my former home (i.e., the place where I used to live).'

(17)   *bayachó=us*   *aj*   *wa:so*
       break:TR=3M.A   ART.N   glass
       'He (absent) has broken the (present) glass.'

While this shows that the applicability of nominal past-tense marking independently of clausal tense is restricted in Movima, the examples presented so far have shown that in principle, Movima nominal tense marking is indeed of the independent type. However, the following section shows that it is frequently employed for the marking of clausal tense.

4.   Nominal past-tense marking encoding clausal tense

Under certain circumstances, the existence of the referent at the time of speaking is disregarded and the past-tense article is used to mark clausal past tense. This occurs on a regular basis with nouns referring to absent non-human entities (cf. 4.1). Furthermore, even in the case of referents present at the speech situation and human referents, the article is occasionally employed for the marking of clausal tense (cf. 4.2).

4.1   Reference to absent non-human entities in past-tense contexts

When in a past-tense context reference is made to an absent, non-human entity, this is done by a past-tense NP, no matter whether the referent is still in existence or not. For example, the car referred to by the past-tense NP in (18) still existed at the actual time of speaking:

(18)   *jayna*   *lista*   *n-oj*   *joyaj-wa=oj*   *awto jayna*
       already   ready(F)   O-ART.N.P   arrive-NMZ=ART.N.P   car   already
       '[She] was ready when the car arrived.'

It can be assumed that nouns referring to non-human entities can be marked irrespective of the existence of the referent because the existence of a non-human entity which played a role in a past event is less relevant than that of a person or an absolute concept. With an absent non-human referent, therefore, the article can be used to indicate clausal tense.

    The following example shows that the possibility of past-tense marking is not related to the grammatical relation encoded by the NP. Transitive subjects can be marked for past tense, too:

(19) *nanará=oj*   *son↓-poy*   *di' pa:ko oj*   *charki*
      let.loose=ART.N.P other-BR:animal REL dog   ART.N.P dried.meat
      'The other dog let go of the dry meat.'

4.2 Nouns denoting present entities or humans

The past-tense article can be used for clausal tense marking even with the effect
that the restrictions imposed by the presence or animacy of the referent are
overridden. For some speakers and under certain circumstances, it can be more
important to mark clausal tense than to consider the existence of the referent,
even when it is human, as in (20), or when it is present at the speech situation,
as in (21) and (22).

(20) *n-asko*   *elaná=uj*   *pa'*   *isnoj   ma'*
      O-PRO.N.A leave=ART.M my.father ART.F.P my.mother
      'At that (time) my father left my mother.' [both absent, but alive]

(21) *jiwa:wa=y'ɬi n-oj*   *asna=y'ɬi*   *jayna*
      come=1EXCL O-ART.N.P home=1EXCL already
      'We came home already [where we are now].'

(22) *jayna   n-oj*   *imayni jayna   tivijni oj*   *chodo:wi*
      already O-ART.N.P night   already hurt   ART.N.P my.stomach
      'Then in the night, my stomach hurt.'

This shows that there is a certain liberty in the use of the past-tense article.
Speakers can employ the past-tense article as a marker of clausal tense, irrespective of the existence or non-existence of the nominal referent. As a result, the
marking of clausal tense is a major function of the past-tense article.

5. Towards an explanation

We have seen that the possibility of marking nouns for past tense depends to a
large extent on the actual existence of the referent at the time of speaking, which
shows that the scope of Movima nominal tense marking is principally over the
noun phrase. However, the criterion for past-tense marking is less clear-cut
than might, at first, be thought: the kind of concept denoted by the noun, its
animacy, and its presence or absence with respect to the speech situation do also
play a role. These factors can be arranged on a gradual scale according to their
influence on the possibility of nominal tense marking, as in Figure 1.

Thus, the possibility of past-tense marking of a noun cannot be predicted
exclusively on the basis of the existence or non-existence of the referent.
Depending on certain other properties of the referent, such as absence and
inanimacy, the past-tense article can just be employed as a device for marking

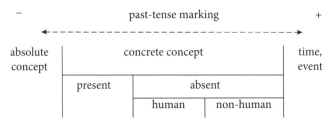

Figure 1. Possible past-tense marking according to the type of referent

clausal past tense. Apart from that, discourse-pragmatic devices can play a crucial role: speakers can use the past-tense article in order to mark propositional past tense, whereby the criteria presented in Figure 1 can be overridden.

From this it is evident that Movima nominal tense marking must be determined by more factors than just by properties of the referent. The following is an attempt to propose a model which captures these factors.

It has become apparent at various points in the above description that the spatial and temporal categories encoded by the Movima article are closely connected: only absent referents can be encoded by a past-tense NP; with temporal and action nouns, the absentive article marks a tense category; and nouns denoting "absolute" concepts are not only unmarked with respect to tense, but also with respect to space.

Under the assumption that the Movima article does not really separate space and time, I want to postulate that it marks nouns according to the (physical and temporal) "presence" and "accessibility" of their referents, be they concrete or abstract, in the perception of the speaker. With the example of the neuter article, which displays most distinctions since it is combined with concrete as well as abstract nouns, this is schematized in Table 2.

Table 2. The article as a marker of perceived presence and accessibility

oj	koj		aj
−present −accessible	−present +accessible	+present −accessible	+present +accessible

The features [+present] and [+accessible], which can only be expressed by the unmarked article, apply to the speaker's physical surroundings, on the spatial level, and to the time span from the moment of speaking into the future, on the temporal level. Hence, it can be said that Movima categorizes future events as accessible. (The encoding of absolute concepts is not characterized by this scheme because these concepts are not subject to deictic criteria.)

The absentive article indicates that something is perceived as either present or accessible, but not both. On the spatial level, it can be applied to entities which are within the surroundings of the speaker, but not accessible (e.g. invisible), or, as was illustrated above, which are outside the surroundings of the speaker, but in existence and therefore perceived as accessible.[8] On the temporal level, the absentive article marks the time span on the same day, but before the moment of speaking, as is reflected by its function with temporal and action nouns (cf. 3.2). Apparently, events that have occurred within this time span are perceived as accessible, even though they do not continue at the time of speaking.

The category encoded by the past-tense article, finally, indicates that the referent is not present and, furthermore, that it is perceived as neither spatially nor temporally accessible. This is the reason why it can appear in past-tense contexts, irrespective of the referent's existence: many entities that played a role in the past are not perceived as accessible at the moment of speaking, even though they may still be in existence. By contrast, an entity that has simply lost its function can still be physically present at the moment of speaking, in which case it is not encoded by a past-tense NP (cf. 3.4). The accessibility feature, furthermore, helps to understand why in Movima, past tense only covers the time span up to the previous evening: what has occurred the day before usually does not affect us as much as what has occurred on the same day, and can therefore be perceived as inaccessible.

While this is only a tentative analysis of the system, it provides a clue why independent and propositional tense are difficult to tease apart in Movima. The article is applied not only according to a measurable property of the nominal referent, but also according to the larger context of reference. Thus, we are not dealing with grammatical tense marking here, but with a temporal interpretation of a complex pragmatic category.

Notes

* I wish to thank my Movima consultants in Santa Ana del Yacuma, Bolivia. Furthermore, my thanks go to Mily Crevels, Rik van Gijn, Andrej Malchukov, Pieter Muysken, Rachel Nordlinger, and an anonymous *LIN* reviewer for their comments. All disclaimers apply.

1. My analysis is based on texts I recorded in Santa Ana del Yacuma, Bolivia. All examples are from these texts and from my field notes. In their representation I basically follow the Leipzig Glossing Rules.

2. Definiteness is not a category of the article. It is expressed by the demonstratives, which form a different paradigm.

3. The letter *j* represents the sound [h], which is in allophonic variation with [s].

4. The term "surroundings" means that the referent is perceived as being somewhere close by, e.g. in the same house or compound as the speaker.

5. Under certain circumstances, e.g. when a transitive subject is encoded by a NP in postverbal position, the article is encliticized to the predicate. This is only a phonological effect of the constituent order and does not mean that the article belongs morphologically to the verb.

6. Due to space limitations, the arguments for the exact delimitations of the temporal categories cannot be given within this paper.

7. There does not seem to be any direct relationship between the aspectual adverb *jayna* 'already' and nominal tense marking.

8. The feature pairs indicate that the absentive article is also a marker of evidentiality. Empirical evidence supports this.

Abbreviations

1EXCL = first person plural exclusive; 1SG = first person singular; A = absential; ABS = absolute state; ART = article; BR = bound root; CL = classifier; DEF = definiteness marker; DUR = durative; F = feminine; IMP = imperative; IN = incorporated noun; INC = inchoative; INT = intensifier; INTR = intransitive; LOC = locational; LV = linking vowel; M = masculine; N = neuter; NMZ = action nominalizer; NSTD = non-standing; O = oblique; P = past; PL = plural; POSS = possessive; PRD = predicative; PRO = personal pronoun; PRS = presentive; REAS = reason; REL = relativizer; S = intransitive subject; TR = transitive

Reference

Nordlinger, R. and Sadler, L. (2003) 'Nominal tense in cross-linguistic perspective'. Ms. University of Melbourne/University of Essex.

The perceptual development
of a British-English phoneme contrast
in Dutch adults

Willemijn Heeren
Utrecht University

1. Introduction

The world's languages differ in their phoneme inventories. While learning a
first or second language, a listener must acquire such a set of phonemes. In the
continuous flow of speech sounds, however, two instances of one phoneme may
show great diversity, due, for example, to speaker characteristics or speech rate.
Moreover, two acoustically similar speech sounds may actually be realizations
of two different phonemes. Native listeners tend to put sharp boundaries
between phoneme categories in their language. Generally, discrimination of
utterances taken from different sides of the phoneme boundary is higher than
discrimination of within-category tokens. Assuming that this discrimination
pattern is a native listener's end state, this would also be what a language learner
is trying to achieve. But how does one learn to perceive novel phonemes?

Early studies that tried to change phoneme perception through laboratory
training were not very successful (see Strange and Jenkins 1978 for a review).
Later studies, however, have shown that nonnative phoneme contrasts can be
learnt through relatively short laboratory training (e.g. Jamieson & Morosan
1986; Lively, Logan & Pisoni 1993). But there are also nonnative contrasts for
which training is unnecessary. Best et al. (2003) showed that nonnative phoneme contrasts that do not fall within the acoustic range exploited by one's
native language can be discriminated quite well.

To study the perceptual development of novel phoneme contrasts, we start
from two opposing hypotheses that have been posed to test learning of native
phonemes (Liberman, Harris, Kinney & Lane 1961): Acquired Distinctiveness
and Acquired Similarity. Both hypotheses deal with the degree to which within-

Linguistics in the Netherlands 2004 21 (2004), 91–101.
ISSN 0929–7332 / E-ISSN 1569–9919 ©Algemene Vereniging voor Taalwetenschap

category and between-category differences can be discriminated by a listener. The first hypothesis, Acquired Distinctiveness, says that listeners learn to perceive differences between those speech sounds that they are trained to categorize differently, although they were unable to hear any differences before learning this new phoneme contrast. After training, discrimination of stimuli on different sides of the phoneme boundary has improved. In support of this hypothesis, a training study by Jamieson and Morosan (1986) reported increased discrimination at the phoneme boundary without within-category improvement.

The second hypothesis, Acquired Similarity, states that both within-category and between-category speech sounds can be distinguished well before training. As a result of training, however, perceptual sensitivity to speech sounds that are categorized together decreases, such that only above-chance discrimination of the stimuli straddling the phoneme boundary remains. This way of learning seems similar to the way infants treat speech sounds during their first year of life (Pisoni 1991). Werker and Tees (1984a), for example, have shown that infants of 6 to 8 months of age can discriminate a natural speech contrast that their language environment does not contain, and that is not discriminated by adults from that language. But, after about 10 to 12 months these infants lose the ability to discriminate these phoneme pairs. It is not probable, however, that the infants' representations lie at a phonemic level.

The question this paper aims to answer is: how do Dutch listeners learn the British English /θ–s/ contrast, as /θ/ is not a phoneme of Dutch. Do Dutch adults learn the /θ–s/ contrast in accordance with Acquired Distinctiveness or Acquired Similarity? We tried to answer this question by means of a laboratory training study, run with Dutch adult listeners. Both before and after training, the perception of the nonnative phoneme continuum was assessed in absolute identification and discrimination tests. A control group that did not participate in training sessions, was also tested.

A subquestion that was addressed in the present study is whether the availability of knowledge of the language one is learning influences perceptual learning. Since most Dutch have learnt some English in primary and secondary school, the /θ–s/ contrast may not be entirely new to the participants. However, knowing that /θ/ is a different sound than /s/ does not imply that a Dutch listener can differentiate the two acoustically. Furthermore, the Dutch often produce /s/ when trying to pronounce /θ/ (Collins & Mees 1999), which shows that they have difficulties with the English phoneme. We want to find out whether listeners who are told which language they are learning, benefit from this knowledge, as opposed to learners who are left in the dark as to what language they are learning.

2. Method

2.1 Materials

Eight-stimulus continua were synthesized for the British-English phoneme contrast /θ–s/ by means of linear spectral interpolation (van Hessen 1992). The phonemes occurred in the onset position of a pair of (both in Dutch and in English) nonsense words: *thif – sif.* Nonsense words were used to exclude word frequency effects or lexical bias (cf. Ganong 1980). The phoneme continua were based on speech from six speakers of Standard English, both males and females. The location of the phoneme boundary in each continuum had been determined from a classification study with 31 native British-English listeners.[1]

2.2 Participants

Thirty-four students participated in the test. None of them studied English. All were native speakers of Dutch and reported normal hearing. Half of the subjects received training between pretest and posttest. The other half, the control group, participated only in pretest and posttest, with a time interval of approximately a week.

2.3 Design

The experiment was a pretest-posttest design. In both pretest and posttest four interval AX (4IAX) discrimination and absolute identification with speech from one male speaker were administered. At the end of the posttest a short questionnaire was given. In contrast with earlier training studies, we did not present written labels to our participants, but introduced the categories by means of pictures. This forced the listeners to figure out the acoustic differences by themselves.

On each trial of 4IAX discrimination, two different stimuli A and B were presented in one of eight possible orders: AB–AA, AA–BA, BA–AA, AA–AB, BB–AB, BB–BA, AB–BB or BA–BB. The listener had to indicate whether the first or the second pair consisted of the same stimuli. From the eight stimuli in the continuum, pairs A,B were chosen at either a one-step or a three-step distance. For example, a possible three-step trial is: 14–11. Learning by Acquired Distinctiveness would become most apparent in the one-step test, since the discrimination level in this test was low from the beginning. On the other hand, learning by Acquired Similarity would show in the three-step test, since its initially high discrimination levels could fall as a result of training. The 4IAX discrimination test was expected to reflect both phonemic and auditory perception of the stimulus pairs (Pisoni 1975; Gerrits 2001).

In absolute identification the listener has as many response options as there are stimuli. Since the listener is asked to indicate exactly which stimulus he heard, this test gives us insight into the listeners' control over the continuum.

For training, a classification design with trial-by-trial feedback on the correctness of the participants' responses was used. Classification was preferred over discrimination, since it directs the participants' attention towards the existence of two categories (e.g. Jamieson & Morosan 1986). The training materials consisted of phoneme continua from five speakers, both males and females, other than the test speaker. Speaker variation was included to encourage robust category formation (Lively et al. 1993).

2.4 Procedure

Listeners were tested individually. Half of them were told that they would hear English nonsense words, the other half of the participants were told that they would hear words from a foreign language. All experiments were run in a relatively quiet room at the Utrecht Institute of Linguistics OTS. A laptop computer was used both to present the stimuli at random and to register responses. Stimuli were presented over Beyerdynamic DT 770 headphones at a comfortable listening level.

The pretest was completed on the first day. On subsequent days, training sessions were run until the listener classified the new phoneme contrast correctly in at least 85% of the trials. On each training session, one to four training tests of 480 trials each were run. On the final day the posttest took place. This test was of a similar content as the pretest, apart from a short questionnaire that was given after the listening tests. In this, the listeners were asked about the spelling of the newly learnt words and their experience with foreign languages. The following subsections will discuss the procedures of the listening tests in more detail.

2.4.1 4IAX discrimination

The first test administered during pretest and posttest was 4IAX discrimination. This test was given twice, once with one-step stimulus pairs (i.e. 1–2, 2–3, …, 7–8) and once with three-step stimulus pairs (i.e. 1–4, 2–5, …, 5–8). The order of these tests was balanced across subjects.

Listeners received written instructions in which they were asked to indicate whether the first or the second word pair they heard consisted of the same stimuli. It was stressed that differences could be small. Responses were given by striking one of two keys on the computer's keyboard. A short task introduction was given, consisting of eight four-step stimulus pairs from the same continuum. Inter-stimulus intervals were set at 300 ms, inter-pair intervals at 500 ms, and response times were unlimited. The eight different orders per stimulus pair were each presented four times, resulting in 224 trials for the one-step test ($=4$ repetitions $\times 7$ stimulus pairs $\times 8$ possible orders) and 160 trials in the three-step test ($=4$ repetitions $\times 5$ stimulus pairs $\times 8$ possible orders). Trial order was randomized and there were three short breaks at regular intervals.

2.4.2 *Absolute identification*

The second test in pre- and posttest was absolute identification. Listeners received written instructions, telling them to indicate exactly which stimulus they had heard from the continuum. The instructions included a picture of a row of eight buttons numbered 1 to 8 from left to right. Over the first and eighth buttons, pictures of a man wearing differently colored headphones were shown. It was explained that each button hid a unique word. The words changed in steps from the name of the first man (behind button 1) to the name of the second man (behind button 8). Next, the stimuli were introduced five times in increasing, decreasing and random sequences. Listeners were instructed to listen very carefully and to try to remember which button corresponded to which word. During testing, stimuli were presented 20 times in random order, which resulted in a total of 160 trials. Listeners responded by mouse-clicking one of eight on-screen buttons. Response times were unlimited and there were two short breaks at regular intervals.

2.4.3 *Classification training with feedback*

During training, a classification design was used. The categories were represented by the pictures of the men and were introduced as the men's names. The listeners had to reach a mean score of at least 85% correct identifications over two subsequent training tests before proceeding to the posttest. The test was introduced by the pronunciation of both endpoint stimuli by each of the five training speakers.

Listeners received immediate feedback on each trial, informing them of the correctness of their choice. After every quarter of the total number of trials a break was given. During each break, and also at the end of a training test, the percentage of correct responses so far was shown. The training tests each contained 12 repetitions per stimulus, resulting in 480 trials ($=5$ speakers $\times 8$ stimuli $\times 12$ repetitions).

3.   Results

Training results were represented as percentages of *sif*-responses per stimulus for each of the five speakers. Next, the phoneme boundary was determined at the 50%-point for each of the five speakers in the training set and for each listener separately. Also, boundary widths were determined by calculating the

25–75% range. Boundary widths reflect the steepness of the boundary. For 4IAX discrimination, percentages of correct responses were determined per stimulus. From absolute identification results, the mean responses to each of the stimuli and their variances were determined.

3.1 Training

The participants' results from the first and the last training session were compared to the English norm defined by 31 native listeners. The mean boundaries in the first and last training sessions differed significantly from those defined by the English listeners (F[1,221]=7.9, p=.005 and F[1,222]=7.7, p=.006, respectively). Post-hoc analyses showed, however, that the mean boundary of only one speaker differed from the English norm in both training sessions. The Dutch listeners perceived more stimuli as /s/. In addition, the boundary value of one more speaker in the last training differed from that of the English. Listeners again judged more stimuli as /s/.

The results from the first training session did not lead to boundary width values in 36% of the cases: usually, no 25%-points were found, which means that listeners did not consistently choose the /θ/ category for stimuli at that end of the continuum. In the last training session, this number had decreased to only 6.3%, approximately equal to the number of cases the natives missed (6.5%). The boundary widths of the listeners for whom the ranges were defined differed significantly from the native English ones in the first training session (F[1,186]=52.4, p<.001). In the last training session, however, these differences were no longer present.

3.2 4IAX discrimination

For one-step 4IAX discrimination, a repeated measures ANOVA was run with within-subjects factors Test (2) and Stimulus Pair (7), and between-subjects factors Listener Group (2) and Language (2). The results are shown in Figure 1.

First of all, a main effect of Test was found (F[1,30]=14.9, p=.001). Listeners gave more correct answers in the posttest than in the pretest. Secondly, a main effect of Stimulus Pair was found (F[6,180]=10.2, p<.001). This means that listeners were not equally good at distinguishing all pairs of stimuli.

No main effect of Listener Group or Language was found. The absence of these effects means that the test listeners did not perform considerably better than the controls, and that listeners in the English condition did not benefit from their knowledge of what language they were attending. A post-hoc ANOVA on just the posttest data did reveal an effect of Listener Group (F[1,224]=7.5, p=.007): the trained listeners scored better than those in the control group.

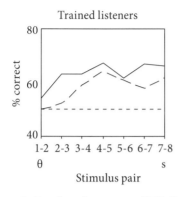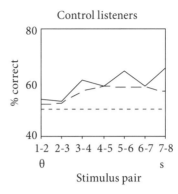

Figure 1. Results of one-step 4IAX discrimination of pretest (dashed) and posttest (solid) with a reference line at chance level.

Three-step 4IAX discrimination showed similar results. A repeated measures ANOVA resulted in main effects of Test ($F[1,30]=13.4$, $p=.001$) and Stimulus Pair ($F[3.4,101.4]=9.3$, $p<.001$). Again, no main effect of Listener Group of Language was found. A post-hoc ANOVA on the posttest data showed that trained listeners performed better than the controls ($F[1,155]=10.8$, $p=.001$).

3.3 Absolute identification

A repeated measures ANOVA was run on the mean responses with within-subjects factors Test (2) and Stimulus (8) and between-subjects factors Listener Group (2) and Language (2).

Firstly, a Test × Stimulus interaction ($F[4.5,136]=3.9$, $p=.003$) was found. At the /θ/-end of the continuum, participants became better at identifying the stimuli, while this was not the case at the /s/-end. This can be seen in Figure 2 by the trend towards the ideal case of absolute identification at the /θ/-end only. Furthermore, main effects of Test ($F[1,30]=28.2$, $p<.001$) and Stimulus ($F[2.6,78.3]=794.1$, $p<.001$) were found. But again, no effects of the between-subjects factors Listener Group and Language were present.

The repeated measures ANOVA on the mean variances showed main effects of Test ($F[1,30]=20.6$, $p<.001$) and of Stimulus ($F[4.3,129.7]=5.5$, $p<.001$). Posttest variances were smaller than those in the pretest, meaning that participants had become better at identifying the stimuli.

In sum, differences between pretest and posttest were clearly present in the three tests. Trained listeners' progress, however, was hard to discriminate from that of control listeners. The fact that some test listeners needed only a few training sessions to reach criterion may partly account for this. In the following subsection this explanation will be investigated.

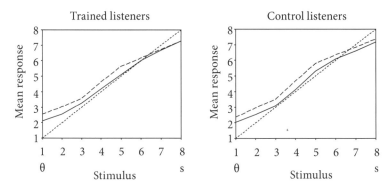

Figure 2. Mean responses to each of the stimuli in pretest (dashed) and posttest (solid). The line of short dashes shows the ideal case of error-free perception.

3.4 The effect of training amount on pretest-posttest differences

The amount of training needed to reach criterion varied among test listeners: some needed only 960 training trials before reaching criterion, while others needed as many as 7680 trials. It is conceivable that those listeners who needed more training also show larger differences between pre- and posttest results. Therefore, the trained listeners' data were tested in repeated measures ANOVA's, this time with Training Amount as a covariate. Only the findings that differ from the effects described in Sections 3.2 and 3.3 will be reported here.

For three-step 4IAX discrimination, a Text × Training Amount interaction was found ($F[1,15] = 4.8$, $p = .044$) as well as a main effect of Training Amount ($F[1,15] = 16.4$, $p = .001$). The rise in correct responses between pretest and posttest tended to be larger as the amount of training increased. The mean variances of the stimuli in absolute identification also showed a main effect of Training Amount ($F[1,15] = 5.5$, $p = .033$).

3.5 Posttest questionnaire

After the perception tests, listeners wrote down the words they had heard as the two extremes during absolute identification. The reported sets varied greatly. From the test group, six listeners reported the correct pair of words, but none of the control listeners succeeded in doing this. Remember that acoustically only the first consonant varied between stimuli *thif* and *sif*. Three types of errors were identified. Listeners (a) replaced target phonemes with other phonemes, (b) added phonemes that were not present in the signal or (c) reported hearing differences between the vowels or between the coda consonants.

In total, participants in the control group made more errors: 55 as opposed to 37 for the trained listeners. The controls made the majority of these, 49%, in their responses to the first consonant, i.e. the target phoneme. They used almost twice as many substitutions, and also additions that resulted in complex onsets such as *stif* instead of *thif*. They also more often replaced the coda consonant with another one as in *striss* instead of *thif*.

4. Discussion

Listeners participated in training sessions until they learnt the contrast to the predetermined level of 85% correct. The training results showed that the phoneme boundaries were already close to the English norm during the first training session. But the widths of the phoneme boundaries became much smaller and even indistinguishable from the English norm as a result of training.

The pre- and posttest revealed main effects of Test for both discrimination and absolute identification tests. However, the absence of Test × Listener Group interactions showed that listeners — whether in the test or control group — all performed better when they did the tests for the second time. Differences between the test and control groups were only present within the posttest data of three-step discrimination and of the variance results in absolute identification. As for three-step discrimination, test listeners performed better than controls, especially at the /θ/-end of the continuum in the posttest. Response variances in absolute identification were smaller for the test group.

By taking into account the amount of training participants received, we found that listeners who completed many training sessions showed a larger difference between their pretest and posttest results for three-step discrimination and for the variances in absolute identification. For these results, our assumption that the more training a listener needs, the more improvement will be found, was borne out.

The main research question of this paper was: do Dutch adults learn the British-English /θ–s/ contrast in a way compatible with Acquired Distinctiveness or with Acquired Similarity? We found no support for learning by Acquired Similarity. In that case, perceptual sensitivity to speech sounds that belong to the same category should decrease, but we found no such effects at all. On the contrary, the improvement we found for the discrimination tests mainly occurred within instead of between categories. So these findings do not strongly support our other hypothesis, Acquired Distinctiveness, either.

Despite the progress during training, little evidence of an increase in discrimination levels at the phoneme boundary was found, contrary to earlier findings (Jamieson & Morosan 1986). This may have been caused either by the nature of the tasks used in pre- and posttest, or by the participants' high pretest levels. Firstly, the tasks used may have directed the listeners' attention too much towards the acoustic differences between the stimuli by testing auditory instead of phonemic perception. However, we expected to find a combination of these listening levels in our results (Gerrits 2001; Pisoni 1975). Secondly, most participants performed already quite well in the pretest (see, for example, Figure 2). The space left for improvement as a result of training was thereby restricted and possibly difficult to distinguish from improvement by task repetition. We also think that the pretest was a training in itself due to its length, which helped control listeners to improve their scores in the posttest. Most earlier studies however, did not test a control group (e.g. Strange & Dittmann 1984; Logan, Lively & Pisoni 1991) and could therefore only report the test group's progress.

An explanation that may account for a portion of the errors made by the participants in reporting which words they had heard, is 'verbal transformation' (Warren 1961a). When listeners are repeatedly confronted with the same syllable, word or sequence of words, they start hearing differences that are not present in the signal. The types of changes found in this study are consistent with the types of misperceptions reported by Warren (1961a). But, control listeners made more errors than test listeners. We assume that the speaker variation that was available to the trained participants helped them to form the correct representations more often in comparison with the control group.

A sub-question that was addressed in the present study was whether the availability of knowledge of the language you are learning influences perceptual learning. We found that participants who knew they were listening to English did not benefit from this knowledge. So either listeners in both the English and the Foreign Language conditions used their knowledge of English equally, or neither of the groups accessed this knowledge.

5.   Conclusion

Dutch listeners improved their perception of British-English /θ–s/ during training. Trained listeners performed better in the posttest than in the pretest and in several respects they also did better than the control group. Their improved performance excluded Acquired Similarity, but did not strongly support Acquired Distinctiveness either. This effect was thought to be due to both the high pretest performances of our participants and the nature of the tests used in pretest and posttest. Furthermore, control listeners, who received no training, also improved by simply performing the tests in pretest and posttest twice. These results show that it is important to include a control group into the design of a phoneme training study, which has often not been the case. Finally, listeners who knew that they were listening to British-English did not benefit from this knowledge opposed to listeners who were told they were listening to a foreign language.

Note

1. This work was supported by the Netherlands Organisation for Scientific Research (NWO).

References

Best, C. T., Traill, A., Carter, A., Harrison, K. D. & Faber, A. (2003) !Xóõ click perception by English, Isizulu, and Sesotho listeners. *Proceedings of the 15th ICPhS, Barcelona*, 853–856.

Collins, B. S. & Mees, I. M. (1999) *The phonetics of English and Dutch*. Brill, Leiden.

Ganong, W. F. (1980) Phonetic categorization in auditory word perception. *Journal of Experimental Psychology: Human Perception and Performance* 6(1), 110–125.

Gerrits, E. (2001) *The categorisation of speech sounds by adults and children*. Doctoral Dissertation, Utrecht University.

Hessen, A. J. van (1992) *Discrimination of familiar and unfamiliar speech sounds*. Doctoral Dissertation, Utrecht University.

Jamieson, D. G. & Morosan, D. E. (1986) Training non-native speech contrasts in adults: acquisition of the English /ð/–/θ/ contrast by francophones. *Perception & Psychophysics* 40, 205–215.

Liberman, A. M., Harris, K. S., Kinney, J. A. & Lane, H. (1961) The discrimination of relative onset-time of the components of certain speech and nonspeech patterns, *Journal of Experimental Psychology* 61(5), 379–388.

Lively, S. E., Logan, J. S. & Pisoni, D. B. (1993) Training Japanese listeners to identify English /r/ and /l/. II The role of phonetic environment and talker variability in learning new perceptual categories. *Journal of the Acoustical Society of America* 94, 1242–1255.

Logan, J. S., Lively, S. E. & Pisoni, D. B. (1991) Training Japanese listeners to identify English /r/ and /l/: A first report. *Journal of the Acoustical Society of America* 89, 874–886.

Pisoni, D. B. (1975) Auditory short-term memory and vowel perception. *Memory & Cognition* 3, 7–18.

Pisoni, D. B. (1991) Modes of processing speech and nonspeech signals. In I. G. Mattingly & M. Studdert-Kennedy (eds.): *Modularity and the motor theory of speech perception*. Lawrence Erlbaum Associates, Hillsdale NJ, 225–238.

Strange, W. & Dittmann, S. (1984) Effects of discrimination training on the perception of /r–l/ by Japanese adults learning English. *Perception & Psychophysics* 36, 131–145.

Strange, W. & Jenkins, J. J. (1978) Role of linguistic experience in the perception of speech. In R. D. Walk & H. L. Pick (eds.): *Perception and experience*. Plenum Press, New York, 125–169.

Warren, R. M. (1961a) Illusory changes of distinct speech upon repetition-the verbal transformation effect. *British Journal of Psychology* 52, 249–258.

Werker, J. F. & Tees, R. C. (1984a) Cross-language speech perception: evidence for perceptual reorganization during the first year of life. *Infant Behavior and Development* 7, 49–63.

Phonetic or phonological contrasts in Dutch boundary tones?

Vincent J. van Heuven and Robert S. Kirsner

University of Leiden / University of California at Los Angeles

1. Introduction

Linguistic categorisation of sound. A basic problem of linguistic phonetics is to explain how the infinite variety of speech sounds in actual utterances can be described with finite means, such that they can be dealt with in the grammar, i.e. phonology, of a language. The crucial concept that was developed to cope with this reduction problem is the sound category, or — when applied to the description of segmental phenomena — the phoneme.

Categorisation of sounds may proceed along several possible lines. First, many differences between sounds are simply too small to be heard at all: these are subliminal. The scientific discipline of psycho-acoustics provides a huge literature on precisely what differences between sounds can and cannot be heard with the naked ear. Moreover, research has shown that our hearing mechanism has developed specific sensitivities to certain differences between sounds and is relatively deaf to others. An important concept in this context is the notion of categorical perception. This notion is best explained procedurally in terms of a laboratory experiment.

Imagine a minimal word pair such as English *back* ~ *pack*. The onset of voicing in *back* coincides with the plosive release, whilst the voice onset in *pack* does not start until some 50 ms after the release. We create a series of exemplars by interpolating the voice onset time of a prototypical *back* (0-ms delay) and that of a prototypical *pack* (70-ms delay) in steps of 10 ms, yielding an 8-step continuum ranging over 0, 10, 20, 30, 40, 50, 60, and 70 ms. These eight exemplars are played in random order to English listeners for identification as either *back* or *pack*. The 0-ms voice delay token will yield exclusively *back*-responses (0% *pack*); the 70-ms token will have 100% *pack*-responses. But what results will be obtained for the intermediate exemplars? If the 10-ms changes in voice delay are perceived *continuously*, one would predict a constant, gradual increase in %-*pack* responses for each 10-ms increment in the delay, i.e., the psychometric function (the line that captures the stimulus-response relationship) is essentially a straight line (open symbols in Figure 1B). The typical outcome of such experiments, however, is non-continuous. For the first part of the continuum all exemplars are perceived as *back*-tokens, the rightmost exemplars are near-unanimously perceived as *pack*. Only for exemplars in the middle of the continuum do we observe uncertainty: here the responses are ambiguous between *back* and *pack*. The psychometric function for this so-called categorical perception is sigmoid, i.e., has the shape of an S (big solid symbols in Figure 1B). In the idealized case of perfect categorical perception we would, in fact, expect a step-function jumping abruptly from 0 to 100% *pack*-responses somewhere along the continuum (thin black line with small solid symbols in Figure 1B).

The *category boundary* (at 35-ms VOT in Figure 1B) is defined as the point along the stimulus axis where the responses are completely ambiguous, i.e., 50–50%. For a well-defined *cross-over* there should be a point along the stimulus axis where 75% of the responses agree on one category, and a second point where there is 75%-agreement on the other. The *uncertainty margin* is the distance along the stimulus axis between the two 75%-points.

Although a pronounced sigmoid function is a clear sign of categorical perception, researchers have always been reluctant to consider it definitive proof. Listeners, when forced to, tend to split any continuum down the middle. Therefore, two conditions should be met: (i) identification should show a clear sigmoid, and (ii) discrimination should show a local peak for stimuli straddling the category boundary.

The discrimination function is determined in a separate experiment in which either (i) identical or (ii) adjacent tokens along the stimulus continuum are presented pair-wise. Listeners then decide whether the two tokens are 'same' or 'different'. Two kinds of error may occur: a physically different pair may be heard as 'same', and a pair of identical tokens may be called 'different'. The results of a discrimination task are best expressed as the percentage of correct decisions obtained for a 'different' stimulus pair minus the percentage of errors for 'same' pairs constructed from these stimuli (the latter percentage is often called the response bias). In the case of true categorical perception the discrimination scores show a pronounced peak for the stimulus pair straddling the category boundary, whilst all other pairs are discriminated at or only little above chance level (see panel A in Figure 1). Physically different sounds that fall in the same perceptual category, are hard to discriminate. In the case of continuous perception, there is no local peak in the discrimination function.

Categorical nature of intonational contrasts? By intonation we mean the pattern of

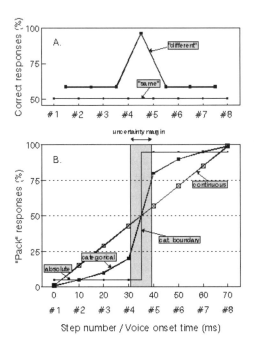

Figure 1. Panel A. Hypothetical discrimination function for physically same and different pairs of stimuli (one-step difference) reflecting categorical perception. Panel B. Illustration of continuous (open squares) versus categorical (big solid squares) perception in the identification and discrimination paradigm. Category boundary and uncertainty margin are indicated (further, see text).

rises and falls in the time-course of the pitch of spoken sentences. Speech melodies can be parameterized cross-linguistically and described in much the same way as has been done for the segmentals in language: a set of distinctive features defines an inventory of abstract units, which can be organized in higher-order units subject to well-formedness constraints. Moreover, intonational contrasts are used to perform functions that can also be expressed by lexico-syntactic means, such as turning statements into questions, and putting constituents in focus. For these reasons it has become widely accepted that intonation is part of the linguistic system (Ladd, 1996:8). Yet, there have always been adherents of the view that speech melody should be considered as something outside the realm of linguistics proper, i.e., that intonation is a paralinguistic phenomenon at best, to be treated on a par with the expression of attitudes or emotions. Typically, the communication of emotions (such as anger, fear, joy, surprise) or of attitudes (such as sarcasm) is non-categorical: the speaker shows himself more or less angry, fearful, or sarcastic in a continuous, gradient fashion.

A relatively recent insight, therefore, is that a division should be made in melodic phenomena occurring in speech between linguistic versus paralinguistic contrasts. Obviously, only the former but not the latter type of phenomena should be described by the grammar and explained by linguistic theory. This, however, begs the question how the difference can be made between linguistic and paralinguistic phenomena within the realm of speech melody. Ladd & Morton (1997) were the first to suggest that the traditional diagnostic for categorical perception should also be applicable to intonational categories. Only if a peak in the discrimination function is found for adjacent members on a tone continuum straddling a boundary between tonal categories, are they part of the linguistic system, i.e., phonological categories. If no categorical perception of the tone categories can be established, the categories are 'just' the extremes of a paralinguistic or phonetic tonal continuum. Ladd & Morton tested the traditional diagnostic on a tone continuum between normal and emphatic accent in English and noted that it failed.

Remijsen & van Heuven (2003) tested the traditional diagnostic on a tone continuum between 'L%' and 'H%' in Dutch, and showed that indeed there was a discrimination peak for adjacent members along the continuum straddling the boundary. At the same time, however, we had to take recourse to listener-individual normalization of the category boundary, a complication that is not generally needed when dealing with contrasts in the segmental phonology. Moreover, our relatively weak categorical effects could have been the result of an incorrect subdivision of the 'L%' to 'H%' tone range. Van Heuven & Kirsner (2002) showed that Dutch listeners were perfectly able to categorize final pitches in terms of three categories, functionally denoted as 'command' intonation, 'continuation', and 'question' (see §3). However, we did not run the full diagnostic involving both identification and discrimination. Also, we asked our listeners to choose between three response alternatives, viz. command, conditional and question. Although the extremes of the range, i.e. command versus question, are unchallenged linguistic categories, the conditional may well be non-distinct from the question type. After all, in the grammar developed by 't Hart, Collier & Cohen (1990) any type of non-low terminal pitch falls into the same category, indicating non-finality. It occurred to us that we should take the precaution to run the experiment several times, using different response alternatives, such that two separate binary ('command' ~ 'no command' and 'question ~ 'no question') response sets as well as our original ternary response set ('command' ~ 'conditional' ~ 'question') were used by the same set of listeners. If the intermediate 'conditional' response category does constitute a clearly defined notion in the listeners' minds, the binary and ternary divisions of the stimulus range should converge on the category boundaries. The present paper seeks to remedy our earlier infelicities.

We conclude this introduction by summarizing our research questions:

1. Are there three phrase-final boundary tones in Dutch: low for 'command' (also used for 'statement'), intermediate for 'conditional', and high for 'question' or just two, lumping the latter two together into a single category 'non-terminal'?

2. Where along the continuum are the category boundaries between the two or three boundary tones?

3. Are the category boundaries at the same positions irrespective of the binary versus ternary response mode?

4. Are the boundaries truly categorical in the sense that there are discrimination peaks for adjacent stimulus pairs straddling the category boundaries?

2. Methods

A male native speaker of standard Dutch read the sentence *Neemt u de trein naar WAgeningen?* with a single 'H*L' accent on the first syllable of *Wageningen.* The utterance was recorded onto digital audio tape (DAT) using a Sennheiser MKH 416 unidirectional condenser microphone, transferred to computer disk (16 kHz, 16 bits) and digitally processed using the Praat speech processing software (Boersma & Weenink, 1996). The intonation pattern of the utterance was stylized by hand as a sequence of straight lines in the ERB by linear time representation. Nine intonationally different versions were then generated using the PSOLA analysis-resynthesis technique (e.g. Moulines & Verhelst, 1995) implemented in the Praat software. The nine versions were identical up to and including the 'H*L' configuration on *Wageningen*. From that point onwards the nine versions diverged into two falls and seven rises. The terminal frequencies of the nine versions were chosen to be perceptually equidistant, i.e., the difference between any two adjacent terminal frequencies was equal in terms of the ERB scale.[1] The terminal pitch of version 1 equaled 80 Hz, the increment in the terminal frequency for each following version was 0,25 ERB, as shown in Figure 2.

For the **discrimination** task, which was the first task imposed on the subjects, stimuli were presented in pairs that were either the same or one step apart on the continuum. In the latter case, the second can be higher or lower than the first (hereafter AB and BA, respectively). The eight AB stimulus types ran from pair {1,2} to {8,9}; the eight corresponding BA types from {2,1} to {9,8}. This yielded 9 identical pairs and 2 × 8 = 16 different pairs, which occurred in random order, yielding a set of 25 trials in all, which was presented to each listener four times in different random orders, preceded by five practice trials. Stimuli within pairs were separated by a 500-ms silence, the pause between pairs was 3000 ms. For the **identification** task listeners responded to individual stimuli from the 9-step continuum by classifying each either in terms of a binary or a ternary choice:

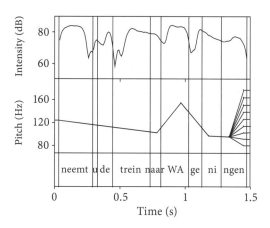

Figure 2. Steps 1 through 9 along resynthesized continuum differing in terminal pitch by 0,25 ERB increments.

(1) 'Command' ~ 'no command'. In one task the listeners were instructed to decide for each stimulus whether they interpreted it as a command or not.
(2) 'Question' ~ 'no question'. An alternative task involved the decision whether the stimulus sounded like a question or not.
(3) 'Command' ~ 'condition' ~ 'question'. The third task was identical to the task imposed in van Heuven & Kirsner (2002).

Half of the listeners first performed task (1), the other half of the listeners began with task (2). Task (3) was always the last identification procedure in the array of tests. For each task, the set of nine stimuli were presented five times to each listener, in different random orders, and preceded by five practice items, yielding sets of 50 identification stimuli per task.

Ten male and ten female Dutch listeners took part in the experiment on a voluntary basis. Participants were university students or members of their families. Subjects listened to the stimuli at a comfortable loudness level over Quad ESL-63 electrostatic loudspeakers, while seated in a sound-treated lecture room. They marked their responses on printed answer sheets, always taking the discrimination task first and the identification tasks last.

3. Results

Figures 3 and 4 present the results obtained in the binary identification tasks, i.e., the forced choice between 'command' ~ 'no command' (Figure 3) and between 'question' ~ 'no question' (Figure 4). The psychometric function for the 'command' responses is very steep. The category boundary between 'command' and 'no command' is located at a step size of 2.7, and the margin of uncertainty runs between 2.2 and 3.7, i.e., a cross-over from 75% to 25% 'command' responses is effected by an increase in the terminal pitch of the stimulus of 1.5 step (i.e., 0.37 ERB). A complete cross-over is also found for the 'question' ~ 'no question' task. The category boundary finds itself at a stimulus value of 3.6, whilst the margin of uncertainty runs between 2.3 and 4.9, i.e., an interval of 2.6 increments of 0.25 ERB. The category boundaries in the 'command' and 'question' tasks do not coincide, but diverge by almost a complete step: 2.7 versus 3.6 step. Note, once more, that none of the subjects had been alerted to the possible existence of an intermediate category between 'command' and 'question'. Therefore, the emergence of the interval between the 'command' and the 'question' boundaries might be taken in justification of an intermediate category.

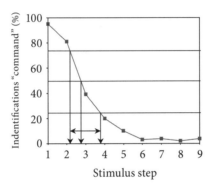

Figure 3. Percent 'command' responses as a function of stimulus step in binary identification of 'command'~'no command'.

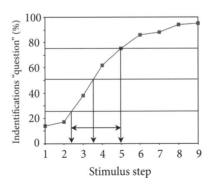

Figure 4. As Figure 3, but for 'question' ~ 'no question'

Let us now turn Figure 5 for the results of the ternary identification task, in which the same listeners were required to classify the nine stimulus types as either 'command', 'conditional subclause' or 'question'. The boundary between 'command' and 'continuation' is at 2.8; this is hardly different than the 'command' ~ 'no command' boundary that was found in the binary response task. This, then, would seem to be a very robust boundary, showing that at least 'command' intonation has well-defined linguistic status. The boundary between 'continuation' and 'question' is less clearly defined. Also, the maximum scores in these two categories are around 80% rather than 90% or more. Although there is no ambiguity in the listeners' minds whether a stimulus is a command or something else, the choice between 'continuation' and 'question' seems more ambiguous, leaving room for a minority response in the order of 20%. This would indicate to us that we are dealing here with a continuum rather than with a dichotomy. Finally, we may note that the (soft) category boundary between 'continuation' and 'question' is located at a stimulus value of 7.2. The boundary, then, that sets off 'question' from 'no question' responses proves unstable: there is a shift from the binary response task (3.6) to the ternary task (7.2) of no less than 3.6 points along the stimulus continuum. It would seem, then, that the 'command' category is highly stable and well-established in the minds of the listeners. The 'question' boundary, however, is rather poorly defined.

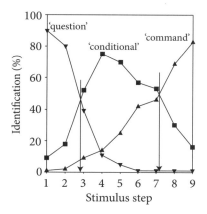

Figure 5. Ternary identification of stimuli as 'command', 'conditional clause' or 'question'. Category boundaries are indicated.

Figure 6 presents the mean percentage of successfully discriminated stimuli that were actually different (hereafter 'hits'), and the percentage of false alarms, i.e. 'different' responses to (identical) AA stimuli. The false-alarm rate is roughly 20% across the entire stimulus continuum. This value can be seen as a bias for responding 'different'. Generally, an increment of 0.25 ERB is discriminated above the 20% bias level, with the exception of the difference between stimulus steps 5 and 6. The discrimination function shows two local peaks. The first one is very large, and is located between stimulus steps 2 and 3. This peak obviously coincides with the stable category boundary found between 'command' and the non-command responses (whether binary or ternary). A

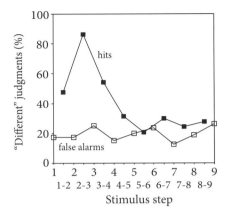

Figure 6. Percent 'different' judgments to nine identical stimulus pairs (false alarms) and eight pairs differing by one step (hits).

much smaller second discrimination peak may be observed between stimulus steps 6 and 7, which location may well reflect the rather poorly defined category boundary between 'continuation' and 'question'.

Using the so-called Haskins formula $D_{pred} = \frac{1}{2} \times (1 + (P_1 - P_2)^2)$ to predict correct discrimination of different stimulus pairs from the identification scores obtained for each of the stimulus steps along the continuum, we find very high correlations between predicted and observed discrimination for 'command' identification: $r = .949$ ($p < .001$) in the ternary and $r = .932$ ($p = .001$) in the binary task. Prediction of discrimination behavior from 'question' identification is only just significant in the binary task: $r = .710$ ($p = .049$) but negative (and insignificant) in the ternary identification task: $r = -.545$ ($p = .163$). These statistics, again, suggest that only the 'command' ~ 'no command' contrast is categorical.

4. Conclusions and discussion

Let us now try to formulate answers to the research questions in §1.2. The first question was whether the domain-final boundary tones are contiguous categories along a single tonal dimension, and map onto the command, continuation and question meaning in a one-to-one fashion. The results of our experiments clearly indicate that this is indeed the case. Our listeners had no difficulty in using the three response alternatives provided to them. When the terminal pitch was lower than the preceding pivot point in the contour the responses were almost unanimously for 'command'. When the final pitch was higher than the preceding pivot point, the incidence of 'continuation' responses increased up to and including step 4, and decreased for higher terminal pitches which were more readily identified as questions as the terminal pitch was higher.

Although there was always some ambiguity between the 'continuation' and 'question' alternatives, the results clearly indicate that 'continuation' is signaled by moderate final pitch, and question by (extra) high pitch.

The latter finding suggests that asking a question involves a higher degree of appeal by the speaker to hearer than asking the listener's continued attention. We may also note that our result clashes with Caspers (1998). She found that the intermediate final pitch (or high level pitch in her experiment) was unambiguously identified as continuation; extra high final pitch ambiguously coded either continuation or question. Comparison of Caspers' and our own results is hazardous since the utterance-final tone configurations differ, not so much at the underlying tone level, but at the surface. It seems to us that the discrepancy between Caspers' and our own findings can be resolved if we accept the possibility that Caspers' extra high terminal pitch was simply not high enough to elicit the 80% 'question' responses that we got in our experiment.

The results so far concur with van Heuven & Kirsner (2002). However, we may now go on to consider the second, third and fourth questions, which asked where the category boundaries are located along the final pitch continuum between low, intermediate and high, in the binary and ternary response tasks, and to what extent the boundaries coincide with a peak in the discrimination function. The results obtained in the binary ('command' ~ 'no command') and ternary ('command' ~ 'continuation' ~ 'question') identification tasks are virtually the same, yielding the same location of the boundary (at step 2.7) separating the 'command' category from the rest of the stimulus continuum. However, a very unstable boundary is found in the binary 'question' ~ 'no question' task (at step 3.6), which is reflected in the poorly defined boundary separating the 'continuation' and 'question' categories in the ternary response task (at step 7.2). Moreover, we have seen that the category boundary between 'command' and 'no command' coincides with a huge peak in the discrimination function. Although there is a modest local maximum in the discrimination function that may be associated with a boundary between 'continuation' and 'question', this peak is not very convincing.

We take these findings as evidence that there is a linguistic, or phonological, categorization of the final boundary tone continuum in just two types, which is best characterized as low and non-low. The low boundary tone signals dominance or superiority on the part of the speaker. This is the boundary tone that is suited for issuing statements and commands. The non-low boundary tone signals subservience of the speaker to the hearer; the speaker appeals to the hearer for his continued attention or for an answer to a question.

The non-low part of the boundary opposition, however, represents a gradient, paralinguistic continuum between a moderate appeal (asking for the hearer's continued attention) and a stronger appeal (asking the hearer for a verbal reply to a question). Here the lower terminal pitches are associated with weaker degrees of appeal (or subservience), and the higher levels with strong appeal, but in a continuous, gradient, non-phonological manner.

Our results indicate that earlier findings reported by Remijsen & van Heuven (2003) are to be viewed with caution. We now know that the listeners' task should not be to decide whether the stimulus is a statement (or a command) versus a question. If binary response alternatives are required, the categories should be 'statement' versus 'no statement' but a better procedure would be to ask the listener to choose from three categories: 'statement' (equivalent to 'command' in our experiments) ~ 'continuation' ~ 'question'. Had such precautions been taken by Remijsen & van Heuven, their category boundary would have been much better defined with less listener-individual variation.

Methodologically, the classical identification-cum-discrimination paradigm is a useful diagnostic tool in intonation research which allows linguists to decide experimentally whether a melodic contrast is categorical and therefore part of the phonology, or continuously gradient and therefore phonetic or even paralinguistic.

Notes

1. The experiments reported in this article were run by Suzanne Strik and Josien Klink in partial fulfillment of the course requirements for the Experimental Phonetics Seminar 2003/04 taught by the Linguistics Programme at Universiteit Leiden.

2. The ERB scale (Equivalent Rectangular Bandwidth) is currently held to be the most satisfactory psychophysical conversion for pitch intervals in human speech (Hermes & van Gestel, 1991). The conversion from hertz (f) to ERB (E) is achieved by a simple formula: $E = 16.6 \times \log(1 + f/165.4)$.

References

Boersma, P. and Weenink, D. (1996). Praat, a system for doing phonetics by computer. *Report of the Institute of Phonetic Sciences Amsterdam*, 132.

Caspers, J. (1998). 'Who's next?' The melodic marking of question vs. continuation in Dutch. *Language and Speech* 41, 375–398.

Hart, J. 't, Collier, R. and Cohen, A. (1990). *A Perceptual study of intonation. An experimental-phonetic approach to speech perception.* Cambridge: Cambridge University Press.

Hermes, D.J. and Gestel, J.C. van (1991). The frequency scale of speech intonation. *Journal of the Acoustical Society of America* 90, 97–102.

Heuven, V.J. van and Kirsner, R.S. (2002). Interaction of tone and particle in the signaling of clause type in Dutch, in H. Broekhuis, P. Fikkert (eds.). *Linguistics in the Netherlands 2002*, Amsterdam/Philadelphia: John Benjamins, 73–84.

Ladd, D.R. (1996). *Intonational phonology.* Cambridge: Cambridge University Press.

Ladd, D. R. and Morton, R. (1997). The perception of intonational emphasis: continuous or categorical? *Journal of Phonetics*, 25, 313–342.

Moulines, E. and Verhelst, E. (1995). 'Time-domain and frequency-domain techniques for prosodic modification of speech'. In W. B. Kleijn and K. K. Paliwal, eds., *Speech coding and synthesis*. Amsterdam: Elsevier Science, 519–555.

Remijsen, A. C. and Heuven, V. J. van (2003). Linguistic versus paralinguistic status of prosodic contrasts, the case of high and low pitch in Dutch, in J. M. van de Weijer, V. J. van Heuven, H. G. van der Hulst (eds.): *The phonological spectrum. Volume II: Suprasegmental structure*. Amsterdam/Philadelphia: John Benjamins, 225–246.

Alles is fleurich, ik bin it mei

On the comitative particle *mei* in Frisian and its counterparts in the other Germanic languages

Jarich Hoekstra
Christian-Albrechts-Universität

1. Introduction

All Germanic languages, except English, possess a comitative particle homo-phonous with the comitative adposition. Until now the comitative particle has not received much attention in the grammatical literature. In this paper I will outline the syntactic and semantic properties of this element in the various Germanic languages, taking West Frisian *mei* as my starting point. On the basis of this description I will propose a tentative analysis of the comitative particle.

2. The comitative particle *mei* in West Frisian

In this section I will give a description of the use and the distribution of the comitative particle *mei* in West Frisian in syntax and in word formation. Note that I will refer to *mei* and its counterparts in other Germanic languages as a *comitative* particle although, as we will see, it has some other functions next to the purely comitative one.

The comitative particle *mei* in Frisian may modify the maximal projections of all lexical categories (N, A, P, V). First consider its use with NPs. As the examples in (1) show, the particle always follows the NP it modifies:

(1) a. Hwa't trochsette en him hwat skikke koe waerd [$_{NP}$ Fries <u>mei</u>]
[J. J.Kalma, *Om Gysbert Japiks hinne* 73 (1963)]
'Who didn't give up and could adapt himself somewhat became a Frisian with the Frisians'

Linguistics in the Netherlands 2004 21 (2004), 114–124.
ISSN 0929–7332 / E-ISSN 1569–9919 © Algemene Vereniging voor Taalwetenschap

    b.   In âlder of in skoalmaster moat faek [$_{NP}$ bern <u>mei</u>] wêze
        [*Wurdboek fan de Fryske Taal* 2, s.v. *bern* I, 1]
        'A parent or a schoolteacher must often be a child with the children'

In (1) *mei* can be roughly paraphrased with a full PP. Thus, instead of *Fries mei* in (1a) it would be possible to say *Fries mei de Friezen* 'a Frisian with the Frisians'. The particle expresses identification or integration and we might speak of the *integrative* function of *mei* here. The noun heading the modified NP typically denotes a member of a category of people (nationality, age group, profession, etc.).

    In the example in (2) it is less easy to give an acceptable paraphrase of *mei* with a full PP. A clumsy paraphrase of *in reden mei* would be something like *in reden mei oare reden* 'a reason with (in addition to) other reasons', i.e. 'one (further) reason'. The particle has an *additive* function here. The *dat*-clause complement of *reden* 'reason' has probably been extraposed in (2).

    (2)   Dit wier den ek al [$_{N^*P}$ in reden t_i <u>mei</u>], dat Klaes Heechflecht nea safier buwten
        'e poarte wêst hie as er nou komme scoe$_i$
        [S. K. Feitsma, *For sprekkers en lêzers* 18 (1888)]
        'This was then one reason why Klaes Heechflecht had never been so far outside
        the gate as he would get now'

The expression *in reden mei* is slightly lexicalised. If it occurs in sentence-initial position the indefinite article may be deleted by some kind of sentential aphaeresis (cf. *It wie suterich waar.* [*Reden* <u>mei</u>], *dat er in min sin hie* 'The weather was lousy. One reason why he had a bad temper').

    The difference between (1) and (2) may be that in (1) *mei* modifies the bare NP, whereas in (2) it modifies the nominal projection headed by the indefinite article, which I have represented by N*P to show that we are dealing with a nominal (functional) projection structurally higher than NP (possibly Number Phrase). A clear example of the additive use of *mei* is also found in the partitive construction (here the *fan*-PP has presumably been extraposed):

    (3)   a.   Dat is [$_{N^*P}$ ien t_i <u>mei</u>] fan 'e bêste fersen fan Obe Postma$_i$
              'That is one of the best poems by Obe Postma'
        b.   Dat binne [$_{N^*P}$ guon t_i <u>mei</u>] fan 'e bêste fersen fan Obe Postma$_i$
        c.   Dat binne [$_{N^*P}$ *pro* t_i <u>mei</u>] fan 'e bêste fersen fan Obe Postma$_i$
              'Those are some of the best poems by Obe Postma'

In (3) the comitative particle modifies an NP headed by an indefinite pronoun. The occurrence of *mei* is dependent on the presence of a superlative in the *fan*-phrase (cf. *ien (*mei) fan 'e fersen* 'one of the poems'). The use of the particle seems to be somewhat pleonastic here ('one, among others, of the best poems').

    In combination with APs the comitative particle also follows the AP it modifies. Compare the examples in (4):

(4)   a.   Heit en mem kipen ek ris efkes yn en waerden [$_{AP}$ jong mei] en songen ek,
              det it davere [S. Kloosterman, *Ut 'e gielgoerde II* 62 (1944)]
              'Dad and Mom dropped in as well and got young with the young people
              and also sang at the top of their voice'
       b.   Mar it binne ek sokke fleurige skutters en den wirdt men ommers sels [$_{AP}$
              fleurich mei] [R. Brolsma, *Pension "Nij Frisia"* 38 (1936)]
              'But they are such merry people and then one gets merry with them, doesn't
              one?'

As in the case of NP modification *mei* has an integrative function here: *jong mei*
means something like 'young with the young ones'.

The comitative particle can further combine with PPs. In this case, however,
it precedes the PP it modifies. The PP can be a normal preposition phrase (5a),
a pronominal adverb (with possible movement of the R-pronoun) (5b) or an
intransitive preposition (directional adverb) (5c):

(5)   a.   Ik ha [$_{PP}$ mei op begraffenis] west
              'I came along to the funeral'
       b.   Hja siet der$_i$ [$_{PP}$ mei t$_i$ yn]
              'She was in it along with some other person(s)'
       c.   Hy is [$_{PP}$ mei werom] kommen
              'He has come back along with some other person(s)'

In combination with the directional (predicative) PPs in (5), *mei* has a purely
comitative function. It can, however, appear with adjunct PPs as well, in which
case it has an additive function:

(6)   [$_{PP}$ Mei fanwegen in útskuorde ferkearing] hie se in oare baan socht
       'Partly because of a broken-off relationship she had looked for another job'

Finally, the comitative particle may occur with VPs. As with PPs, it precedes the
VP it modifies. In combination with a VP *mei* may have a purely comitative
function, as in (7):

(7)   a.   Hja hat [$_{VP}$ mei dit bedriuw grut makke]
       b.   Hja hat dit bedriuw$_i$ [$_{VP}$ mei t$_i$ grut makke]
              'She has made this company big with some other person(s)'

The particle may either precede the direct object or the verb (or complex predicate). Since in both cases the particle takes scope over the whole VP, I assume
that the word order difference results from scrambling of the direct object.

The comitative function may fade into an additive one. Compare the examples
in (8), where it is hard to decide whether the particle is comitative or additive:

(8)   a.   Dat leau ik mei
              'I believe that too'
       b.   Ik sil der mei om tinke
              'I will also keep an eye on it'

In its additive function *mei* may also precede either the direct object or the verb:

(9)   a.   Hy hat [$_{V*P}$ mei it stek ferve]
        b.   Hy hat it stek$_i$ [$_{V*P}$ mei t_i ferve]
            i.   'He has also painted the fence (in addition to some other person(s))'
           ii.   'He has also painted the fence (in addition to, e.g., mowing the lawn)'
          iii.   'He has also painted the fence (in addition to, e.g., painting the shed)'
          vi.   'He has also painted the fence (in addition to, e.g., repairing it)'

Additive *mei* in (9) may have four different scopal interpretations, partly dependent on the stress (on *hy* in reading (i), on *it stek* in reading (ii) and (iii), on *ferve* in reading (iv)). Additive *mei* clearly occupies another, higher structural position (represented here by V*P) than purely comitative *mei*, since it obligatorily precedes the latter (which, as we will see below, is strictly bound to the edge of VP):

(10)   Hy hat [$_{V*P}$ mei (juster) [$_{VP}$ mei it stek ferve]
        'He has also painted the fence with some other person(s) (yesterday)'

Summarizing, we have seen that in syntax the comitative particle *mei* in Frisian may modify NP (N*P), AP, PP and VP (V*P). It can have an integrative function (with NP and AP), a purely comitative function (with predicative PP and VP) and an additive function (with N*P, adjunct PP and V*P). In Frisian the particle *mei* follows NP (N*P) and AP (the [+N] categories), whereas it precedes PP and VP (V*P) (the [−N] categories).

    The comitative particle also appears as the first part of a compound. As such it may precede nouns (11a), adjectives (11b) and verbs (11c), in the latter case as a separable verb particle:

(11)   a.   meieigner 'co-owner', meipassasjier 'co-passenger'
        b.   meiskuldich 'also guilty, accessory to', meiferantwurdlik 'jointly responsible'
        c.   meiride 'to travel with some other person(s)', meisjonge 'to join in singing'

The 'bound' use of the particle clearly contrasts with its 'free' use. Compare, for example:

(12)   a.   Hy is meidirekteur   'He is the co-director'
        b.   Hy is [$_{NP}$ direkteur mei]   'He is director with the director (e.g. the janitor)'
        c.   Hy is [$_{VP}$ mei direkteur]   'He is the director with some other person(s)'
        d.   Hy is [$_{V*P}$ mei direkteur]   'He is also the director (he has some other
                                          function(s) as well)'

Let us now have a look at the other Germanic languages and see how the comitative particle behaves there.

3.   The comitative particle in other Germanic languages

The only Germanic language that does not seem to have developed a comitative particle from the comitative adposition is English. English has only full comitative *with*-PPs (cf. *I come with *(you) to the cinema*) and it does not form compounds with *with* (verbs like *withdraw* and *withstand* preserve the old meaning of *with*, 'against, back'). One might want to relate this to the fact that Modern English has lost the etymological counterpart of Frisian *mei*, Dutch *me(d)e*, German *mit*, Danish *med* etc. (also Old English *mid*!). Note, however, that Icelandic has the preposition *með*, but no 'free' comitative particle, although it has the verb particle in *Hann kemur/fer með* 'he comes/goes along' etc. (Halldór Sigurðsson, p.c.). On the other hand, Faroese has the preposition *við*, like English, but developed at least the additive variant of the particle (cf. *Eg hugsi so við* 'I think so too').

We turn to the remaining Germanic languages. First consider German. The German comitative particle *mit* has been discussed in some detail by Zifonun (1996/1997, 1999). As in Frisian (cf. (2)), the comitative particle may occur with an indefinite noun phrase (N*P), but other than in Frisian, it precedes this noun phrase:

(13)   Das war [$_{N*P}$ mit ein Grund, weshalb sie gekündigt hatte]
       'That was one reason why she quit the job'

This is also the case in the partitive construction in (14), which compares to the Frisian example in (3a):

(14)   Das ist [$_{N*P}$ mit eins der schönsten Gedichte von Rilke]
       'That is one of the most beautiful poems by Rilke'

As I noted in connection with the Frisian example, the comitative particle in the partitive construction is dependent on the presence of a superlative. A superlative is also obligatorily present in the partitive constructions in (15), where *mit* modifies a following DP (15a) or DegP (15b):

(15)   a.   Das ist [$_{DP}$ mit das schönste Gedicht von Rilke]
         'That is one of the most beautiful poems by Rilke'
     b.   Dieses Gedicht von Rilke ist [$_{DegP}$ mit am schönsten]
         'This poem by Rilke is one of the most beautiful'

Whereas *mit* in (14) (like *mei* in (3)) seems to be more or less pleonastic, *mit* in (15) clearly triggers the partitive interpretation of the DP and the DegP (cf. also Zifonun 1996/1997-II: 24).

The comitative particle may stand before predicative PPs (cf. (16)), i.e. in its purely comitative function, but not before adjunct PPs, i.e. in its additive function (compare Frisian *mei út namme fan myn frou* 'also on behalf of my wife' with German *auch im Namen meiner Frau*).

(16) Antje ist [$_{PP}$ <u>mit</u> in die Stadt] gefahren
      'Antje came along to town'

The comitative particle can also modify VP (cf. (17)) and V*P (cf. (18)). As
with Frisian *mei*, an object may either follow or precede *mit* in these cases:

(17) a. Hans hat [$_{VP}$ <u>mit</u> die Veranstaltung vorbereitet]
      b. Hans hat die Veranstaltung$_i$ [$_{VP}$ <u>mit</u> t_i vorbereitet]
          'Hans organised the event with some other person(s)'

(18) a. Sie haben [V*P <u>mit</u> das Klavier hinaufgetragen]
      b. Sie haben das Klavier$_i$ [V*P <u>mit</u> t_i hinaufgetragen]
          'They also carried the piano upstairs'

Finally *mit-* may compound with nouns, adjectives and (as a separable particle)
with verbs, e.g. *Mitdirektor* 'co-director', *mitverantwortlich* 'jointly responsible',
mitfahren 'to travel with some other person(s)'.

In Dutch the comitative particle is not as productive as in Frisian and
German, but Dutch is interesting because it formally distinguishes a preposition
met and a postposition/particle *mee* (cf. *Hij ging <u>met</u> zijn vader <u>mee</u>* 'He went
with his father'). Only the latter form occurs as a comitative particle. In
addition *mee* has a by-form *mede*. In Dutch the comitative particle can only
modify PPs and VPs. In its purely comitative function before directional
(predicative) PP and VP it appears as *mee* (cf. (19a,c)), in its additive function
before adjunct PP and V*P as *mede* (cf. (19b,d)). In word formation *mee-*
combines with verbs, *mede-* with nouns and adjectives (cf. (19e)). Compare:

(19) a. Kees ging [$_{PP}$ <u>mee</u>/*<u>mede</u> naar de kerk]
          'Kees came along to the church'
      b. Ik feliciteer je [$_{PP}$ <u>mede</u>/*<u>mee</u> namens de kollega's]
          'I congratulate you also on behalf of the colleagues'
      c. Ze heeft het projekt$_i$ [$_{VP}$ <u>mee</u>/*<u>mede</u> t_i opgezet]
          'She organised the project with some other person(s)'
      d. Hij heeft [$_{V*P}$ <u>mede</u>/*<u>mee</u> de telefoon uitgevonden]
          'He has also invented the telephone'
      e. <u>mee</u>rijden/*<u>mede</u>rijden   'to drive with some other
                                                         person(s)'

          <u>mede</u>directeur/*<u>mee</u>directeur   'co-director'
          <u>mede</u>verantwoordelijk/*<u>mee</u>verantwoordelijk 'jointly responsible'

The use of the comitative particle with VP seems to be somewhat more restricted in Dutch than in Frisian and German: comitative *mee* can only stand
immediately before the verb (or complex predicate), i.e. the object is obligatorily scrambled.

Finally, let us have a quick look at the mainland Scandinavian languages,
taking Danish as an example. The sentences in (20) (from the ODS), show that
the comitative particle *med* follows N*P (20a,b), precedes (predicative) PP (20c)

and follows VP (20d) and V*P (20e). The verb particle *med* follows the verb, whereas *med-* is prefixed to nouns and adjectives (20f):

(20)   a.   Da jeg nu formodede, at Skiørbug var [$_{N^*P}$ en Aarsag med], gav jeg ham ... Skiørbugs-Kløver [ODS 13 s.v. *med*,1154]
'Since I suspected that scurvy was one of the causes, I gave him scurvy-clover'

  b.   En stor Deel af disse Folk, endog [$_{N^*P}$ nogle t_i med] af de ... tapreste iblant dem$_i$ leve paa denne Maade [ibid. 1150]
'A large part of these people, even some of the bravest among them, live like that'

  c.   Manden ... skulle have Paalægsmad [$_{PP}$ med paa Arbejdspladsen] [ibid. 1153]
'The man should take sandwiches with him to work'

  d.   Vill du [$_{VP}$ drikke The med]? [ibid. 1150]
'Will you have tea with us?'

  e.   Saadann har man [$_{V^*P}$ klaget i England med] [ibid. 1154]
'So did they complain in England too'

  f.   køre med   'to travel with some other person(s)'
meddirektør   'co-director'
medansvarlig   'jointly responsable'

4.   Towards an analysis of the comitative particle

After this survey of the use of the comitative particle in Frisian and the other Germanic languages, I will present the basic ingredients for an analysis. I will depart from the hypothesis that there is only one particle *mei* etc. that has different functions according to the phrase type with which it is combined (although some language-specific provisos may be necessary). The basic distinction seems to be between the comitative function (comprising the purely comitative as well as the integrative function) and the additive function (compare the formal reflex of this dichotomy in Dutch *mee*/*mede*!). In its comitative function the particle modifies the bare lexical projections NP, AP, PP and VP used as predicates, in its additive function it modifies functional projections (N*P, V*P and, in German, DP and DegP) and non-predicative PP. (An anonymous reviewer claims that N*P and D*P have to be predicates when combined with the comitative particle, but even though they are normally used in predicative position, they can be arguments too, cf. German *Mit ihm haben wir* [*mit einen der besten Forscher auf diesem Gebiet*] *gewonnen* 'With him we managed to win one of the best researchers in the field'.) In the following I will focus on the comitative use of the particle, but at the end I will make a few remarks on its additive use.

Until now I tacitly assumed that the comitative particle and the XP it modifies form one constituent. A topicalisation test suffices to show that they actually do:

(21) a. [$_{NP}$ Fries mei] is er nea rjucht wurden
          'He never really became a Frisian with the Frisians'
     b. [$_{AP}$ Jong mei] wurdt men yn 'e boarterstún
          'On the playground one gets young with the young ones'
     c. [$_{PP}$ Mei nei Grins ta] gie allinnich myn broer
          'Only my brother came along to Groningen'
     d. [$_{VP}$ Mei it stek fervje] docht er mar komselden
          'He seldom paints the fence with some other person(s)'

In her study of comitative *mit* in German, Zifonun does not seem to distinguish PP-modifying from VP-modifying *mit*. It is clear, however, that the particle may form one constituent with a PP. Even a full comitative PP may, as (22) shows:

(22) [$_{PP}$ Mei ús heit nei Grins ta] gie allinnich myn broer
      'Only my brother came along to Groningen with my father'

I assume that the comitative particle heads a PP that is right- or left-adjoined to the XP constituent it modifies. Note that the separable verb particle can also be a maximal projection; as (23) shows, it may be topicalised:

(23) [$_{PP}$ Mei] gie er suver nea
      'He practically never came along'

I will have nothing to say here on the possible internal structure of the PP containing *mei* (for some arguments against ellipsis of a prepositional object or the presence of an empty pronoun, see Zifonun (1996/1997-II: 20–23)).

   Observe further that comitative *mei* is frozen at the edge of the XP it modifies and that it may not be stranded; it nor XP can be extracted. In (24) this is illustrated for PP-modifying *mei* (note that (24a) is marginally acceptable in a not-intended reading in which *nei Grins ta* is an adjunct and *meinimme* a particle verb):

(24) a. *Nei Grins ta$_i$ hat er syn broer [$_{PP}$ mei t_i] nommen
     b. *Mei$_i$ hat er syn broer [$_{PP}$ t_i nei Grins ta] nommen
          'He took his brother with him to Groningen'

The example in (25) shows that a VP-modifying comitative particle, unlike a full comitative phrase, may not be scrambled over adverbs; it is strictly bound to the edge of VP:

(25) a. Bouke hat {juster mei / *mei juster} it stek ferve
          'Bouke painted the fence yesterday with some other person(s)'
     b. Bouke hat {juster mei Sjoukje / mei Sjoukje juster} it stek ferve
          'Bouke painted the fence yesterday with Sjoukje'

Note by the way that the frozenness and unstrandability of the comitative particle implies that in the last line of Waling Dykstra's popular song 'Simmer-moarn' (Summer Morning) in the title of this paper the particle can only be VP- or V*P-modifying *mei* (cf. (26b,b')). The alternative interpretation as AP-modifying integrative *mei* could only be derived by illicitly stranding *mei* (cf. (26a,a')).

(26) a.   Alles is fleurich, ik bin$_i$ [$_{AP}$ fleurich mei] t_i
      a'. *Alles is fleurich, ik bin$_i$ it$_j$ [$_{AP}$ t_j mei] t_i
      b.   Alles is fleurich, ik bin$_i$ [$_{V*P/VP}$ mei [fleurich t_i]]
      b'. Alles is fleurich, ik bin$_i$ it$_j$ [$_{V*P/VP}$ mei [t_j t_i]]
           'Everything (in nature) is happy, I am happy with it/too'

This considered, let us assume that comitative *mei* is a syntactic affix that is used to comitative-mark a predicate, i.e. to indicate that the action, process or state expressed by the predicate is jointly performed/undergone/possessed by the agent/theme and some other person(s). Like a morphological affix, the comitative particle may not be separated from its base.

The comitative particle can in principle appear adjoined to VP or incorporated in the verb. In the case of complex predicates, i.e. a copula verb and a secondary predicate, the particle may be adjoined to the secondary predicate, to NP, AP or PP, and in this way comitative-mark the whole complex predicate.

Something fascinating occurs in the case of complex predicates consisting of a motion or transport verb and a directional PP. Here the comitative particle is either adjoined to the PP (27a) or attached to the verb (27b,c). In the latter case the directional PP must be extraposed, probably because the verb particle *mei* fills the structural position otherwise occupied by this PP. Strikingly, however, extraposition does not force the normal adjunct interpretation of PPs in extraposition in Frisian. In fact, (27a) and (27c) are more or less synonymous; in both cases the particle seems to comitative-mark the whole complex predicate.

(27) a.   Hy is mei nei Grins ta riden
           'He traveled with some other person(s) to Groningen'
      b.   *Hy is nei Grins ta meiriden
      c.   Hy is meiriden nei Grins ta

Another interesting phenomenon occurs with the verb *nimme* 'to take'. If this verb forms a complex predicate with a directional PP, this PP is obligatorily comitative-marked. Here as well, the comitative marker can appear either on the PP or on the verb, again comitative-marking the whole complex predicate:

(28) a.   Hja hie de kat *(mei) op bêd nommen
           'She took the cat to bed with her'
      b.   *Hja hie de kat op bêd meinommen
      c.   Hja hie de kat meinommen op bêd

With *nimme* comitative-marking is probably obligatory, because *nimme* is goal-oriented, i.e. the inherent goal of *nimme* is the agent. If it is combined with a secondary predicate, denoting the goal of the theme, speakers may feel urged to explicitly express that agent and theme land at the same place. This is done by adding the comitative particle *mei* (which has a reflexive interpretation here) or some other comitative PP like *by har* 'with her'. Note that also in this case English is different: in English the comitative PP is not obligatory with the verb *take* (cf. *She took the cat to bed (with her)*).

The order of the comitative particle with respect to the predicate seems to reflect the canonical position of (PP-)adjuncts. In the contential West Germanic OV-languages adjuncts normally follow nominal and adjectival projections, whereas they precede prepositional and verbal projections. For Frisian this is shown in (29):

(29) a. it hûs [op 'e pôle]　　　　　'the house on the island'
　　　 b. lokkich [sûnder dy]　　　　'happy without you'
　　　 c. [mei de boat] nei Amearika　'by boat to America'
　　　 d. [by 't hjerst] de hage knippe　'to trim the hedge in autumn'

The VP-final position of the comitative particle in the VO-language Danish (cf. (20d)) tallies with the general position of adjuncts in languages with a right-branching VP (Danish *vente på toget i en time* 'to wait for the train for one hour').

Note further that in Danish and in North Frisian, which have a right-branching particle phrase with the directional particle preceding the PP (e.g. Danish *ud i køkkenet* 'out to the kitchen', North Frisian (Fering-Öömrang) *iin uun dörnsk* 'into the livingroom'), there has been a tendency to adjoin the comitative particle to the right of prepositional secondary predicates (cf. Hoekstra 2000):

(30) a. De unge Damer (*kan maaske*) drages [$_{PP}$ ind <u>med</u>] (nowadays: <u>med</u> ind)
　　　　　 [ODS 13 s.v. *med*,1154]
　　　　　 'The young ladies could possibly be dragged in'
　　　 b. Hi as ei [$_{PP}$ tüs <u>mä</u>] kimen　　　　(Fering-Öömrang)
　　　　　 'He didn't come home with some other person(s)'

I have nothing much to say on the additive use of the particle. As a V*P-modifier it is comparable to focus particles like *ek* 'also'. As an N*P-modifier in Frisian and Danish, it resembles postnominal adjuncts like Frisian *deropta* (e.g. *50 euro deropta* '50 euro extra') or Danish *til* (*fem minuter til* 'another five minutes'). An interesting question is of course why the use with N*P seems to be restricted to nouns denoting reason or cause and to the partitive construction.

That German has the particle before N*P, unlike Frisian and Danish, may have something to do with the fact that additive *mit* also precedes DP (and DegP) in German. In its use before DP *mit* might occupy the specifier position of a pre-DP quantifier phrase (cf. Giusti 1991). The construction reminds one of partitive constructions in the older stages of the Germanic languages in which a DP with an adjective in the superlative is preceded by a numeral. Compare the following example from Old Frisian:

(31)   tria dae beste hinx dyer [*Oudfriesche Oorkonden* II 248, l. 61]
        'three of the best horses (lit. three the best horses)'

If *mit* before DP is in the specifier of a high quantifier phrase, *mit* before N*P might occupy the specifier position of a lower quantifier phrase in German (possibly Number Phrase).

5.   Concluding remarks

In this article I have given a description of the comitative particle *mei* in West Frisian and compared it to its counterparts in the other Germanic languages. Needless to say that my analysis of the comitative particle only scratches the surface. Future research will have to answer many questions of principle and detail that could not be exhaustively treated here. Among the former are the question of the historical development of the comitative particle, the question of its semantics, and the question of the relevance of apparently word order-sensitive elements like the comitative particle for directionality, in particular the antisymmetry hypothesis (Kayne 1994).

References

Giusti, Giuliana (1991) 'The Categorial Status of Quantified Nominals', *Linguistische Berichte* 136, 438–454.

Hoekstra, Jarich (2000) '*Versandete Präpositionen*' (*Preposition Wrap*) *und die Struktur der Partikelphrase im Nordfriesischen*. Ms. Fach Friesische Philologie, Christian-Albrechts-Universität, Kiel.

Kayne (1994) *The Antisymmetry of Syntax*. MIT Press, Cambridge, Mass.

ODS = *Ordbog over de Danske Sprog*. Gyldendalske Boghandel/Nordisk Forlag, København (1932, 1968²).

Zifonun, Gisela (1996/1997) 'Ungewöhnliche Verwendungen von *mit* (I, II)', *Deutsch als Fremdsprache* 33/4, 218–222; 34/1, 20–25.

Zifonun, Gisela (1999), 'Wenn *mit* alleine im Mittelfeld erscheint. Verbpartikeln und ihre Doppelgänger im Deutschen und Englischen', in: Heide Wegener (ed.), *Deutsch kontrastiv. Typologisch-vergleichende Untersuchungen zur deutschen Grammatik*. (Studien zur deutschen Grammatik 59) Stauffenburg Verlag, Tübingen, 211–235.

Does the chronology principle operate on sentence level?
Evidence from the distribution of adverbial PP's[*]

Frank Jansen
Utrecht University

1. Introduction

One of the possible factors that govern the order of constituents in written Dutch is the chronology principle, which states that the order of constituents in the sentence corresponds to the temporal succession of the events they refer to.[1,2] Jansen and Wijnands (2004) try to demonstrate the relevance of this principle on sentence level by comparing the following text fragment with variant (1a), in which the *na*-PP is postponed:

(1) (Het systeem-Berlijn, geïntroduceerd in een oefenwedstrijd tegen AS Roma in Duitsland, bood Adriaanse een uitweg (nl. uit de problemen met Ajax FJ)). Na de zege op Feyenoord won Ajax achtereenvolgens van FC Twente, AZ, Sparta en, gisteren, FC Groningen. (*Volkskrant* 1–10–01)
(The Berlin system, introduced in a training match against AS Roma in Germany, gave Adriaanse a way out (viz. of the problems with Ajax (FJ)). After the victory Ajax beat respectively FC Twente, AZ, Sparta, and, yesterday, FC Groningen.
a. ?Ajax won achtereenvolgens van FC Twente, AZ, Sparta en, gisteren, FC Groningen na de zege op Feyenoord.

Example (1a) is stylistically marked in comparison to (1). In both variants, the reader has the task build up a mental representation of the correct order of events, in this case, the victories of Ajax. In (1), the sentence initial *na*-PP gives the reader a strong signal that the victory on Feyenoord is the starting point of the consecutive events. In (1a) the reader first has to process the series of events from the victory on FC Twente until that on Groningen. After that, after processing *na de zege op Feyenoord*, he realizes that he has to reconstruct his

Linguistics in the Netherlands 2004 21 (2004), 125–133.
ISSN 0929–7332 / E-ISSN 1569–9919 © Algemene Vereniging voor Taalwetenschap

mental representation of the time order, because the victory on Feyenoord precedes all the others.

So, (1) gives more service to the reader building up his mental representation than (1a), and that might be the explanation of the deviancy of (1a). In the absence of other more plausible explanations, I take the difference in acceptability of (1) and (1a) as anecdotic evidence that the chronology principle operates for PP's on sentence level, at least for some kinds of sentences.

In the remainder of this paper I will try to assess the relevance of chronology for constituent order. First, I will give some a priori evidence for and against chronology (Section 2). Then I will present the results of a corpus investigation of temporal PP's (Section 3). Since the results are negative, I will first discuss how we can better explain the distribution of temporal PP's (Section 4). In the last section (4) I will try to reconcile the negative results with the positive evidence presented in this section and the next sections.

2.   A priori evidence for and against chronology on sentence level

2.1 The order of elements in conjunctions is conditioned by the chronology principle

The chronology principle is certainly operative on the level of narrative texts: independent asyndetic sentences of narrative texts are interpreted as referring to successive events (Labov and Waletzky 1967; Thompson 1987). The same holds for the interpretation of conjoined phrases, like

(2)   Jan   at een appel en   een ei
       John ate an apple and an egg

Besides the irrelevant reading in which there is no specific claim about the order of events, example (2) has at least two possible readings: the events are simultaneous ('John ate the apple and the egg at the same time'), or consecutive chronologically ('John ate first the apple and then the egg'). There is one impossible reading: consecutive anti-chronologically ('John ate first the egg and then the apple').

If two temporal PP's are coordinated the chronology principle operates as well. At least that is how I can explain the deviancy of (3a) compared with (3) (both constructed by myself (FJ)):

(3)   Voor zijn afstuderen en na zijn pensioen heeft Peter veel gereisd
       Before graduating and after his retirement, Peter travelled a lot
    a.   ?Na zijn pensioen en voor zijn afstuderen heeft Peter veel gereisd

When the conjunction consists of two temporal prepositions the order is obligatorily chronological: *voor en na de oorlog* 'before and after the war' (*na en voor de oorlog*).[3]

2.2 The order of PP's in a complex PP is conditioned by the chronology principle

Adverbial phrases are sometimes a combination of two PP's, for example *van 10 uur tot half drie* 'from ten o'clock until two thirty'. If in PP's like this (henceforth complex PP's) the two PP's refer to two distinct time events, the internal order is conditioned by the chronology principle: the first PP obligatorily refers to the earlier event and the second PP to the subsequent event. This is the case for idiomatic expressions like *van begin tot eind* 'from the beginning till the end' (**tot eind van begin*), *van 's morgens vroeg tot 's avonds laat* 'from the early morning till the late evening' (**tot 's avonds laat van 's morgens vroeg*). However, more relevant for our goal are cases like (4) where the order of the elements is not frozen:

> (4) In de Finse hoofdstad werden vanaf vrijdag tot en met gisteren de volgende minima gemeten: (…). (*Trouw* 27–2–01)
> In the Finnish capital from Friday till yesterday the following minimum temperatures were measured: (…).

The complex PP *vanaf … gisteren* is easily split up (4a), but a reversed order of the PP's (like in (4b,c)) gives an odd impression:

> (4) a. Vanaf vrijdag werden in de Finse hoofdstad tot en met gisteren de volgende minima gemeten: (…).
> b. ?In de Finse hoofdstad werden tot en met gisteren vanaf vrijdag de volgende minima gemeten: (…).
> c. ?Tot en met gisteren werden in de Finse hoofdstad vanaf vrijdag de volgende minima gemeten: (…)

The same applies to complex PP's with the prepositions *van … tot*, and complex PP's marking the beginning and endpoint of a path:

> (5) Het ziekteverzuim onder het personeel is teruggebracht van 12 naar 8 procent. (*Volkskrant* 8–11–2003)
> a. ?Naar 8 procent is het ziekteverzuim onder het personeel teruggebracht van 12.

From this and the preceding section I conclude that there are cases where an anti-chronological constituent order is unacceptable or at least highly marked.

2.3 Contra-evidence: The distribution of temporal clauses is not chronological

In Jansen, Troost and Sanders (MS), we discuss the chronological conditioning of temporal clauses in relation to the embedding sentence, like for example

> (6) a. Voordat Piet een taart bakte, braadde Carla het vlees
> Before Peter baked a cake, Carla roasted the meat

      b.   Carla braadde het vlees voordat Piet een taart bakte
            Carla roasted the meat before Peter a cake baked

(7) a.   Nadat Joost afgewassen had, zette Johanna koffie
            'After Joost had cleaned (sc. the dishes), Johanna made coffee'
      b.   Johanna zette koffie nadat Joost afgewassen had

The chronology principle predicts that the chronological order of (6b) and (7a) will occur more frequently than the anti-chronological order of (6a) and (7b). However, a quantitative analysis of the temporal clauses in three corpora (policy documents, culinary recipes and chatbox conversations) demonstrated that this prediction was not born out by the facts, as the chronological orders did not occur more frequently in the texts than the antichronological orders. We conclude that there is no evidence that chronology is involved in the distribution of temporal clauses. So at least one type of temporal adverbial phrase is not conditioned by the chronology principle.

3.   A corpus investigation of the distribution of temporal adverbial PP's

3.1 Hypotheses

In the light of the mixed results of the previous section, we need more evidence before we can decide on the relevance of the chronology principle on sentence level. Therefore I did a corpus investigation of temporal PP's, which is presented in this section. I included three types of PP's:

1. PP's with prepositions expressing chronological consecution: *na* 'after', *sinds* 'since' and *vanaf* 'from'. The chronology principle predicts that these PP's predominantly have a sentence initial position. So we expect the order in for example (8) to be significantly more frequent in texts than (9):

    (8)   Na de oorlog werd hij hoogleraar economie aan de VU (*Parool* 27–12–2001)
         After the war he became an economics professor at the VU

    (9)   De Engelse acteur Nigel Hawthorne, (…), is gisterochtend op 72-jarige leeftijd overleden na een hartaanval. (*NH* 27–12–2001)
         The English actor Nigel Hawthorne, (…), died yesterday morning after a heart attack

2. PP's with prepositions expressing anti-chronological consecution *voor* 'before', *voorafgaande aan* 'preceding' and *tot* 'until'. Chronology predicts here a preference for the sentence final position. We expect the order exemplified by (10) to occur more frequently than the order in (11)

    (10) Maar hij bleef preken, bijna elke zondag, tot aan het einde (*NH* 13–11–2001)
         But he kept preaching, nearly every Sunday, until the end

a. Tot vlak voor zijn dood gaf hij cursussen aan beginnende kamerleden
(*Trouw* 12–12–2001)
Until just before his dead he gave courses to beginning members of the
parliament.

3. PP's with prepositions expressing (partial) simultaneity: *tijdens, gedurende*
and *onder*, all translatable by 'during'. Chronology predicts a position
somewhere in the middle of the sentence, like in:

(11) Ivanova veroverde tijdens de Winterspelen van Serajewo een bronzen medaille.
(*Volkskrant* 22–12–2001)
Ivanova conquered during the winter games of Serajewo a bronze medal

3.2 Material and method

I used the corpus of the *Krantenbank*, an electronic database comprising all
articles of the Dutch journals *Algemeen Dagblad, NRC Handelsblad, Het Parool,
Trouw* and *de Volkskrant*. I selected obituaries, a narrative genre, in 2001.[4] The
investigation was limited to adverbial PP's in non-elliptical independent
declarative clauses. PP's that could be analysed as complements of an NP were
excluded. I took at least 25 examples of every preposition into account. The
distribution was analyzed by classifying the PP's in three positions: sentence
initial, sentence final and in the middle of the sentence.

3.3 Results

In Table 1 the distribution of the PP's in the corpus is presented.

When we compare the distribution of *na*-type, *tijdens*-type and *voor*-type
PP's, we see that the predictions of the chronology hypothesis seem to hold for
the na-type and *tijdens*-type, as they occupy most frequently the first and
middle position respectively. However, PP's of the *voor*-type occupy also the
sentence initial position, and not the expected sentence final position. Furthermore, a statistical evaluation of the differences in distribution between the types
revealed that none of the differences between the *na*- and the *voor*-type was
statistically significant ($p > .05$). The distribution of the *tijdens*-type PP's
differed from that of the *na*-type ($\chi^2 = 14.14$, $p < .001$) and from that of the
voor-type ($\chi^2 = 12.17$; $p < .001$). However, this is a difference that cannot be
attributed to chronology.

The lack of success of the chronology hypothesis deteriorates when we
compare the distributions of individual prepositions. The chronology hypothesis predicts that the prepositions of one chronological type, like *tijdens* and
gedurende, na and *sinds*, and *voor* and *tot* have a rather similar distribution
pattern, but this is hardly the case.[5] Conversely, we see two prepositions that are
opposites of each other *na* and *voor*, do have similar distribution patterns.

Table 1. Distribution of three types of temporal PP's in obituaries

	position			total
	sentence initial	middle	sentence final	
Na-type	40 (49%)	10 (12%)	32 (39%)	82
na	16 (62%)	4 (15%)	6 (23%)	26
vanaf	15 (50%)	4 (13%)	11 (37%)	30
sinds	9 (34%)	2 (8%)	15 (58%)	26
Tijdens-type	29 (35%)	35 (43%)	18 (22%)	82
tijdens	13 (43%)	10 (33%)	7 (24%)	25
gedurende	8 (31%)	15 (58%)	3 (9%)	26
onder	8 (31%)	10 (38%)	8 (31%)	26
Voor-type	39 (48%)	13 (16%)	30 (36%)	82
voor	15 (60%)	2 (8%)	8 (32%)	25
voorafgaand aan	12 (55%)	5 (15%)	8 (30%)	27
tot	9 (30%)	7 (23%)	14 (45%)	30

3.4 Conclusion

The conclusion seems inevitable that the distribution of temporal PP's in Dutch narrative texts is not conditioned by the chronology principle. And taken into account the results of the temporal clauses discussed in Section 2.3, we would like to make a wider claim: chronology is irrelevant on sentence level. Or, if it is justified to consider the distributional facts as an indication of preferences of the reader: a reader can build up a mental representation of the time order of two events in a sentence, one in an adverbial PP and the other in the embedding sentence, irrespective of the position of that PP.

4.   How to reconcile the negative evidence of the corpus investigation with the positive a priori evidence for chronology?

Since chronology turns out to be not the norm at all, the fragments we started with in the Sections 1, 2.1 and 2.2, which were the very reason for assuming that chronology is relevant, turn into a problem: why are they so exceptionally sensitive to chronology?

I assume that the chronological interpretation of asyndetic independent sentences and of coordinated phrases (see examples (2), (3) and (i) in note 3) is caused by the chronology principle. If a reader is confronted with two successive expressions with the same function and hierarchical position, he will assume that their order reflects the time order of the events.

Next, the examples in 2.2 (see (4) and (5)) seem to have something in common in that there is mention of two lexical expressions of the order of events in both of them. Both expressions give the reader instructions how to build up a correct mental representation of the time order of the events referred to in the PP's and the event of the embedding clause. I conjecture that this is no problem for the reader if he can simply add the information provided by the second PP to the information provided the first PP. However, if a simple addition will not do, because the reader has to change his interpretation of the first PP as well, the sentence becomes less acceptable.

At this point one might wonder how example (1) (here repeated for convenience) fits into this explanation.

(1)   Na de zege op Feyenoord won Ajax achtereenvolgens van FC Twente, AZ, Sparta en, gisteren, FC Groningen
  a.   ?Ajax won achtereenvolgens van FC Twente, AZ, Sparta en, gisteren, FC Groningen na de zege op Feyenoord.

At first sight, one might think that the temporal expressions *achtereenvolgens* and *na* pose the same reinterpretation problems to the reader as the two expressions in (4) and (5). However, if we delete *achtereenvolgens the sentence remains* awkward:

(1)   b.   ?Ajax won van FC Twente, AZ, Sparta en, gisteren, FC Groningen na de zege op Feyenoord.

I surmise that the enumeration *FC Twente … FC Groningen* itself is another device for signalling the time order. As the parts of enumerations are coordinated, the chronology hypothesis is operative. So the reader gets a powerful signal that the time order of the events is: first a victory on FC Twente, then on AZ, etc. The reader of (1) will add this information to the victory on Feyenoord. The reader of (1a) has to do some reconstruction work before he has built up the time order of events right.

The *na*-PP in (1) functions as a setting for the event depicted in the remainder of the sentence. Therefore it can be considered as a case of linear modification, the fact that a preceding phrase affects the semantic interpretation of the following phrases (see Pardoen 1998; and Jansen 2002 and the references cited there).

I hold Linear Modification also responsible for two other results of this investigation: the fact that we did not find mirror-image examples of (1) with *voor*-PP's and the fact that the distribution of *na* and *voor* turns out to be similar (see Table 1).

Example (1) stands not alone. I found more examples like it, with a sentence initial *na* or *sinds*-PP that could not easily be postponed. However, I did not find any mirror image example with PP's of the *voor*-type group: A sentence with a sentence final *voor*-PP that resisted preposing. And even worse (for the chronology hypothesis) some of the non-sentence final *voor*-PP's (which should be odd because they are anti-chronological) resist postponing to the last position:

(12)   (…) en nu wilde hij (een stervende sprookjesverteller), voor zijn dood, nog een kabouter zien, een werkelijke kabouter. (*Algemeen Dagblad* 22–12–2001)
(…) and now he (a dying fairy-teller (FJ)) wished, before his dead, to see a gnome, a real gnome

a.   ?en nu wilde hij nog een kabouter zien voor zijn dood, een werkelijke kabouter.

The problem with (12a) seems to be that it asserts that the subject wants something to happen before his death, which is obvious and therefore rather ridiculous, while the *voor*-PP in (8) gives only the setting of the event.

Voor-PP's might be even more fit for linear modification than *na*-PP's for a semantic reason. By the very meaning of the preposition *na*, *na*-PP's only assert a chronological series of events, which is expected: events follow each other. However, a *voor*-PP is different. When a writer inserts it in a sentence, it is to warn his readers that their chronological expectations are thwarted: something happened **before** the events they expected. I contend that this unexpected type of information is very suitable for settings. If this is correct I conclude that the astonishing similarity in distribution of PP's of the *na*-type and the *voor*-type is caused by opposed forces: sentence initial *na* is preposed to adjust to the chronology principle and sentence initial *voor* is preposed to emphasize the antichronology of the events.

Notes

* This paper has profited from the helpful comments by prof. dr. Theo Janssen, drs. Jacqueline Evers-Vermeul and dr. Jan ten Thije during the discussion, an anonymous reviewer and dr. Henk Pander Maat, and from an e-mail exchange with dr. P-A. Coppen.

1. Jansen and Wijnands (2004) gives a survey of nine non-grammatical factors that may affect the order of constituents in written Dutch. Jansen (2002) is a more detailed discussion of the relevance of the factor 'Linear Modification'.

2. I use the term *events* here in the ordinary sense of all types of 'occurrences', by consequence also the 'states' and 'processes' in discourse representation theory terminology (see De Swart 1998 for example) are called *events* in this paper.

3. If two during-PP's are conjoined which refer to nonsimultaneous events, the result is a little less awkward than (3a):

(i)   ?Gedurende zijn pensionering en tijdens zijn studietijd en heeft Peter veel gereisd
During his retirement and during his student years, Peter travelled a lot.

It is tempting to attribute the relative unacceptability of (3a) to the opposite signals that *na* and *voor* give to the reader (see Section 4).

4. At 1–1–04 the Krantenbank was taken over by another publishing company, and the tools changed for the worse as it became impossible to select genres. Therefore, I decided to select obituaries by combining in my queries forms of the verb *overlijden* 'to pass away' and the prepositions under investigation.

5. An anonymous reviewer suggests that the difference in distribution pattern between *na* and *sinds*, (and perhaps the same holds for *voor* and *tot*) to a difference in aspect: *na* being perfective and *sinds* being imperfective. This topic awaits further investigation in the future.

References

De Swart, H. (1998) Aspect shift and coercion. *Natural language and linguistic theory* 16, 347–385.

Jansen, F. (2002) Preposed adverbial phrases in Dutch texts. Evidence for the Left-Right Principle or for Linear Modification? In: H. Broekhuis & P. Fikkert (eds) *Linguistics in the Netherlands 2002*. Amsterdam/Philadephia: John Benjamins: 97–106.

Jansen, F., Troost, C. & Sanders, T. (ms) Order of mention in written Dutch coordinated and subordinated clauses.

Jansen, F. & Wijnands, R. (2004) 'Doorkruisingen van het Links-Rechtsprincipe. *Neerlandistiek* 0401/pdf, 1–38.

Labov, W. & Waletzky, J. (1967) 'Narrative analysis: oral versions of personal experience'. In: J. Helm (ed.) *Essays on the Verbal and Visual Arts*, Proceedings of the Annual Spring Meeting of the American Ethnological Society. Seattle: University of Washington Press: 12–44.

Pardoen, J. A. (1998) *Interpretatiestructuur*. Dissertation VUA, Amsterdam.

Thompson, S. A. (1987) '"Subordination" and narrative event structure'. In: R. Tomlin (ed.) *Coherence and grounding in Discourse*. Amsterdam: John Benjamins, 435–454.

Seven years later

The effect of spelling on interpretation[*]

Anneke Neijt, Robert Schreuder and Harald Baayen
University of Nijmegen / Max Planck Institute for Psycholinguistics

1. Introduction

The spelling of linking elements in Dutch compounds such as *boekenkast* 'bookScase' and *slangenbeet* 'snakeSbite' has been an issue since the introduction of an extensive set of rules in De Vries and Te Winkel (1884), the publication that received legal status in 1947 and offers the foundations of present-day Dutch orthography. Though most of De Vries and Te Winkel's spelling system is still in force today, their spelling of linking elements no longer is. This aspect of Dutch spelling was changed in 1954 and in 1995, cf. the overview of words changed and not changed since 1884 in (1).

(1) a. *Not changed*:
zonneschijn 'sunshine', gebarentaal 'sign language'

b. *Changed in 1954*:
vrouwebeeld > vrouwenbeeld 'woman's picture'
aspergenbed > aspergebed 'asparagus field'

c. *Changed in 1995*:
pannekoek > pannenkoek 'pancake'
gedachtengang > gedachtegang 'line of thoughts'

d. *Changed twice*:
zotteklap > zottenklap > zotteklap 'fool's talk'
hondenhok > hondehok > hondenhok 'doghouse'
bessensap > bessesap > bessensap 'currant juice'

The spelling rules of 1884 were primarily based on plural meaning. In a compound with a modifier that lacks plural meaning, for instance *zonneschijn*, the linking schwa is written as *-e* because *zonne* refers to one sun only. In a

Linguistics in the Netherlands 2004 21 (2004), **134–145.**
ISSN 0929–7332 / E-ISSN 1569–9919 © Algemene Vereniging voor Taalwetenschap

compound with a modifier that has plural meaning such as *gebarentaal* 'language with signs', the linking schwa is written as *-en*. This part of De Vries and Te Winkel's rules applies to the examples (1a–d) except to words of the type *hondenhok* which followed a spelling rule based on pronunciation. In earlier stages of Dutch, linking schwa was followed by [n] in hiatus position, i.e. before [h] and before vowels. As the standard pronunciation of linking elements had become schwa in all phonological contexts, this rule was no longer part of the prescriptions of 1954.

The rules of 1954 specified that the linking *-en* should be used only when a plural interpretation of the modifier of the compound is inevitable. As *hond* and *bes* in *hondenhok* and *bessensap* (1d) are not necessarily plural, they should be written with *-e*. Moreover, when the modifier refers to human beings, cf. *vrouwebeeld* (1b) and *zotteklap* (1d), the linking element should be written with *-en*. A third change in 1954 is that rules only apply to words with a plural form ending in *-en* or *-n* and not to words such as *asperge* (1b), that take only a plural *-s* ending. In 1995, the rules based on semantic features such as ⟨+plural⟩ and ⟨+human⟩ have been replaced by morphological criteria, such that the linking element schwa should be written as *-en* after words that take plural *-en* but not plural *-s*. This created the changes in (1c), since *pannen* is the only plural form for *pan*, whereas the plural form of *gedachte* is either *gedachten* or *gedachtes*. Similarly, it reintroduced the old forms *hondenhok* and *bessensap* (1d). For reasons unclear to us, *zotteklap* (1d) regained its old spelling.

The new spelling rules reflect a change in the linguistic analysis of the linking schwa. The older system was based on the conviction that this schwa expressed plurality in compounds such as *gebarentaal* and *gedachtengang*, and that it expressed a meaningless old ending in compounds such as *zonneschijn* and *pannekoek*. The new spelling system regards the schwa in all compounds as a meaningless linking phoneme that by convention is written in the same way as the plural suffix.

In 1996 we investigated the effect of writing the linking schwa as *-e* or *-en* on language processing (Schreuder et al. 1998) for two sets of words. The first set contained compounds such as *boekenkast*, boek+en+kast 'bookcase', with a modifier that has inevitably a plural interpretation. The second set contained compounds such as *slangenbeet*, slang+en+beet 'snake bite', that until then were written as *slangebeet* because its modifier has no plural interpretation. In experiments, we manipulated the presence of *-n* in both groups of words. A first experiment showed that perceptual identification was not affected by whether the linking schwa was realized as *-en* or *-e*. While changing the spelling of the vowel of the modifier of compounds severely affected their string familiarity and led to longer identification latencies, no such effect could be observed for changing the spelling of the linking schwa. A second experiment showed that changing the orthographic realization of the linking schwa from *-e* to *-en* in the group of words formerly spelled without -*n* induced the activation of plural semantics. We concluded that writing the linking schwa in the orthographic form of the plural suffix led to the activation of plural meaning caused by the automatic parsing of the suffix -*en* and its interpretation as a plural marker. A third experiment showed that in the set of words for which the linking schwa is realized as -*en* both in the old and in the new spelling system (type *boekenkast*), leaving out -*n* has no effect. We hypothesized that these compounds, which traditionally are interpreted (and taught) to have plural interpretation for the modifier, have intrinsic plurals as their left-hand members and are stored in the mental lexicon as plurals. A final experiment, plurality rating, investigated speakers' intuitions concerning the plurality of the modifiers in Dutch compounds as a function of the presence or the absence of the -*n*. This experiment again showed the two sets of words to be different. Judgments for the set *slange(n)beet* were influenced by the presence or absence of -*n* more than judgments for the set *boeke(n)kast*. See below for details.

These experimental results support our hypothesis of a dual-route model of morphological processing as outlined by Schreuder and Baayen (1995) and Baayen et al. (1997). In this model, the parsing route and the direct access route operate in parallel. The stored meaning representation of compounds is invoked irrespective of the parsed elements, which explains the different response latencies and plurality ratings for forms with and without -*n* in both types of compounds.

The experiments also show that plural semantics is activated in the mental lexicon when the linking schwa is written as the plural suffix -*en*. We concluded that -*en* is not a meaningless phoneme. Rather, it is the plural suffix itself. We expected that plural interpretation of modifiers will eventually become commonplace for compounds with a linking schwa. In this way, the process of the functional reinterpretation of the schwa as a plural suffix instead of as a (meaningless) relic of the obsolete morphological system of medieval Dutch would be completed (Schreuder 1998: 568).

This paper presents the results of plurality rating experiments with the same word materials but new participants. These experiments took place in 2003, seven years after the original studies were conducted.

2.   Plurality Rating: 1996 *versus* 2003

To see why a scale for plurality makes sense for the issue of determining the meaning of linking schwa, consider the compounds in (2):

(2)   *mierenhoop*   'anthill'
      duiventil   'dovecote'
      hondenhok   'doghouse'
      slakkenhuis 'snail shell'

For anthill, it is fairly obvious that it houses many ants. Less pigeons but presumably more than one will be present in a dovecote. A doghouse could very well be owned by a single dog. But a snail shell definitely is owned by a single snail. The spelling of 1954 opted for the plural interpretation of *mierenhoop* and *duiventil*, but a singular interpretation of *hondenhok* and *slakkenhuis*. In our experiment, we investigated speakers' intuitions concerning plurality as a function of the presence or absence of -*n* in compounds such as *boekenkast* and *slangenbeet* that used to be written with or without -*n* on the basis of their plural or singular meaning.

There are two factors that might influence the plurality rating. The first is the presence or absence of the -*n*. The presence of -*n* will lead to higher plurality ratings for both word types. The second factor concerns the stored meaning of the compound, which, according to our findings in the experiments of 1996, contained the semantics of plurality for the modifier of words of the type *boekenkast* only. Hence, processing *boekenkast* or *boekekast* will activate plural semantics by the direct route. The parsing routes for *boekenkast* and *boekekast* will have the same effect, since they also lead to a mental representation in which plurality is stored. For *slangenbeet*, however, the stored semantic representation is one in which the modifier is viewed as a natural singular. Here, parsing the new form *slangenbeet* will affect plurality ratings, because -*en* signals plurality. We predict that this effect will be smaller in 2003 than in 1996, because the use of -*en* in spelling has changed the semantics of words of this type. Apart from this, we expect that -*en* will have less cue validity, because it is present in all compounds.

Participants. In 1996 and 2003, thirty-three resp. thirty-eight undergraduate students of Dutch linguistics at Radboud University participated. All were native speakers of Dutch.

Materials. Forty-eight compounds of the type *slangenbeet* were selected as experimental items, and 29 compounds of the type *boekenkast*, see appendix. Each of these compounds was presented in two forms: with and without the -*n*. A given participant saw 24 compounds of the type *slangenbeet* with the -*n* and 24 compounds without the -*n*. Similarly, each participant saw 15 compounds of the type *boekenkast* with the -*n* and 14 compounds without the -*n*. A participant was never exposed to spelling variants of the same compound.

Procedure. Participants were asked to rate on a 7-point scale their estimation of the plurality of the modifier of the compounds. A rating of 1 indicated "certainly singular" and a rating of 7 "certainly plural". The participants received explicit instructions to ignore spelling and spelling errors, and to concentrate purely on the semantics of the modifier.

Results and Discussion. Mean plurality ratings are presented in Table 1.

Table 1. Mean plurality ratings on a 7-point scale in 1996 and 2003. The examples *boeke(n)kast* represent compounds that used to be spelled with ⟨n⟩ in the former spelling. The examples *slange(n)beet* represent compounds that used to be spelled without ⟨n⟩.

1996		Compounds actually presented		Difference
		with *-en*	with *-e*	
Word type, based on former spelling	with *-en*	5.72 *boekenkast*	4.60 *boekekast*	1.12
	with *-e*	3.92 *slangenbeet*	2.35 *slangebeet*	1.57

2003		Compounds actually presented		Difference
		with *-en*	with *-e*	
Word type, based on former spelling	with *-en*	5.63 *boekenkast*	5.01 *boekekast*	0.62
	with *-e*	3.48 *slangenbeet*	2.89 *slangebeet*	0.59

In 1996, we observed that removal of the *-n* in *boekenkast* resulted in a smaller decrease in plurality (1.12) than dropping the *-n* from *slangenbeet* (1.57). This interaction was significant by participants as well as by items in an analysis of variance with spelling variants as within-item factor. Significant main effects of actual spelling and word type were also observed. See Schreuder (1998: 566).

On the basis of the new rules for writing linking schwa and our hypothesis of a dual route model of morphological processing, we predicted that the autonomous parsing route for *slangenbeet* will have the effect that the modifier of these types of compounds will be considered plural. In other words: the fact that plural semantics is activated by spelling *-en* will lead to storage of plural meaning. We predicted that in due time, the linking schwa would become completely identical to the plural suffix. A comparison of the two experiments shows that in 2003 speakers' intuitions have changed in the direction predicted. In general, participants judged the plurality of the modifiers to be higher than in 1996 (linear effect model with experiment as factor: $t(4725) = -4.4$, $p = 0.000$).

Our new experiment shows also that the plurality ratings for *boeke(n)kast* and *slange(n)beet* will not become similar, cf. the significant main effect of word type that is also present in the experiment performed in 2003 (linear mixed effect model with subject as error stratum; word type: $t(4725) = 6.2$, $p < 0.000$). The semantic difference on which De Vries and Te Winkel based their rule for the spelling of linking elements is still valid and it seems that this difference is robust.

A main effect of spelling is still present in 2003: $t(4725) = -24.4$, $p < 0.000$. Interestingly, the plurality ratings for *slangenbeet* are lower and those for *slangebeet* are higher in 2003 ($t(4725) = 2.2$, $p < 0.03$) and the effect of manipulating the spelling of linking elements is smaller in both groups of words (for *boeke(n)kast* $1.12 > 0.62$ and for *slange(n)beet* $1.57 > 0.59$; $t(4725) = 4.8$, $p = 0.000$). These changes can be explained on the basis of the new spelling conventions as follows. The new rules are similar for all types of compounds, which leads to similar effects of the experimental manipulation. Because *-en* is conventionally the spelling of linking elements, it has less cue validity in the context of compounds. In other words, since language users no longer have the opportunity to express plurality in compounds, they assign less value to the presence or absence of *n*.

3.   Plurality Rating: Heterogeneous *versus* homogeneous

One of the universals put forward to explain language behavior is the One Meaning One Form Principle that dates back to Wilhelm von Humboldt (1836), cf. Vennemann (1972: 183) and Anttila (1972: 181). In the Dutch linguistic community this universal has become known as Von Humboldt's Universal since the debate between Geert Koefoed, Jaap van Marle and Albert Sassen twenty years ago. Koefoed and Van Marle (1980) used Von Humboldt's Universal to explain language change, whereas Sassen (1981) doubted its usefulness, because polysemy and homophony are abundantly present in languages, and languages need flexibility rather than strict form-meaning relations. Our experiment offers the possibility to test this principle.

The One Meaning One Form Principle defines a reciprocal relation between meaning and form. In our study, we investigated the effect of form differences on meaning, for which the principle predicts that similarity of form will stimulate the language user to find meaning similarities, and that variation of form will stimulate the language user to find meaning differences. The fact that similarity of form leads to similarity of interpretation has been illustrated by the outcome of our experiments: when a linking schwa is written as a plural marker, plurality ratings are higher.

Our experiments thus far also showed that variation of form stimulates the language user to find meaning distinctions: the effect of leaving out *-n* in the spelling is significant. Another question is whether the conceptual difference between the two types of words is autonomously present, irrespective of context. The differences in plurality ratings might decrease or disappear completely when form variation is no longer present. In order to answer this question we performed experiments with our list of compounds in two versions: either all linking elements were written with -*en* or they were written with -*e*.

Participants. Thirty-seven undergraduate students of Dutch linguistics at Radboud University participated. Eighteen participants received compounds written with linking -*en* and nineteen participants received compounds written with linking -*e*. All were native speakers of Dutch.

Materials and Procedure. Similar to the experiment of 1996.

Results and Discussion. Mean plurality ratings were calculated by participants and by items, as well as the mean difference scores for each word type, as shown in Table 2 "homogeneous". For ease of comparison, the relevant part of Table 1 is copied under "heterogeneous".

Table 2. Mean plurality ratings for heterogeneous or homogeneous stimuli in 2003. See for details Table 1, but observe that in the homogeneous setting one group of participants rated compounds actually presented with -*en* and another group of participants rated compounds with -*e*.

2003, heterogeneous		Compounds actually presented	
		with -*en*	with -*e*
Word type, based on former spelling	with -*en*	5.63 *boekenkast*	5.01 *boekekast*
	with -*e*	3.48 *slangenbeet*	2.89 *slangebeet*

2003, homogeneous		Compounds actually presented	
		all with -*en*	all with -*e*
Word type, based on former spelling	with -*en*	5.57 *boekenkast*	5.04 *boekekast*
	with -*e*	3.42 *slangenbeet*	3.10 *slangebeet*

A comparison of the data of both experiments shows hat the pattern of results for the four cells in both experiments is the same ($F(2,5665) = 2.2$, $p < 0.11$). A detailed comparison of the rating patterns of each of the four cells of both experiments shows no differences. This experiment shows that the meaning distinctions between the two groups of words that used to be spelled differently is robust. Even in a context in which the form suggests that all modifiers of the compounds are plural or all are singular, participants react in a similar way.

4.   Family size

For the complete set of words in the experiments of Table 2, we investigated a number of covariates: frequencies and family sizes (Schreuder and Baayen 1997). Token frequencies of the compound, of the modifier and of the head are no predictors of plurality judgments (linear mixed effect model, compound frequency: $t(4658) = -0.77$, $p = 0.44$; modifier frequency: $t(4658) = -0.82$, $p = 0.41$ and head frequency: $t(4658) = -0.31$, $p = 0.75$), but there is an effect of family size of modifier and head.

A larger family size of the modifier correlates with a lower rating ($\beta = 0.15$, $t(4660) = -4.45$, $p = 0.000$). Our tentative explanation runs as follows. Modifiers with a large family size occur in a large number of morphological contexts. The chance for such modifiers to be used in contexts with different interpretations is higher and the user will be less certain about their meaning (cf. Moscoso 2003). Both plural and singular contexts will be available, which leads to vagueness, that translates in lower plurality ratings. (Examples may clarify this point. The family of *boek* consists of words such as *boekenkast, handboek, omboeken, boeking, boekje* etc. This family is larger than the family of *slang*, that includes *slangenbeet, slangenleer, tuinslang, slangetje* etc. Given a larger family, the contexts in which *boek* occurs are more diverse than the contexts in which *slang* occurs.)

Also, a correlation of the family size of the head was found, but only in words of the type *slangenbeet* ($\beta = -0.21$, $t(4660) = 5.62$, $p = 0.000$). When the family size of the head of these compounds is larger, plurality ratings for the modifiers are higher. The difference between words of the type *slangenbeet* and words of the type *boekenkast* can be explained on the basis of form-meaning relations, which are different for both types of words. In words such as *boekenkast* the linking schwa and the grapheme *en* are appropriate, but in words such as *slangenbeet* they are inappropriate, since the meaning of these modifiers is singular rather than plural. The context of the modifier (in our experiment: the head of the compound) is the only clue for the interpretation of the, questionable, plural form of the modifier. The influence of the head on the interpretation of the modifier hence will be more important in this type of compounds. Along the line of reasoning presented above, a larger family size leads to vagueness, in which case the influence of the head on the interpretation of the modifier will be less, and the information provided by the form of the modifier will be more important. Given that this form suggests plurality, the ratings will be higher.

5.   Conclusion

The experimental studies before and after Dutch spelling reform show that language behavior is influenced by visual patterns in writing and by spelling conventions. Spelling the linking element in compounds as -e or as -en affects plurality ratings both in the old and in the new spelling. The new spelling conventions however, lead to higher overall plurality ratings, a smaller effect of leaving out the -n and a similar effect of leaving out the -n in the two types of compounds included in the study (e.g. compounds such as boekenkast that used to be written with -en on the basis of the plural meaning of the modifier and compounds such as slangenbeet that used to be written with -e on the basis of the singular meaning of the modifier). In sum: writing -n has less cue validity in the new spelling. However, the difference in meaning on which the former difference of spelling was based, is still present, even in a context where all compounds are written with or without n.

Our experiments can be explained partly by the One Meaning One Form Principle. Similarity of form leads to similarity of interpretation: spelling the linking elements as plural endings leads to higher plurality ratings. It is not true, however, that the meaning distinctions on which the older spelling conventions were based completely disappeared, nor is it true that the interpretation of linking elements is influenced by a context in which all forms are presented with -e or all forms are presented with -en.

It turns out that language use is sensitive to spelling conventions, which may drift away from meaning, as is the case when alphabetic writing forces a categorical distinction for meaning oppositions such as number that are scalar rather than privative. We conclude that Bloomfield is both right and wrong when he claims that "Writing is not language, but merely a way of encoding language by means of visible marks" (1933:21). Writing is a way of encoding language. But it is not *merely* a way of encoding language, since language behavior can be changed by spelling reforms. The De Vries and Te Winkel spelling explicitly taught the language user to interpret the linking elements as plural markers in appropriate contexts, and the new spelling teaches the language user to rely on morphology, and not to use semantic distinctions. As shown by our experiments, both conventions affect interpretation. However, the meaning distinctions that formed the basis of the De Vries and Te Winkel spelling seem to remain intact.

Note

* We thank Jaap van Marle and Henk Schultink for helpful comments.

References

Anttila, R. (1972) *An introduction to historical and comparative linguistics*. The Macmillan Company, New York and Collier-Macmillan Ltd, London.

Baayen, R.H., Dijkstra, T., and Schreuder, R. (1997) 'Singulars and plurals in Dutch: Evidence for a dual parallel route model'. *Journal of Memory and Language* 37, 94–117.

Bloomfield, L. (1933) *Language*. Holt, Rinehart and Winston, New York.

Humboldt, Wilhelm von (1836) *Ueber die Verschiedenheit des menschlichen Sprachbaues und ihren Einfluss auf die geistige Entwicklung des Menschengeschlechts*. Translated by G.C. Buck and F.A. Raven (1971) Linguistic Variability and Intellectual Development, University of Miami Press, Coral Gables, Florida.

Marle, J. van, and Koefoed, G. (1980) 'Over Humboldtiaanse taalveranderingen, morfologie en de creativiteit van taal'. *Spektator* 10, 111–147.

Moscoso del Prado Martín, F. (2003) *Paradigmatic Structures in Morphological Processing*. PhD Thesis Nijmegen.

Sassen, A. (1981) 'Sprachveränderung und Wilhelm von Humboldts Universale'. In S. Sondereger and J. Stegeman (red.) *Niederlandistiek in Entwicklung*, Martinus Nijhoff, Leiden, 81–92.

Schreuder, R. and Baayen, R.H. (1995) 'Modeling morphological processing'. In L.B. Feldman, ed., *Morphological aspects of language processing*. Lawrence Erlbaum Associates Inc, Hillsdale, NJ, 131–154.

Schreuder, R. and Baayen, R.H. (1997) 'How complex simplex words can be'. *Journal of Memory and Language* 37, 11–139.

Schreuder, R., Neijt, A., van der Weide, F. and Baayen, R.H. (1998) 'Regular Plurals in Dutch Compounds: Linking Graphemes or Morphemes?' *Language and Cognitive Processes* 13, 551–573.

Vennemann, T. (1972) 'Phonetic analogy and conceptual analogy'. In T. Vennemann and T.H. Wilbur, eds., *Schuchardt, the Neogrammarians, and the Transformational Theory of Phonological Change*. Athenäum Verlag, Frankfurt, 181–204.

Vries, M. de, and Te Winkel, L.A. (1884) *De grondbeginselen van de Nederlandsche spelling*. De Gebroeders Van Cleef, 's-Gravenhage (first edition 1863).

Appendix

Words used and mean plurality ratings (resp. mean in 1996, heterogeneous or homogenous in 2003)

The type SLANGENBEET
bananenschil (banana peel) 2.92/2.16/2.11; bananeschil 1.50/1.74/2.47; beddengoed (bedclothes) 4.17/4.26/4.33; beddegoed 3.67/2.58/3.68; berenmuts (bearskin) 3.42/3.16/3.06; beremuts 1.42/2.32/2.58; bokkensprong (goat's jump) 4.17/2.42/2.89; bokkesprong 1.75/2.37/2.58; brillenglas (spectacle-glass) 3.42/3.68/3.17; brilleglas 1.75/2.16/2.83;

dennenboom (fir tree) 4.08/3.21/3.28; denneboom 1.67/3.21/3.84; druivensuiker (grape sugar) 5.58/5.53/5.17; druivesuiker 4.00/3.95/4.42; eikenhout (oak wood) 3.50/2.79/3.56; eikehout 2.33/3.16/2.89; flessenhals (bottle neck) 3.58/3.42/2.22; flessehals 1.17/2.16/2.47; ganzenveer (goose feather) 3.08/2.89/2.44; ganzeveer 1.25/2.16/2.74; geitenkaas (goat's cheese) 4.83/4.89/3.83; geitekaas 2.42/2.95/3.16; hanenkam (cock's comb) 2.17/2.68/2.44; hanekam 2.00/1.68/2.47; hartenwens (heart's desire) 3.00/2.84/3.11; hartewens 1.58/1.74/1.53; hazenlip (hare-lip) 2.33/2.21/2.39; hazelip 1.25/2.32/2.21; hertenleer (venison leather) 4.08/4.37/4.29; herteleer 2.58/2.89/2.89; hondenpoep (dog-dirt) 3.08/2.47/3.39; hondepoep 2.58/2.68/2.89; karrenspoor (cart track) 4.50/3.16/4.24; karrespoor 2.92/2.11/3.33; kattenkwaad (mischief) 4.58/3.21/3.61; kattekwaad 2.33/3.11/3.32; kerkenraad (church council) 4.67/4.89/3.72; kerkeraad 3.00/2.68/3.53; kersenpit (cherry stone) 2.92/2.53/2.53; kersepit 1.67/2.05/2.47; kippenvel (hen skin) 4.08/3.63/3.56; kippevel 2.75/2.63/3.16; konijnenhok (rabbit hutch) 4.58/4.47/4.72; konijnehok 2.75/4.42/4.00; krullenbol (curly head) 6.75/6.21/5.28; krullebol 4.00/4.68/4.95; kurkentrekker (corkscrew) 4.58/4.26/4.44; kurketrekker 3.33/2.89/3.79; lampenkap (lampshade) 2.75/2.74/2.39; lampekap 1.50/1.84/2.53; leeuwendeel (lion's share) 4.00/3.63/3.59; leeuwedeel 1.92/2.68/2.84; mottenbal (mothball) 4.58/4.47/4.44; mottebal 4.17/3.37/4.21; notendop (nutshell) 2.50/2.53/3.41; notedop 1.50/1.79/2.21; ossenkop (ox head) 2.00/2.79/2.72; ossekop 1.58/1.68/2.42; paardenbloem (dandelion) 3.58/3.21/2.71; paardebloem 1.92/2.79/2.84; pannenkoek (pancake) 2.58/2.68/2.56; pannekoek 2.58/2.58/2.74; pennenlikker (quill-driver) 3.33/4.84/4.00; pennelikker 2.08/3.11/3.05; pottenkijker (nosy) 4.43/3.95/3.72; pottekijker 2.75/3.05/4.05; ruggengraat (backbone) 2.33/2.89/2.56; ruggegraat 1.42/2.16/2.26; ruitenwisser (screen wiper) 3.50/4.00/3.67; ruitewisser 2.17/2.74/4.47; schapenmelk (sheep's milk) 4.75/4.53/3.67; schapemelk 3.17/4.42/4.58; schroevendraaier (screwdriver) 5.33/5.16/4.82; schroevedraaier 4.00/4.32/4.37; slakkenhuis (snale shell) 3.08/2.68/3.00; slakkehuis 1.67/2.00/2.21; slangenbeet (snakebite) 2.67/2.58/2.24; slangebeet 1.42/2.05/2.68; speldenknop (pin's head) 3.67/2.53/2.39; speldeknop 1.25/2.05/2.21; spinnenweb (spider's web) 3.00/2.84/3.22; spinneweb 1.50/2.16/2.84; vlaggenstok (flag-staff) 3.17/2.68/3.00; vlaggestok 1.42/2.00/2.42; vossenhol (fox hole) 5.58/4.95/4.61; vossehol 3.25/3.16/4.26; zielenpoot (pitiful person) 2.33/3.00/2.72; zielepoot 1.42/2.26/1.95; zwijnenstal (cesspit) 6.58/4.84/5.13; zwijnestal 2.50/4.21/4.05.

The type BOEKENKAST
bessenstruik (currant bush) 6.42/6.63/6.06; bessestruik 5.67/5.37/5.68; boekenrek (book rack) 6.75/6.58/6.50; boekerek 5.50/5.63/5.95; brievenbus (letter box) 6.17/5.79/5.89; brievebus 4.25/5.37/5.05; dierentuin (animal garden) 6.83/6.53/6.50; dieretuin 6.33/6.05/5.74; druiventros (bunch of grapes) 6.58/6.21/6.22; druivetros 4.83/5.89/5.11; duiventil (pigeon loft) 6.75/6.53/5.88; duivetil 5.58/5.42/6.00; erwtensoep (pea soup) 6.08/5.89/5.56; erwtesoep 4.42/5.42/5.39; gebarentaal (gesture language) 6.67/6.56/5.71; gebaretaal 5.92/4.84/5.42; gevarenzone (danger zone) 3.92/4.63/3.83; gevarezone 3.50/4.00/3.89; kaartenbak (card tray) 6.75/6.47/6.44; kaartebak 5.33/4.84/5.84; kleurenfoto (colour photograph) 5.25/4.95/5.67; kleurefoto 3.67/5.16/4.58; kolenschop (coal shovel) 5.83/6.05/5.28; koleschop 2.83/4.84/5.21; ladenkast (chest of drawers) 5.33/5.26/5.44; ladekast 4.58/4.84/4.79; lappenpop (ragdoll) 5.50/5.05/4.78; lappepop 3.33/3.74/4.05; lippenstift (lipstick) 3.33/3.95/5.06; lippestift 2.83/3.53/3.37; mierenhoop (ant hill) 7.00/6.53/6.06; mierehoop 5.92/5.94/6.05; plankenkoorts (stage fright) 5.08/4.21/4.18; plankekoorts 4.33/3.68/3.84; platenspeler (record player) 5.08/5.68/5.65; platespeler 4.00/4.84/5.00; rattenvanger (rat catcher) 5.50/5.32/6.11; rattevanger 6.25/5.67/5.42; rokkenjager (woman chaser) 5.33/5.37/5.22; rokkejager 4.17/4.00/4.74; rollenspel (role-play) 5.00/5.58/5.72; rollespel 4.92/5.05/5.21; schoenendoos (shoebox) 5.00/5.68/5.11;

schoenedoos 3.25/5.21/4.68; sterrenbeeld (constellation) 4.08/4.32/4.89; sterrebeeld 4.42/3.95/4.47; takkenbos (faggot) 6.00/6.47/5.44; takkebos 5.42/5.26/5.79; tandenstoker (toothpick) 6.00/5.37/5.00; tandestoker 2.75/4.74/4.79; tentenkamp (tents encampment) 6.42/6.37/6.06; tentekamp 4.42/5.89/5.63; toetsenbord (keyboard) 5.75/6.05/6.06; toetsebord 5.58/5.21/5.26; vlammenzee (sea of flames) 6.75/6.16/6.35; vlammezee 4.67/5.37/5.68; warenhuis (department store) 4.50/5.74/5.35; warehuis 4.58/4.84/4.63; wolkendek (cloud cover) 5.83/6.47/5.76; wolkedek 5.17/5.58/5.26; woordenstrijd (verbal combat) 6.25/5.26/6.06; woordestrijd 5.17/5.63/5.72; zakenleven (business life) 5.08/4.53/4.28; zakeleven 2.42/3.42/2.95.

Multi-level OT

An argument from speech pathology

Dirk-Bart den Ouden
University of Groningen

1. Introduction

Since the early 1990s, Optimality Theory (OT) has quickly gained ground in phonology. Its main appeal lies in two characteristics: the focus on well-formedness of the output and the softness of constraints, where a constraint can be violated in order to satisfy more important requirements.

A conspicuous characteristic of classic OT is that all constraints on the output should compete with each other at all times. This basically means that the 'construction' of the output occurs in one step. OT is therefore minimally derivational, the only derivation being that from the input to the output. Mainly on the basis of data from aphasic speakers, I argue that the 'one-step' variant of OT lacks psychological validity and that it is better to assume that the OT algorithm plays a role in determining (phonological) structure at different cognitive levels of processing, at least in production.

2. Single-level OT

One of the criticisms of OT has been based on phonological processes of which it is argued that they simply cannot be adequately described without making reference to some notion of cyclicity or multiple levels of processing.

Such criticism has led to a number of adaptations to the original theory (Prince & Smolensky 1993), all aimed at giving satisfactory descriptions of morphophonological processes in which the output form seems to be opaque, and in which certain constraints appear to have been applied only to specific substrings of the eventual output form. Examples of such tools that aim to maintain the one-step evaluation are Output-Output Correspondence (McCarthy and Prince 1995), in which the optimal output form wants to be as similar as possible to other output forms it is related to, and Sympathy Theory (McCarthy 1998), in which the optimal output form wants to resemble a fairly arbitrarily chosen other output candidate.

Other optimality theorists have chosen to abandon the one-step derivation altogether and to incorporate some type of sequentiality in OT, allowing multiple levels of evaluation, with constraints that apply only to specific stages in the derivation (Booij 1997; Rubach 2000). Crucially, the 'founding fathers' of OT, Prince and Smolensky (1993:79), did not put an absolute restriction on the theory as having only one level of evaluation, although the current practice is such that multiple levels of evaluation are considered a weakness.

3. Multi-level cognitive processing

Beside this formal discussion stands a large body of evidence for multiple levels of processing, from the fields of psycho- and neurolinguistics (e.g. Levelt 1989). Imaging studies of brain activity during language processing, as well as lesion studies, show that different parts of the brain are involved in the performance of different language functions (Démonet 1998; Whitaker 1998). Results of studies into temporally successive brain activity point towards a 'phonological loop' (Baddeley 1986) in which abstract and articulatory levels are distinct, though possibly mutually influential.

Of course, a formal theory of grammar, such as OT, is not *designed* for the purpose of reflecting the psychological reality of language performance. It is specifically meant to reflect competence, so one might argue that any knowledge (however limited) about what actually goes on during speech production and the building of language structure is irrelevant to the formal grammar. However, OT does rely on support from sources external to the grammar, such as language acquisition data and arguments of learnability. It will be hard to maintain that these factors are not rooted in the reality of language use. As such, OT does make claims to psychological reality, which means it is bound by logic to all relevant aspects of this reality.

4. The coda-observation in fluent and nonfluent aphasia

4.1 Experiment

Ten fluent and ten nonfluent Dutch aphasic speakers were tested with a monosyllabic repetition task, on order to investigate the influence of positional markedness within syllables on their paraphasic output (Den Ouden 2002). From language acquisition data, language change and typology, it is known that certain syllable positions are more prone to error than others. For example, in onset clusters, sonorant consonants will be deleted sooner than obstruents. The question was whether this pattern might be related to a phonological or a phonetic level of speech output (planning).

In the absence of extralinguistic factors, such as dysarthria, nonfluent patients with distorted phonological output are claimed to suffer from difficulty in the timing and co-ordination of articulatory movements (Blumstein et al. 1980). This is related to a deficit at a cognitive phonetic level of processing (Code 1998), peripheral to the language processing system, but still considered linguistic. These nonfluent speakers have apraxia of speech.

Fluent aphasic patients presenting with literal paraphasias have unimpaired articulation, but suffer from a deficit in the appropriate selection of phonemes. The label of fluent aphasia covers a range of traditional syndromes, such as Wernicke's aphasia and conduction aphasia. What these disorders have in common is that they yield incorrect phonological plans. This may be caused by incorrect lexical access or representations, or by incorrect phonemic sequencing, i.e. the mapping of speech sounds and features onto metrical frames (phonological encoding). The difference, then, between fluent and nonfluent aphasic speakers is that fluent aphasics create an erroneous phonological plan that may be correctly executed phonetically, whereas nonfluent aphasics phonetically implement incorrectly a correct phonological speech plan.

The subjects repeated 114 Dutch monosyllabic words. Their segment deletions were counted per syllable position, defined on the basis of a template. Following this template, in example word *sprints* the boldface positions (p, i and t) are strongest, i.e. least prone to deletion. Results showed that the deletion patterns of fluent and nonfluent speakers were largely similar, with the positions stipulated as relatively weak in the template indeed being deleted more often than their stronger neighbours. However, in coda clusters, the pattern was not so clear, which is why a further analysis was done, specifically aimed at clusters.

4.2 The coda observation

For this analysis, only 41 items from the original task were analysed. These were the items with complex onsets or complex codas which did not violate the sonority slope, meaning that the sonority value of segments rose from the margins to the peak. The clusters all consisted of one obstruent (C[−son]) and one sonorant (C[+son]) segment.

Results are visualised in figure (1), where the black bars show the mean (proportionate) number of deletions of obstruents and the grey bars those of the sonorants.

(1)   Deletions in onset and coda clusters for fluent and nonfluent speakers

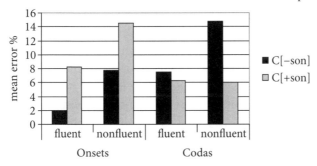

The patterns of deletions are equal for both groups in onsets, but not in codas, where only the nonfluent patients delete the sonorant coda position significantly more often than the nonsonorant coda position. For example, the nonfluent patients' rendition of the target word *print* /prɪnt/ will characteristically be [pɪt], while the fluent patients, as a group, will turn it into either [pɪn] or [pɪt], in a seemingly random fashion.

Apparently, the positional markedness relations yield similar output patterns in the paraphasic syllable onsets produced by fluent and nonfluent aphasic speakers, but different patterns in codas. This 'coda observation' leads to a different analysis of the data, this time in terms of conflicting types of markedness, segmental vs. syllabic (or 'positional').

4.3 Segment vs. Syllable Markedness

According to a hierarchy of segmental markedness going back to Jakobson (1941), consonants are less marked if they are less sonorant. This segmental markedness applies non-contextually; it does not take into account the position of a segment within a syllable. Note that it can account for the error pattern of the nonfluent patients, but not for the coda observation in fluent patients' errors.

If we do look at segments in the context of prosodic structure, however, a different picture emerges. Clements (1990) argues that the preferred sonority slope of syllables has a steep rise in sonority pre-vocalically and a slow decline in sonority postvocalically. This Sonority Cycle allows us to formulate a second markedness hierarchy, viz. syllable markedness, according to which onsets want to be nonsonorant and codas want to be sonorant.

Syllable markedness alone cannot account for the pattern of deletions observed in fluent patients' paraphasias. However, segmental and syllable markedness reinforce each other in onsets, whereas they are in opposition in codas. It is this combination of the two types of markedness, or rather the crucial conflict between them, that may account for the fluent patients' error pattern, which is a 50–50 distribution of deletions in coda clusters.

The full analysis of the presented data is that nonfluent aphasics have a deficit at a phonetic level of processing, at which the markedness of individual segments, or feature combinations, is an influential factor. The impairment allows this type of markedness to become dominant, which means that when clusters of consonants are reduced, the nonsonorant, segmentally least marked consonant will come out as the winner, irrespective of its position within a syllable. But before this phonetic level of processing, constraints on sonority sequencing, i.e. on preferred syllable structure, are active beside constraints on segmental markedness. At the affected level(s) of processing in fluent aphasic patients, the conflict between segmental markedness constraints and syllable markedness constraints emerges, as structure preserving constraints lose control over the output of the speech production process. For fluent aphasics, this yields a pattern of errors in which onsets are relatively systematically reduced to nonsonorant segments, while codas are reduced on a seemingly random basis to either sonorant or nonsonorant segments, as the constraints are in direct conflict over what is a preferred segment in coda position.

5.   An OT analysis

The tools of OT seem particularly suited to give a representation of the conflict between markedness constraints with opposing output goals, such as described above. However, the application of OT to language pathology is only in its infancy, so a number of choices have to be made and argued for in this domain.

5.1 Aphasia

Aphasia is generally characterised by a prominence of unmarked structures. Compared to speakers without brain damage, the aphasic speaker is less faithful to the input, the input here being the lexicon or, for example, utterances to be repeated. The most straightforward way of representing this in OT is by a lowering of faithfulness constraints, relative to markedness constraints.

Note that it is theoretically also possible that input representations themselves are disturbed, so that the correct constraint ranking works on incorrect input, or that the number and/or type of output candidates that are generated is in some way restricted. In OT, however, these options do not directly account for the prominence of the unmarked, as observed in aphasic speech. Any systematic way of constricting the input or the output candidates would somehow have to incorporate extra markedness constraints on these domains. This would come down to an extratheoretical add-on for which there is no evidence or argument in nonpathological natural language. I assume that language impairment is focal breakdown of the normal language system, crucially within its own terms. The impairment will not add new features to the normal system. The aphasic patients in this study show markedness effects in their impaired output, and the OT representation of the impairment consists of the lowering of faithfulness constraints, allowing markedness constraints to have greater influence on the selection of the optimal output candidate.

Aphasic data are never homogeneous. There is much noise and variability, which is precisely why statistics are used to determine whether some structures are really used more often than others, or whether differences might be due to chance. Variation, or optionality, can be represented by 'switching' of adjacent constraints (e.g. Tesar and Smolensky 1998). The *Gradual Learning Algorithm* of Boersma and Hayes (2001) is even able to capture statistical differences in the frequency of occurrence of certain forms. Constraints have moving ranges along the hierarchical scale, which are interpreted as probability distributions, i.e., they are normal distributions with the ranking value as their peak. These ranges may overlap. At one particular moment of evaluation, the position of a constraint on the ranking scale, i.e. its selection point, is less likely the further it is from this constraint's ranking value. Through this, one is able to calculate the probability of a certain ranking of constraints at the moment of constraint evaluation.

Of course, the output of aphasic speakers is not consistently erroneous either. Depending on the severity of their impairment, aphasic speakers will often produce the correct (target) output form. In these cases, it is assumed that the selection point of the relevant faithfulness constraint is above the relevant markedness constraints. The scope of FAITHFULNESS, therefore, should at least partially overlap with that of these markedness constraints. In the analysis provided in the following section, I will focus on the constraint rankings underlying paraphasic output.

5.2 Constraints and tableaux

The constraints required for the analysis presented here are given in (2).

(2) *Markedness*
    *C[+SON]   Do not allow sonorant consonants
    HONs (Onset Harmony)   No sonorant material in onsets
    HCOD (Coda Harmony)   No nonsonorant material in codas
    Faithfulness
    PARSE   Preserve input material

As discussed above, segmental markedness seems to be prominent in the paraphasias of the nonfluent aphasic speakers, who have an impairment at the cognitive phonetic level of speech planning. This is represented in Tableau (3), where *C[+Son] is ranked higher than PARSE. The markedness constraint here picks out the only relevant candidate that does not violate it.

(3)   Tableau nonfluent patients /prɪnt/ → /pɪt/

/prɪnt/	*C[+son]	Parse
prɪnt	** !	
pɪnt	* !	*
☞ pɪt		**
pɪn	* !	**
rɪt	* !	**
rɪn	** !	**
rɪnt	** !	*
prɪt	* !	*
prɪn	** !	*

The fluent patients turn example word *print* into either [pɪn] or [pɪt]. This is because of a competition between a constraint on the preferred sonority value of the syllable constituent coda and the segmental markedness constraint that disallows sonorant consonants. With respect to HCod and *C[+Son], two rankings are possible, with different results, as shown in Tableaux (4a) and (4b).

(4)   a.   Tableau fluent patients /prɪnt/ → /pɪt/

/prɪnt/	*C[+son]	HCod	HOns	Parse
prɪnt	** !	*	*	
pɪnt	* !	*		*
☞ pɪt		*		**
pɪn	* !			**
rɪt	* !	*	*	**
rɪn	** !		*	**
rɪnt	** !	*	*	*
prɪt	* !	*	*	*
prɪn	** !		*	*

b. Tableau fluent patients /prɪnt/ → /pɪn/

/prɪnt/	HCOD	*C[+SON]	HONS	PARSE
prɪnt	* !	**	*	
pɪnt	* !	*		*
pɪt	* !			**
☞ pɪn		*		**
rɪt	* !	*	*	**
rɪn		** !	*	**
rɪnt	* !	**	*	*
prɪt	* !	*	*	*
prɪn		** !	*	*

Note that the specific ranking of HONS is irrelevant here, as it is not in conflict with the other markedness constraints. I have represented it in the tableaux, because HONS is linked strongly to HCOD, both being similar types of constraints on syllable content. The reason for ranking it below HCOD is that codas are generally more marked than onsets, so it seems reasonable to assume that restrictions on coda content are more important than restrictions on onsets.

5.3 Level-specific constraints vs. large-scale reranking

The data of the fluent aphasic speakers come about by the switching of positions between HCOD and *C[+SON] and, of course, the lowering of PARSE, with respect to its 'normal' position above these markedness constraints. Apparently, then, at the level of deficit of the fluent patients, HCOD and *C[+SON] are so closely ranked that their ranges overlap almost 100%. What we could do now, is to say that at the level of deficit of the nonfluent patients, the ranking of these constraints is very different, i.e., their ranking values are much further apart, so that *C[+SON] is always most prominent. This is an undesired situation, as it opens up the possibility of totally different rankings at (or: in the representation of) different levels of processing. A major argument against an analysis in which different types of aphasia are represented through structural reranking of markedness constraints is the fact that aphasic speech errors hardly ever violate the phonotactics of the mother tongue of the speaker, or, indeed, universal restrictions on well-formedness (see Buckingham 1992). This would be unexplained if markedness constraints changed position in the hierarchy on a large scale. The adherence to (mother tongue) phonotactics points towards a lowering of faithfulness constraints only.

However, the variation found in the patterns of paraphasias belonging to different types of aphasia, such as observed in the presently discussed study, acts as an argument *against* the mere lowering of faithfulness constraints in the representation of aphasia. To represent different aphasic symptoms only through different degrees of faithfulness lowering comes down to saying that aphasic 'syndromes', or rather, clusters of symptoms, only differ with respect to the degree of severity of the impairment. This is a view that has indeed been held (e.g. Freud 1891), but detailed (linguistic) analysis of aphasic data lead contemporary aphasiologists to think of different types of aphasia as reflecting impairments at different functional levels of cognitive (if not linguistic) processing. This is also the approach adopted here. At those particular levels, of course, the impairments may still differ in degree of severity.

For these reasons, rather than claiming that the constraints HONs and HCOD are ranked noncompetitively low at the level of impairment of nonfluent aphasics, I argue that they are *non-existent* at this level. In this way, structural reranking of markedness constraints is avoided. This means, then, that the analysis allows different levels of evaluation of constraints, where not all constraints are active (i.e. exist) at all levels. I maintain that, from a psycholinguistic and neurolinguistic perspective, this is the only natural way to conceive of linguistic processing.

In psycholinguistic modelling, it is common practice to minimise the number of levels, modules or stages of processing to those necessary for an accurate representation of empirical findings. A similar principle, Level Minimalism, is formulated by Rubach (2000) for his modification of OT, Derivational Optimality Theory, which allows multiple levels of evaluation. Another principle he formulates to restrict the power of his framework is that of Reranking Minimalism: "[the] number of rerankings is minimal [—] reranking of constraints comes at a cost and needs to be argued for" (Rubach 2000:313). This principle is in line with the present approach of unstable rankings to account for variation and level-specific constraints instead of structural reranking of markedness constraints to account for the influence of different factors at different levels of speech production processing. The idea is that the only difference between the impaired and the healthy system is the lowering of faithfulness constraints at the affected level(s) of processing.

Another treat offered by this analysis is that syllables and constraints on their structure are only relevant as organising units at phonological levels of processing and not at the cognitive phonetic level of processing where articulation is planned. Syllables are not articulatory units (for a discussion of corroborative evidence for this claim, see Den Ouden 2002:89–90).

5.4 OT for unimpaired language

According to the approach presented here, language impairment at specific levels of processing brings to light the factors that are functional at these levels. In OT, these factors are represented by constraints. Some of these constraints will normally, in an unimpaired language system, not be 'relevant', as they are hidden under a layer of faithfulness constraints, except in child language acquisition, when faithfulness constraints are also assumed to be ranked low. Thus, in non-brain-damaged speakers, the same constraints are functional at the same levels of processing as in aphasic speakers (of the type discussed here). However, for non-impaired speakers, faithfulness constraints are ranked sufficiently high at all these levels to ensure 'normal' native language output. Lowering of faithfulness, as in language impairment, causes the 'emergence of the unranked'.

This implies that it is still not *a priori* impossible to represent the grammar of unimpaired language in a single constraint tableau. Even if the process of speech production will work such that the output of one level, or module, serves as the input to the next, the static description of the language system can incorporate the various factors of influence in one representation. It is only when the system breaks down that the individual parts reveal themselves.

6. Conclusion

On the basis of fluent aphasics' and nonfluent aphasics' responses to a monosyllabic real word repetition test, I have argued that there is a difference between the phonological level of speech processing and the phonetic level of processing. In an OT approach, the constraints responsible for preferred syllable content are active only at pre-phonetic levels of evaluation, whereas a constraint on segmental markedness, saying that consonants should be as consonantal as possible (and therefore nonsonorant) is active at the pre-phonetic, as well as at the phonetic level.

Aphasia, in this approach, comprises the lowering of faithfulness constraints at the affected level of processing. The different levels account for the different types of aphasia that are generally recognised. Also, aphasia is characterised by highly variable output caused (or at least represented) by unstable ranking of close (adjacent) markedness constraints. In the approach presented here, the lowering of faithfulness constraints makes visible the unstable rankings that are there in the first place, but which are normally hidden because they do not have an effect on normal speech output.

Language breakdown provides a window on the workings of the language system and linguistic theories should be able to deal with the view thus offered.

It is not sufficient to claim that OT is 'not about' breakdown or psycholinguistic models, or that it does not have to be able to account for evidence of temporal processing or multiple levels of processing as long as there is no straightforward theory of the relation between language, mind and brain. Through such argumentation, phonological theory runs the danger of becoming merely a boundlessly creative method of deriving surface level data (output forms) from hypothesised underlying (input) forms. Therefore, OT should aim at ways to incorporate multiple levels of (phonological) processing, rather than focus on retaining the single evaluation hypothesis. The present paper has discussed one way of dealing with such stages in processing.

References

Baddeley, A. (1986) *Working Memory.* Clarendon Press, Oxford.

Blumstein, S. E., Cooper, W. E., Goodglass, H., Statlender, S. and Gottlieb, J. (1980) 'Production deficits in aphasia: A voice-onset time analysis'. *Brain and Language* 9, 153–70.

Boersma, P. and Hayes, B. (2001) 'Empirical tests of the gradual learning algorithm'. *Linguistic Inquiry* 32, 1, 45–86.

Booij, G. E. (1997) 'Non-derivational phonology meets Lexical Phonology'. In I. Roca, ed., *Derivations and Constraints in Phonology.* Oxford University Press, Oxford.

Buckingham, H. W. (1992) 'Phonological production deficits in conduction aphasia'. In S. E. Kohn, ed., *Conduction Aphasia.* Lawrence Erlbaum Associates, Hillsdale etc.

Clements, G. N. (1990) 'The role of sonority in core syllabification'. In J. Kingston and M. E. Beckman, eds., *Papers in Laboratory Phonology I. Between the Grammar and Physics of Speech.* Cambridge University Press, Cambridge.

Code, C. (1998) 'Models, theories and heuristics in apraxia of speech'. *Clinical Linguistics and Phonetics* 12, 1, 47–65.

Démonet, J. F. (1998) 'Tomographic Brain Imaging of Language functions: Prospects for a New Brain/Language Model'. In B. Stemmer and H. A. Whitaker, eds., *Handbook of Neurolinguistics.* Academic Press, San Diego, 131–142.

Freud, S. (1891) *Zur Auffassung der Aphasien: Eine kritische Studie.* Franz Deuticke, Leipzig and Vienna. In E. Stengel, transl., *On Aphasia: A Critical Study.* International Universities Press, New York, 1953.

Jakobson, R. (1941) *Kindersprache, Aphasie und allgemeine Lautgesetze.* Translation: A. R. Keiler (1968) *Child Language, Aphasia and Phonological Universals.* Mouton, The Hague.

Levelt, W. J. M. (1989) *Speaking: From Intention to Articulation.* MIT Press Cambridge, Massachusetts.

McCarthy, J. (1998) 'Sympathy and phonological opacity', Ms., University of Massachusetts, Amherst.

McCarthy, J. and Prince, A. (1995) 'Faithfulness and Reduplicative Identity'. In J. Beckman et al., eds., *Papers in Optimality Theory*, University of Massachusetts Occasional Papers 18, 249–384.

Ouden, D. B. Den (2002) *Phonology in Aphasia: Syllables and segments in level-specific deficits.* Doc. diss., University of Groningen.

Prince, A. and Smolensky, P. (1993) *Optimality Theory: Constraint interaction in generative grammar.* Rutgers University Center for Cognitive Science Technical Report 2.

Rubach, J. (2000) 'Glide and glottal stop insertion in Slavic languages: A DOT analysis'. *Linguistic Inquiry* 31, 2, 271–317.

Tesar, B. and Smolensky, P. (1998) 'Learnability in Optimality Theory'. *Linguistic Inquiry* 29, 229–268.

Whitaker, H. A. (1998) 'Neurolinguistics from the Middle Ages to the Pre-Modern Era: Historical vignettes'. In B. Stemmer and H. A. Whitaker, eds., *Handbook of Neurolinguistics*. Academic Press, San Diego, 27–54.

The acquisition of definiteness distinctions by L2 learners of French[*]

Petra Sleeman
University of Amsterdam

1. Introduction

In this paper I will be concerned with the acquisition of the pragmatic-syntactic interface by L2 learners of French. For pragmatic features it might be the case that they have a universal character, but the interface with for example syntax has in every case to be learned, both in L1 and in L2 acquisition. Furthermore, for L2 learners it might be necessary to learn that relations between pragmatics and syntax in L2 are different than relations between pragmatics and syntax in L1.

Ferdinand (2002) shows that the acquisition of the French dislocation construction, a pragmatic-syntactic interface structure emphasizing the topic of a sentence, is not difficult for Dutch L2 learners (secondary school pupils in her study), because Dutch also has a dislocation construction with the same pragmatic value as the French one. Ferdinand tries to show that there is a relation between the use in Dutch and in French: the Dutch learners use the dislocation construction in both languages or in neither of the languages. Ferdinand concludes therefore that there is transfer of a style of topic marking from Dutch to French. Sleeman (2004) shows that although transfer may play a role, another aspect is important for the acquisition of the dislocation construction, viz. a stay of some months in France, French dislocation being mainly used in the spoken language.

In this paper I discuss the acquisition of another pragmatic-syntactic interface phenomenon, viz. the syntactic expression by means of the article of new and old information in L2 French. Whereas Dutch also expresses newness by means of the article, so that the pragmatic-syntactic interface relations for the article might be transferred from Dutch to French, Japanese does not have articles, so that transfer is not possible. In this paper I compare the acquisition

Linguistics in the Netherlands 2004 21 (2004), **158–168.**
ISSN 0929–7332 / E-ISSN 1569–9919 © Algemene Vereniging voor Taalwetenschap

of definiteness distinctions by Dutch and Japanese guided L2 learners of French. But before discussing the acquisition by the Dutch and Japanese L2 learners of French, I show how definiteness distinctions are acquired in L1 French.

The paper is organized as follows. In Section 2 the acquisition of definiteness distinctions in L1 French is discussed. The acquisition of definiteness distinctions in L2 French by Dutch and Japanese guided learners is studied in Section 3. In Section 4 the results are discussed, followed by a conclusion in Section 5.

2. The acquistion of the use of the article in L1 French

De Cat (2004) claims that children learning L1 French do not have any problems at all with the acquisition of the syntactic expression of newness in French. Her paper is a reaction to a study by Hickmann et al. (1996) on the acquisition of the article by French L1 learners. In Hickmann et al.'s experiment children from three age groups (on average 4;10, 7;1 and 10;6 years old) were asked to tell two picture stories to a blindfolded person. Hickmann et al. showed that even seven-year-olds regularly used the definite article for a newly introduced referent. Their data suggest that the discourse-internal function of indefinite/definite determiners for the contrastive marking of new/given information is learned late.

According to De Cat however, the data resulting from studies on L1 acquisition of the syntactic expression of newness by means of the article have to be treated carefully. In the first place, in spite of a strong correlation between indefiniteness and information newness, as in (1),

(1) *J'ai   trouvé une noix.*
     I have found a   nut
     'I've found a nut.'

there are cases in which a definite article can be used for a seemingly newly introduced referent, as is the case for a unique instantiation (2)–(3) or associative anaphora (4)–(5):

(2) *[Le/*un] soleil sèche ses habits.*
     the/a   sun dries his clothes
     'The sun dries his clothes.'

(3) *Il rentre à [la/*une] maison.*
     he returns to the/an   house
     'He goes back home.'

(4) *J'ai   acheté une nouvelle voiture mais j'ai déjà   perdu les clés.*
     I have bought a   new   car   but I have already lost the keys
     'I've bought a new car but I've already lost the keys.'

(5) *Il pêchait   bien tranquillement puis tout à coup il est tombé dans la   rivière.*
     he was fishing peacefully   then suddenly   he is fallen in   the river
     'He was fishing peacefully and then suddenly he fell in the river.'

A second reason for treating the data resulting from studies on L1 acquisition of the article carefully, is that children sometimes have another perception of the world than adults. Although in Hickmann et al.'s experiment the listener was blindfolded and could not see the pictures, the children regularly used the definite article for a newly introduced referent. De Cat's interpretation is that children do not always realize that another person, for instance someone they are talking to on the telephone, cannot see everything they see. This might be the explanation for the children's use of the definite article for newly introduced referents in Hickmann's experiment. The children saw the picture book, so for them the referent was not new but present in the physical context, viz. the picture book. The use of the definite article is appropriate in that case. The children forgot, however, that the listener could not see the referent. The erroneous use of the definite article for newly introduced referents by children seems thus to be due to a cognitive problem with respect to shared knowledge.

De Cat suggests thus that Hickmann et al.'s results are due to the experimental techniques used. She found corroborating evidence for this interpretation of Hickmann et al.'s results in the study of children's spontaneous production. De Cat examined the use of the article in her corpora, which contain data from five monolingual French children, who were recorded for a period of 18 months on average, with ages ranging from 1;10 to 3;6, which means that the children throughout the study were younger than even the youngest participants in Hickmann et al's elicitation experiment. De Cat distinguishes three types of errors that the children could make. A Type I error is the use of a new, non-unique definite instead of an indefinite in a focus position in typical referent-establishing constructions like (1).[1] In Hickmann et al.'s study, the children made only a very small number of Type I errors, in De Cat's interpretation of the data. In De Cat's corpora of spontaneous speech the children did not make mistakes of this type and furthermore definiteness distinctions were used in a target-like fashion in the presentational construction from the earliest attested cases, which indicates that children master the structural marking of referent newness at a very early age. A Type II error is the use of an indefinite for a topic, which in the adult language must be definite.[2] If new information and indefiniteness are not inextrincably linked in the mind of children, it can be expected that they use indefinites in dislocated DPs, which are always topics:

(6) **Un clown, il arrive.*
     a   clown he arrives

The children of De Cat's corpora did not make Type II errors: when indefinites are dislocated in their speech, it is with a generic or a D-linked interpretation.

A Type III error occurs when the child uses a definite to introduce a new referent, although this referent is not salient enough to be identifiable by the hearer, for instance as a topic in the dislocation construction:

(7) *Le clown, il arrive.*
     the clown he arrives

According to De Cat, the children in Hickmann et al.'s study especially make Type III errors. Because of the situation, the picture book they can see, they consider a non-salient referent to be salient and encode it as a (definite) topic. In De Cat's corpora of spontaneous speech production, type III errors were not noticed, which indicates again that children master the structural marking of referent newness at a very early age, contra Hickmann et al's claim.

De Cat takes it as uncontroversial that children can distinguish new from old information appropriately from the onset of language production, a point argued for by Baker and Greenfield (1988) among others. What children have to learn, is to use the correct syntactic encodings for the expression of new or old information. According to De Cat children have acquired this at a very early age already.

In the next section I study the acquisition of the syntactic expression of the pragmatic notions of new and old information by adults learning L2 French.

3.   The acquisition of the use of the article in L2 French

In order to see how L2 learners of French acquire the pragmatic-syntactic interface rules that relate the pragmatic notions of old and new information to definite and indefinite DPs, I tested a group of Dutch and a group of Japanese learners of French.

As in Hickmann et al.'s study, the test was an elicitation test based on a picture book. All subjects had the picture book The Frog Story before them and were asked to tell the story in French and, although this was not important for the present research, to use past tenses. The subjects were allowed to quickly leaf through the booklet before telling the story. Words that were supposed to be difficult were given in French, but without the article. These were the French words for almost all referents that had to be used to tell the story properly, apart from the French words for 'boy', 'dog' and 'hole'. Although there was no blind-folded listener, the subjects were told that their story would be recorded on tape, and would be heard later by someone who did not know the story and would not see the pictures.

3.1 Dutch learners of L2 French and the acquisition of definiteness distinctions

The Dutch group was composed of 6 female students studying at Utrecht University. All students had learned French during at least 4 years at school, so that they had had at least 400 hours of instruction in French, and four of them were students majoring in French at university since two, three or four years. One of them had been working in France during one year.

In most cases the Dutch students used the article correctly. There were, however, some incorrect uses, which might just as in Hickmann et al.'s test be attributed to the fact that an elicitation test based on a picture story was used. In (8), *la taupe* 'the mole' is used as a definite topic, although it is newly introduced. This is a Type III error, the only important type of definiteness error the children made in Hickmann et al.'s test, in De Cat's interpretation of the data:

(8)   *Mais **la taupe** mordrait   le jeune garçon.*
      but the mole would-bite the young boy
      'But a mole bit the boy.'

The students made, however, also Type I errors. They used definites for newly introduced referents in focus. The children in Hickmann et al.'s test made very few Type I errors, in De Cat's interpretation of the data. In (9) *le bocal*, 'the jar', is newly introduced, in (10) *le tronc d'arbre* 'the tree-trunk', in (11) *le grand trou* 'the big gap' and in (12) *le cerf* 'the deer':

(9)   *La grenouille est escapée **le   bocal**.*
      the frog   is escaped the jar
      'The frog escaped from the jar (in which he was).'

(10) *Le jeune garçon regardait **le   tronc d'arbre**.*
      the young boy   watched the tree-trunk
      'The boy watched a tree-trunk.'

(11) *Et **le cerf** a   tombé le garçon dans **le   grand trou**.*
      and the deer has fallen the boy   in   the big   gap
      'And the deer has thrown the boy in a big gap.'

(12) *Et il prend dans sa main la tête **du   cerf**.*
      and he takes in   his hand the head of-the deer

The Dutch students did not make Type II errors, i.e. they did not use an indefinite DP for an already introduced or salient referent. They only made some Type I and Type III errors: they used 7 (=7.2%) definite DPs for 96 newly introduced referents in focus (Type I error: 1 occurrence) and in topic position (Type III error: 6 occurrences), which means that there were 1.9% errors for a total number of 370 referential DPs in the Dutch corpus of L2 French utterances. According to De Cat, the children in Hickmann et al.'s test especially made

Type III errors, i.e. they only used definite DPs for newly introduced referents in topic position.

In the previous section it was shown that according to De Cat children have problems with respect to shared knowledge, which might explain the type III errors. They use new referents as topics, i.e. as definite DPs, because for them they are salient. Adults should not have problems any more with respect to shared knowledge. It seems to me therefore that the type I and III errors that the Dutch learners of French make are due to another factor, viz. the fact that they are not telling a story to another person, but are just describing the pictures they see. They are thinking aloud. This favors the use of definite determiners instead of indefinites.

De Cat takes it as uncontroversial that children can distinguish new from old information appropriately from the onset of language production. What children have to learn, is to use the correct syntactic encodings for the expression of new or old information. I interpreted the saliency violations by the Dutch students as being extra-linguistic. The many correct uses of the article in their speech production suggests that they possess the required competence of French to encode new referents appropriately. The question that can be raised is how the adult L2 learners have acquired this competence. Have they learned the correct syntactic encodings in L2 French for the expression of the possibly innate competence to distinguish new from old information or does their L1 play a role? To answer this question I first turn to the acquisition of definiteness distinctions by Japanese L2 learners of French.

3.2 Japanese learners of L2 French and the acquisition of definiteness distinctions

Contrary to Dutch, which has both definite and indefinite articles, Japanese does not have articles. In order to study the acquisition of the syntactic encoding of definiteness by Japanese learners of L2 French, I asked nine Japanese students of French to tell the Frog Story in French. The stories were recorded and analysed. All Japanese students were participating in a French language course for which a minimum of 100 hours of previous guided acquisition was required. Most of the students however had had at least 300 hours of formal instruction and most of them had been living in France for at least four months. Just like the Dutch students, all Japanese students were able to tell the stories in French, with the help of a small list of French words (nouns were presented without the article).

It turned out that the Japanese students had much more difficulties with the syntactic encoding of new and old referents than the Dutch students. As expected, they sometimes left out the article, just as in Japanese, especially after a preposition:

(13) *Grenouille* *est sortie*   *dans le pot.*
      frog   is come out in   the jar
      'The frog had left the jar.'

(14) *Ils cherchaient* **grenouille.**
      they searched   frog
      'They were searching the frog.'

(15) *Et après il s'   est fait tomber par* **cerf.**
      and then he himself is made fall   by   deer
      'And then the deer made him fall.'

They also made Type II errors, i.e. they used indefinites for already introduced referents. The Dutch students did not make these errors. In (16) an indefinite noun is in focus position, in (17) it is in topic position and in (18) it is a dislocated topic:

(16) *Le garçon et le chien a   trouvé la grenouille n' est pas dans* **un pot.**
      the boy   and the dog has found the frog   NEG is NEG in   a   jar
      'The boy and the dog discovered that the frog was not in the jar.'

(17) **Un garçon** *a   ouvert la fenêtre.*
      a boy   has opened the window
      'The boy opened the window.'

(18) *Mais* **un garçon,** *il n' avait pas arrêté   chercher un grenouille.*
      but a boy   he NEG had NEG stopped search a frog
      'But the boy did not stop searching the frog'

Just like the children in Hickmann et al.'s experiment and the Dutch students in my test, the Japanese students made some Type I and Type III errors, i.e. they used definites for newly introduced referents in focus or topic position. But whereas the children and the Dutch students might have made these errors because of the test which was based on a picture story, so that all referents were present in the situational context, the Type I and Type III errors in the speech production of the Japanese students were more numerous and could not always be attributed to the picture task. To see why this should be so, consider (19), which exemplifies a Type I error, a definite DP for a newly introduced referent in focus position:

(19) *Il y avait un garçon et un chien. Ils avaient une grenouille dans* **le pot.**
      there were a boy   and a dog they had   a frog   in   the jar
      'There were a boy and a dog. They had a frog in a jar.'

In Section 3.1 I claimed that the erroneous use of the definite article by the Dutch students was due to the fact that the students were sometimes describing the pictures instead of telling a story. Sentences (8)–(12) can all be seen as oral descriptions of pictures. With the use of (19), however, the Japanese student is not describing a picture, but is telling a story.

Sentence (20) exemplifies the use of a newly introduced referent in a presentational construction, a Type I error that the children in Hickmann et al.'s test never made, according to De Cat:

(20) *Là-bas il y a*   **le** *cerf il y avait* **le** *cerf.*
there   there-is the deer there-was the deer
'There was a deer there.'

An example of a Type III error, a definite for a newly introduced referent in topic position, is given in (21):

(21) *Un petit garçon a*   *trouvé une trou dans le   terre   et*
a   little boy   has found a   hole in   the ground and
soudain **le taupe** *sortit   du   trou.*
suddenly the mole comes-out of-the hole
'The boy found a hole in the ground and suddenly a mole came out of the hole.'

There were no examples of newly introduced referents as a definite topic in dislocated position, but there were examples of the reverse, a newly introduced referent as an indefinite in a typical topic position, the dislocated position. We could call this type of error a Type IV error:

(22) *Et* **un hibou,** *il était sorti   de la   trou dans l'   arbre et*
and an owl   he was went-out of the hole in   the tree and
des   abeilles *ils   ont   commencé attaquer le   chien.*
IND.PL bees   they have begun   attack   the dog
'And an owl came out of the hole and bees began to attack the dog.'

The examples mentioned so far show that the Japanese students have problems with the syntactic expression of newness. They made many mistakes. Furthermore, they corrected themselves sometimes, as the examples (23)–(24) illustrate, which shows that they are not sure about the correct use of the article:

(23) *Ils   avaient un grenouille dans* **le** *pot dans* **un pot.**
they had   a frog   in   the jar in a   jar
'They had a frog in a jar.'

(24) *L' hibou est a   suivi   un petit garçon le   petit garçon.*
the owl is has followed a little boy   the little boy
'The owl has followed the little boy.'

One student almost consistently used the definite article with the dog and the indefinite article with the boy:

(25) *Et* **le chien** *et* **un garçon** *regardent la   grenouille.*
and the dog and a   boy   watch   the frog
'And the dog and the boy watch the frog.'

(26) **Un garçon,** *il avait crié   et* **le chien,** *il regardait dans le   forêt.*
a   boy   he had shouted and the dog he looked in   the forest
'The boy shouted and the dog looked in the forest.'

The Japanese students also used definite determiners different from the definite article, but often in an incorrect way. Whereas in (27) the demonstrative has an antecedent in the immediate context, in (28) this is not the case. Some students seem to overuse the demonstrative determiner and use it where they should use a definite article:

(27)   *Soudainement ce   cerf s'arrêtait. Ce garçon et   son chien sont tombés.*
       suddenly   that deer stopped that boy   and his dog   are fallen
       'Suddenly the deer stopped. The boy and the dog fell.'

(28)   *Tout à coup une taupe s'apparaît et   ce   garçon blessait   son nez.*
       suddenly a   mole appears and that boy   wounded his nose
       'Suddenly a mole appeared and the boy hurt his nose.'

The Japanese students also used a possessive pronoun when there was no antecedent for the pronoun in the immediate preceding context:

(29)   *Ils   ne   peuvent pas le   trouver. Son chien est tombé de le*
       they NEG can   NEG him find   his dog is fallen of the
       fenêtre   et   puis un petit garçon a   aidé   son chien.
       window and then a   little boy   has helped his dog
       'They could not find him. The dog fell out of the window and then the boy helped his dog.'

(30)   *Et   soudain le   taupe sortit   du   trou et   son chien a   trouvé*
       and suddenly the mole comes out of-the hole and his dog   has found
       une maison de abeilles.
       a   house of bees
       'And suddenly a mole came out of the hole and the dog found a beehive.'

The preceding data show thus that the relation between the pragmatic notions 'old' and 'new' referent and the syntactic expression by means of a definite or indefinite DP is much more difficult to acquire for the Japanese L2 students of French than for the Dutch students or for the children learning French as their L1. In the next section I discuss the question as to why this should be so.

4.   Discussion

The fact that Dutch has articles with definiteness distinctions while Japanese does not have articles suggests that L1 plays a role in the acquisition of the syntactic expression of newness by means of the article. This had already been shown by Zobl (1984). Zobl noted that the acquisition of the determiners *a* and *the* in English is faster for L2 learners whose native language also makes a distinction between indefinite and definite determiners (such as French and Spanish) than for those L2 learners whose native language does not make such a distinction (such as Chinese or Russian). For Zobl this meant that there was positive transfer of properties from French and Spanish to English. More specifically, I propose that interface relations between the pragmatic distinction 'new' versus 'old' and its syntactic expression by means of an article can be positively transferred (cf. Ferdinand 2002, who argued that the relation between the pragmatic notion of topic and its syntactic expression as a dislocation construction can be positively transferred from Dutch to French).

Positive transfer is possible from Dutch but not from Japanese. Japanese is a determiner-free language (see e.g. Fukui 1995). Determiners such as *a*, *the* or *some* do not exist. Definiteness is not marked morphologically either. As a means to express definiteness, although not equivalent to *the*, prenominal modifiers expressed by *so*-series in Japanese can be added to serve for deictic use. This might explain the overuse of the demonstrative determiner by some Japanese learners, as noticed in §3.2:

(31) *So-no   otoko-no hito-ga   haitte-ki-ta.*
      that-GEN male-GEN person-NOM enter-come-PAST
      'That/the man entered.'

Since positive transfer of the interface rules for the article is not possible for Japanese learners of L2 French, they have to learn them. This seems to be a very hard task for them. On a total number of 502 referential DPs in the Japanse corpus of L2 French, there were 61 (=12.2%) definiteness errors (23 (=4.6%) type I errors, 34 (=6.8%) type II errors and 4 (=0.8%) type III errors). In addition there were 4 (=0.8%) type IV errors, 12 (=2.4%) wrong uses of the possessive pronoun and 15 (=3%) misplaced uses of the demonstrative pronoun. Furthermore the article was wrongly omitted 33 times (=6.6%).

The conclusion of this section is that if positive transfer is not possible the acquisition of definiteness distinctions, just like other syntactic-pragmatic interface relations (e.g. the distinction between preverbal and postverbal subjects in Italian (Sorace 2003)), seems to be a very difficult task for L2 learners.

5. Conclusion

In this paper I have shown that whereas children learning French acquire the interface relations for the article quite easily, this is not always the case for adult learners of L2 French. Whereas Dutch learners of L2 French seem to positively transfer the interface relations from Dutch, Japanese learners, for whom positive transfer is not possible, have many problems in acquiring the interface rules.

Notes

* This research was done as part of the Interface Issues Program (Petra Bos, Peter Coopmans, Astrid Ferdinand, Ger de Haan, Bart Hollebrandse, Roeland van Hout, Aafke Hulk, Peter Jordens, and Petra Sleeman) funded by the Netherlands Organization for Scientific Research, Council for the Humanities (nr. 360–70–011). I would like to thank 6 Dutch students from Utrecht University and 9 Japanese students who followed a summer course at the University Paris III for having participated in the experiment. I also thank Aafke Hulk and Natascha Müller and an anonymous reviewer for their valuable comments on earlier versions of this paper. All errors are of course mine.

1. Focus is the new information of the sentence and is in the default case on the most embedded element of the VP.

2. The topic of a sentence is that part that serves as a starting point for new information.

References

Baker, Nancy & Patricia Greenfield (1988). 'The development of new and old information in young children's early language'. *Language Sciences* 10.1, 3–34.

Cat, Cécile de (2004). 'A fresh look at how young children encode new referents'. In Petra Bos, Bart Hollebrandse & Petra Sleeman, eds., *IRAL* 42.2, 111–127.

Ferdinand, Astrid (2002). 'Acquisition of Topic marking in L2 French'. In Hans Broekhuis & Paula Fikkert, eds., *Linguistics in the Netherlands* 2002, 49–59.

Fukui, Naoki (1995.) 'The Principles-and Parameters approach: A comparative syntax of English and Japanese'. In Masayoshi Shibatani & Theodora Bynon, eds., *Approaches to Language Typology*. Oxford, Clarendon Press, 327–372.

Hickmann, Maya, Henriëtte Hendriks, Françoise Roland & James Liang (1996). 'Cohesion and anaphora in children's narratives: a comparison of English, French, German and Chinese'. *Journal of Child Language* 26, 419–452.

Mayer, Mercer (1969). *Frog, where are you?* New York, Penguin Putnam.

Sleeman, Petra (2004). 'Guided learners of French and the acquisition of emphatic constructions'. In Petra Bos, Bart Hollebrandse & Petra Sleeman, eds., *IRAL* 42.2, 129–151.

Sorace, Antonella (2003). 'Residual optionality at the syntacs-pragmatics interface in L2 advanced grammars'. Paper presented at the Workshop 'Interface Issues in L1 and L2 acquisition', Free University, Amsterdam, 23–24 October 2003.

Zobl, Helmut (1984): 'Cross-language generalizations and the contrastive dimension of the interlanguage hypothesis'. In A. Davies, C. Criper & A. P. R. Howatt, eds.: *Interlanguage*. Edinburgh University Press.

Exploring Cantonese tense[*]

Rint Sybesma
University of Leiden

1. Background: Chinese tense

Sinitic languages are often claimed to be tenseless. Claims to this effect generally consist of two subclaims, which can be formulated as follows:

(1) a. Sinitic languages have no morphological/semi-lexical or grammatical(ized) means of marking events as past events;[1]
   b. in these languages, the plotting of events on the time axis is administered by means of temporal adverbs or is determined by the context.

The Cantonese sentences in (2) illustrate these claims. They denote past events and there are no markers attached to the verb (subclaim (1a)). Subclaim (1b) is illustrated by the minimal pair in (2b) and (2c): the latter describes a current situation and the former, with the temporal adverb ji^5-cin^4 'formerly', describes a past event. (The superscripts in the Cantonese renderings are tone markers.)

(2) a. ngo⁵ (kam⁴-jat⁶) maai⁵ jat¹-bun² syu¹ ge³-si⁴-hau⁶, …
      1s   yesterday buy one-CL book while
      'when I was buying a book (yesterday), …'
   b. keoi⁵ ji⁵-cin⁴ hai² Rotterdam zyu⁶
      3s   before at   Rotterdam live
      's/he used to live in Rotterdam'
   c. keoi⁵ hai² Rotterdam zyu⁶
      3s   at   Rotterdam live
      's/he lives in Rotterdam'

Reformulation of the claims may still be necessary in view of data such as those in (3) (quite apart from the question where the "present tense" interpretation in (2c) comes from, in the absence of any temporal adverb; see Section 4). The sentences in (3) denote past events, despite the absence of temporal adverbs. What is more, comparing (3a) with (3b) and (3c) with (2c), we must conclude

Linguistics in the Netherlands 2004 21 (2004), **169–180**.
ISSN 0929–7332 / E-ISSN 1569–9919 ©Algemene Vereniging voor Taalwetenschap

that the elements *zo²* and *lei⁴*, morphological or semi-lexical markers by any definition, are responsible for the marking of these events as past events. Indeed, as the obligatoriness of *zo²* in (3d) shows, the presence of a temporal adverb may not always be sufficient.

(3) a. ngo⁵ maai⁵-zo² jat¹-bun² syu¹
         1s   buy-zo² one-CL book
         'I bought a book'
     b. ngo⁵ maai⁵ jat¹-bun² syu¹
         1s   buy   one-CL book
         'I buy/want to buy a book'
     c. keoi⁵ hai² Rotterdam zyu⁶ lei⁴
         3s   at   Rotterdam live LEI⁴
         's/he used to live in Rotterdam'
     d. ngo⁵ kam⁴-jat⁶ maai⁵-*(zo²) jat¹-bun² syu¹
         1s   yesterday buy-zo²   one-CL book
         'I bought a book yesterday'

Taking *zo²* and *lei⁴* as the main focus, this paper aims at exploring Cantonese tense, from a general, theoretical point of view and in view of the claims in (1).

2.   Background: Tense and finiteness

I explore Cantonese tense against the background of widely accepted theories of tense and finiteness. As to tense, I adopt the Reichenbachian idea that there are three time spans as well as two T(ense) nodes, which express the relative order of the time spans (Reichenbach 1947; Klein 1994; Stowell 1996; Hoekstra 1992; a.o.). The time spans are TU, the utterance time; TT ("Topic Time"), the time span the utterance is meant to make a claim about; and TSit, the time of the event denoted by the predicate of the sentence.[2] It is generally assumed that the two T-nodes, T1 and T2, each have two possible settings, [+PST] and [−PST], which enables them to express the relative order of TU, TT and TSit. T1 arranges TU and TT (traditionally a matter of "tense"), and T2 does the same for TT and TSit ("aspect"). How this pens out for English is shown in (4) (cf. Hoekstra 1992 (36)).

(4)   T1   T2
     a. is[−PST]   V -ing[−PST]   TU,TT overlap; TT, Tsit overlap
     b. has[−PST]   V -ed[+PST]   TU,TT overlap; T-Sit precedes TT
     c. was[+PST]   V -ing[−PST]   TT precedes TU; TT,T-Sit overlap
     d. had[+PST]   V -ed[+PST]   TT precedes TU; TSit precedes TT

Presumably, though the claim would be that all sentences contain a T1, not all of them have a T2-node. Whether they do or not depends on several factors, one of them being the type of predicate they contain. Sentences with predicates denoting telic events, for instance, may have both T-nodes, where as sentences with predicates referring to non-telic events will not have a T2. If there is no T2, TSit and TT overlap.

As to finiteness, I adopt the definition of a finite sentence as a sentence with its own temporal reference, a sentence which is able to temporally anchor onto the context (Enç 1987; Guéron & Hoekstra 1995; Bianchi 2002; a.o.). To this end, a finite sentence is equipped with an operator in the C-domain of the sentence, and this operator binds a pronominal variable in T1 — a *pronominal* variable because it has features of itself: [+PST] or [−PST], as we just saw. The operator is the foothold of the context in the sentence, it represents the contextual "here-and-now". The relation between the operator and the [±PST] T1 determines the temporal reference of the sentence in the context.

Note that for a sentence to be finite as just defined does not entail that there must be a finite form. Whether a language has finite forms depends on independent properties of the language, which we will not discuss here (Campbell 1995).

One more note before we look at Cantonese *zo²* and *lei⁴*: in this paper I use the phrase "past event" loosely, referring to any situation in which TSit is located before TU, regardless of what happens to TT.

3. Cantonese *zo²* and *lei⁴*: Differences and similarities

The sentences given above show that Cantonese has three different markers for presenting events as past events, *zo²*, *lei⁴* and a zero-marker. *Zo²* occurred in a sentence with a telic event (see (3a), (3d)), *lei⁴* in one with a state (see (3c)); (2a) and (2b) show that the zero-marker is compatible with both types of events. In the following section we consider the question what determines the distribution of these three elements. In this section, we look at additional facts regarding *zo²* and *lei⁴*, so as to get a more complete descriptive picture.

First, *lei⁴* is not compatible with telic events, with or without *zo²*. Similarly, *zo²* is incompatible with states, with or without *lei⁴*.[3] In contrast, *zo²* and *lei⁴* can both occur with non-telic activities, where they can even cooccur; thus, (5) is well formed as is, but either *zo²* or *lei⁴* can be dropped without affecting the well-formedness (though the interpretation is affected, which we do not go into here). This use of *zo²* and *lei⁴* is not included in the discussions in the remainder of this section; we return to it later on (footnote 6).

(5) keoi⁵ kam⁴-jat⁶ sik⁶-zo² di¹ heung¹-jiu¹ lei⁴
     3s   yesterday eat-zo² CL^pl banana   LEI⁴
     's/he ate some bananas (yesterday)'

The sentence in (5) reveals a further difference between zo^2 and lei^4: whereas the former directly follows V^0, the latter follows the VP as a whole.

To zoom in on their meaning, let's investigate the following sentence pairs.

(6) a. keoi^5 hai^2 Rotterdam zyu^6 lei^4 (= (3c))
        3s   at   Rotterdam live LEI^4
        's/he used to live in Rotterdam'
    b. ngo^5 maai^5-zo^2 jat^1-bun^2 syu^1 (= (3a))
        1s buy-zo^2 one-CL book
        'I bought a book'

(7) a. keoi^5 1989 nin^4 hai^2 Rotterdam zyu^6 lei^4
        3s   1989 year at   Rotterdam live LEI^4
        'in 1989 s/he lived in Rotterdam (for a while)'
    b. ngo^5 kam^4-jat^6 maai^5-zo^2 jat^1-bun^2 syu^1 (cf. (3d))
        1s   yesterday buy-zo^2 one-CL book
        'I bought a book yesterday'

(8) a. keoi^5 1989 nin^4 hai^2 Rotterdam zyu^6
        3s   1989 year at   Rotterdam live
        'in 1989 s/he lived in Rotterdam'
    b. *ngo^5 kam^4-jat^6 maai^5 jat^1-bun^2 syu^1 (cf. (3d))
        1s   yesterday buy one-CL book
        intended: 'I bought a book yesterday'

In (6), both zo^2 and lei^4 express that an event has been completed or concluded. It is irrelevant when they took place, all that is expressed is that we are dealing with events that have been rounded off at the speech time. In the terms introduced in Section 2, we may say that TSit is located before TT and that TT and TU overlap.

The sentences in (7) are minimally different from those in (6), both in form and in meaning. Like their counterparts in (6), the sentences in (7) each denote an event that is explicitly marked as having been completed/concluded at the time of speaking, but now a time adverbial is added to specify when the event took place. In other words, the time adverbials modify TSit. As was the case with the sentences in (6), then, in the sentences in (7), TSit has been dissociated from TT, which overlaps with TU.

In both (6) and (7), it seems to be the case that the dissociation of TT and TSit is administered by zo^2 and lei^4: by explicitly marking the event as having been concluded by a certain time, they locate the event in its entirety, and thus TSit, before that certain time.

The sentences in (8) differ from their counterparts in (7) in two respects. First, the events are not explicitly marked as having been completed or concluded, which means that TSit and TT overlap. Secondly, the time adverbials in (8) do not modify TSit but introduce TT: we want to make a claim about 1989 and yesterday respectively, namely that certain events took place then. The claim is limited to the said time intervals, we don't make claims about any other time spans; thus, whereas the meaning of (7a) implies that the subject no longer lived in Rotterdam in 1990, no such claim is implied in (8a). In any case, due to the use of the time adverbials, in (8a) and (8b) TT has been explicitly moved to prior-to-TU. (The ungrammaticality of (8b) will be addressed below.)

What we observe is that, in principle, time adverbials can do two things (as was discussed in Klein 1994): they can introduce TT and they can modify TSit. When we compare the sentences in (7) and (8), we see that they do the former in the absence of zo^2 and lei^4 and the latter in their presence. However, here we discover a difference between zo^2 and lei^4: whereas in sentences with lei^4, a time adverbial is never interpretable as if introducing TT, in sentences with zo^2 it is possible to get such a reading.

(9)   a. ngo^5 1989 nin^4 bat^1-zo^2-yip^6 laa^3
           1s   1989 year finish-zo^2-tasks SFP
           'I graduated in 1989'
      b. ngo^5 1989 nin^4 ji^5-$ging^1$ bat^1-zo^2-yip^6 laa^3
           1s   1989 year already finish-zo^2-tasks SFP
           'by 1989, I had already graduated'

The sentence in (9a) reports on an event that has been concluded and happened to have taken place in 1989. In contrast, the sentence in (9b) is a claim about 1989: by then, the event had already taken place. The time adverbial in (9a) modifies TSit, in (9b) it introduces TT. As in (6) and (7), in (9a), TT and TU are not dissociated, but in (9b) they are, due to the time adverbial. In both sentences, TSit is dissociated from TT due to zo^2.

In sentences with lei^4, a time adverbial can only be interpreted as modifying TSit. The question is why that should be the case. What is probably relevant in this context is the fact that lei^4, unlike zo^2, cannot be used with ji^5-$ging^1$ 'already', nor can it occur in 'after'-conjuncts, which zo^2 can. Despite some similarities, lei^4 and zo^2 may turn out ot be two very different elements after all.

Finally, I need to mention the "actuality marker" function of lei^4. Addition of lei^4 to a sentence makes the sentence as a whole especially relevant to the context; it says: "the event has happened in the past, but I am telling you about it for a special reason" — the reason most likely being quite obvious in the context.

Here is a summary of the properties of zo^2 and lei^4, mentioned or discussed above. We investigate them further in the remainder of this paper.

zo^2	lei^4
– immediately follows the verb	– follows the VP
– may alternate with zero form, is sometimes obligatory	– may alternate with zero form

– with telic events, with activities, not with states	– with states, with activities, not with telic events
– induces T2 effect	– induces T2 effect
– time adverbials can introduce TT	– time adverbials cannot introduce TT
– compatible with 'already' and 'after'	– incompatible with 'already', 'after'
– no other effects	– actuality marker

4.   Cantonese T1

In Section 1, we found two overt morphological/semi-lexical elements which are used for presenting events as past events, zo^2 and lei^4. From the sentences presented above, it is clear that neither of them instantiates T1, since neither is involved in locating TT relative to TU. This raises questions regarding the nature of T1 in Cantonese. Indeed, do Cantonese sentences have a T1-node at all?

Although Cantonese apparently does not have any overt markers for T1, there seems to be evidence that it does have a T1-node (the following argument is due to Matthewson 2002). To see what the evidence is, let's look at (2c). As I reported above, this sentence has a "present" tense reading. The question is: Where does this reading come from? Significantly, the temporal reading of sentences like (2c) can only be changed with the use of linguistic material, such as adverbs (see (2b)) and *linguistic* context (and lei^4). Non-linguistic information cannot do that job. For instance, if the subject of such a sentence is a deceased person, the sentence is simply infelicitous. The fact that the temporal interpretation in these sentences can only be manipulated with linguistic cues suggests that the present tense interpretation is also linguistically expressed. There is no overt tense marker, but T1 is set at [−PST], as is clear from the interpretation.

There is a theory-internal argument for a T1 node in Cantonese too. If it is right, as the theory summarized in Section 2 says, that the three time spans can be dissociated from each other with the use of the two T-nodes, then the sentence in (9b), in which all three nodes are dissociated, constitutes a piece of evidence supporting the postulation of the T-nodes.

The way we may interpret the situation in Cantonese is that T1 has two settings, [+PST] and [−PST], both with zero-marking. The setting is determined by the linguistic context or an adverbial, that is, adverbials that we got to know as adverbials which introduce TT. If there is no adverbial and no specific context has been introduced, we get a default [−PST] ("here and now"). As in other languages, the relation between the tense operator and the variable in T1 determines the temporal anchoring onto the context. This is essentially what I would like to propose for Cantonese, except for an important amendment to be made in Section 6. The amendment is prompted by the question posed earlier with respect to the use of time adverbials in sentences with lei^4. The question was: Why can't these adverbials introduce TT in sentences with lei^4? Now we can rephrase the question and ask: Why can't they set T1 to [+PST] in such sentences?

5.   The function and structural position of zo^2

In the previous section we established that there are good reasons to assume that Cantonese has a T1-node. We can now move on and ask: How about T2? All along, I have talked about zo^2 and lei^4 as "inducing T2-effects", carefully avoiding saying that they *are* T2 elements, because I don't think they are. For lei^4 this is clear: it only occurs with states and non-telic activities and if sentences with non-telic event predicates have no T2 (Section 2), lei^4 cannot be a T2 element. But how about zo^2? In this section we discuss zo^2, turning to lei^4 in Section 6.

   Zo^2 is the Cantonese counterpart of Mandarin verb-*le*, which is generally acknowledged to be a perfective marker. More specifically, in Sybesma and Vanden Wyngaerd (1997) and Sybesma (1997), it is analysed as a "realization marker", with different interpretational effects for telic and non-telic events. With telics (for non-telics see footnote 6), it is a realization marker in the sense that it indicates that the inherent end point of the event is reached; once the end point has been reached the event as a whole can be seen to have realized. The analysis of Mandarin *le* can be extended to Cantonese zo^2 unproblematically.

   If zo^2 is a realization marker as defined, most of the properties in the summary at the end of Section 3 are explained. The fact that it does not cooccur with states, for instance, is clear: states have no inherent end point, the attainment of which zo^2 would mark. The distributional zo^2-zero alternation pattern also falls out, when we realize that zo^2 is only used in contexts in which the completion of the event is at issue. In (2a) we have a sentence with a telic event, the completion of which is not at issue: as the translation indicates ('when I was buying a book'), we had not reached the end point of the event (when presumably something else happened). That is why zo^2 is not used. On the other hand, zo^2 is obligatory in (3d)/(8b), a main clause sentence with a temporal adverbial referring to a pre-TU time interval. The explanation here is that if one wants to refer to a telic event as having taken place, in its entirety, in the past, one cannot avoid explicit marking of the realization of the end point, which is done with zo^2 (Verkuyl 1972).

   As a realization marker, zo^2 occupies a position inside the VP; more specifically, Sybesma (1997) and Sybesma and Vanden Wyngaerd (1997) argue that it heads a projection inside the small clause which complements V. In the latter paper it is also argued that Mandarin *le* (by extension, Cantonese zo^2) has the same function as the element *ge-* in Dutch past participles. Dutch past participles consist of three parts: realization marker *ge-*, the lexical verbal stem and, as Hoekstra (1992) argues (see (4)), a marker of the past tense. This marker of the past tense is T2. We can conclude from this that if zo^2 has the same status as *ge-*, it is not T2. We may draw a second conclusion, namely that if Dutch *ge-* is always accompanied by a past tense T2, this is possibly the case for Cantonese zo^2 as well, even though it is not marked overtly (not suprisingly: T1 does not seem to ever have any overt marking either). Leaving the second conclusion undiscussed, let's conclude that zo^2 occupies a position inside the VP and that it is not T2.

T1 is in no way influenced by the presence of zo^2. Just like in any other sentence, its value is determined by the linguistic environment or temporal adverbials; the sentence in (9b) illustrates how an adverbial sets the T1 to [+PST]. In other cases, like (6b) and (7b), the setting is [−PST]. These two sentences show that Cantonese is much closer to French and Dutch than to English in that their temporal make up is much more directly reflected in the French *(hier,) j'ai acheté un livre* and the Dutch *ik heb (gister) een boek gekocht*, both using a present perfect (T1[−PST], T2[+PST]), than the English sentence provided as the translation, which uses the simple past.

6.   The function and structural position of lei^4

Turning to lei^4, we have noted that it differs from zo^2 in several respects, suggesting that it does not have the same status as zo^2, structurally and otherwise. For one thing, lei^4 is not a marker which signals that the in-built end point of an event has been reached, because it is only compatible with events that do not involve such an inherent end point. Secondly, it occupies a different surface position: whereas zo^2 is attached to the verb, lei^4 is attached to the end of the phrase. Indeed, lei^4 may even cooccur with zo^2 (see (5)), and in the same way it may cooccur with elements like the so-called experiential marker gwo^3 which itself is in complementary distribution with zo^2. Another reason for assuming that lei^4 is different from zo^2 structurally is related to the actualizing function (see Section 3); in this capacity, lei^4 is in complementary distribution with ge^3.

Ge^3 is known as an assertion marker (Cheung 1972). Taking a wide range of data into consideration, we may more generally call it an actuality marker: it makes the whole sentence it is attached to more relevant to the current context. Here are two examples ((a) based on Fung 2000, 158 (31)). The sentence in (10a) illustrates the use of ge^3 as an assertion marker: the speaker wants to show the hearer that s/he is absolutely sure of what s/he is saying. It is also an actuality marker, because the addition of ge^3 makes the sentence especially relevant to some aspect of the conversational context: due to ge^3, the sentence directly addresses some concern the hearer may have expressed. Without ge^3, the sentence is no more than a neutral statement, without any necessary link to any aspect of the conversation. Similarly, (10b) without ge^3 would simply be a neutral statement of fact, part of a list of someone's abilities, for instance. With ge^3, however, the sentence may be uttered as a reaction to someone's concern regarding the news that the subject of the sentence is going to Berlin. How is he going to find his way around?!

(10) a. go²-di¹-syu¹, aa³-ji⁶-suk¹ wui⁵ luk⁶zuk⁶ gei³-faan¹-lei⁴   (ge³)
          that-CL-book 2nd uncle   will continue send-back-come GE³
          without ge³: 'as to those books, Second Uncle will continue to send them to us'
          with ge³: 'as to those books, Second Uncle will continue to send them to us
          — for sure, don't worry about it'

       b. keoi⁵ sik¹   Dak¹man² (ge³)
          3s   know German   GE
          without ge³: 's/he knows German'
          with ge³: 'don't worry, s/he knows German'

Lei⁴ has the same actualizing function; utterances with *lei⁴* are never completely neutral in the sense that they are always uttered for a reason which is obvious from the conversational context. The sentence in (11) without *lei⁴* would be a neutral statement, but with *lei⁴* the sentence is uttered to explain something, like why s/he did not come to our party last Thursday.

(11) soeng⁶go³-laai⁵baai⁵, keoi⁵ hou² mong⁴ (lei⁴)
       last-week   3s   very busy   LEI⁴
       without lei⁴: 'last week s/he was very busy'
       with lei⁴: 's/he was very busy, last week, you know (no longer is)'

The division of labor between ge^3 and lei^4 is that lei^4 is compatible with past events, while ge^3 takes care of the rest. Ge^3 can cooccur with future modals (as we saw in (10a)), and lei^4 cannot; lei^4 is compatible with sentences that are independently marked as referring to a past event (as we saw in (11)), and ge^3 is not. The question is where the past and non-past readings come from. Are lei^4 and ge^3 responsible for them or are they there independently?

I address this question shortly. Let me first return to the question regarding the structural position of lei^4. Considering (i) that lei^4 and ge^3 have scope over the entire sentence, which suggest that they occupy a peripheral position in the structure; (ii) that Cantonese has no finite forms but still has finite sentences as defined in Section 2; and (iii) that ge^3 and lei^4 make the sentence they are part of especially relevant for the here and now,[4] I propose that lei^4 and ge^3 are possible instantiations of the tense operator in the C-domain of the Cantonese sentence.[5]

In Section 2, I introduced the common idea that in Germanic and Romance languages the head of TP is occupied by a pronominal variable, which is bound by an operator in the C-domain. The [+PST] or [−PST] value of the pronominal variable contributes to the anchoring of the sentence to the extra-sentential time line. In Section 5, I proposed that Cantonese sentences also have this operator in the C-domain, binding a pronominal variable in T1, the value of which is determined by the linguistic context or set by temporal adverbials.

The amendment to this proposal that I promised there to present here is the following. I propose that Cantonese has three different tense operators, and that it is actually the operator which determines the value of the variable in T1. First, it has a tense operator which is phonologically empty; it is the neutral representative of the "here-and-now" and it leaves the value of the T1 as "underspecified". Secondly, there is ge^3. It is less neutral; it expresses something that may be paraphrased as "and this is how it is". The value of the T1 it binds is set at [−PST]. Finally, there is lei^4. Like ge^3 it is not neutral; it adds something like "and this is how it was", with the strong implication that "it is no longer like that now".[6] The value of the T1 lei^4 binds is set at [+PST].

Only in the case of the zero-operator can the value of the T1 node be determined by the linguistic context or an adverbial. In both other cases the value is determined by the operator, ge^3 or lei^4. This explains why time adverbials in sentences with lei^4 can no longer introduce TT and can only modify TSit.

Schematically, this is what we have:

Operator	Value of T1
Ø neutral	underspecified
ge^3 'and this is how it is'	[−PST]
lei^4 'and this is how it was'	[+PST]

The major difference, then, between Cantonese and Germanic-Romance is that, in Cantonese, not the T1-variable is independently specified for [+PST] or [−PST], as it is in Germanic-Romance, but the operator is: the operator binds the variable and determines its value. This makes the relation between the operator and the variable very "Chinese": Chinese languages offer other examples of such a situation, e.g., the variables which come out as *wh*-words or indefinites depending on the operator which binds them (Cheng 1991, Tsai 1994).

7. Tense in Cantonese

In the view presented above, Cantonese is not a tenseless language. Its verbs may not have finite forms, and in some sentences, it does seem to be the case that the adverbials determine the positioning of TT relative to TU, rather than some semi-lexical particle, but ge^3 and lei^4 would certainly count as tense elements. They may not be in T1, but they do determine its value directly.

In view of this analysis, the claims formulated in (1) regarding the alleged tenselessness of Chinese languages need to be reformulated, or it must be made explicit that they do not apply to all Chinese languages in the same way. For Cantonese, subclaim (1a) (Sinitic languages have no grammatical or grammaticalized means of marking events as past events) is correct only if we interpret it as saying that T1 is never marked in any overt way. If I am correct that ge^3 and lei^4 determine the value of T1 as [−PST] and [+PST] respectively, the subclaim in (1a) is not even correct if it is meant to mean that Sinitic has no grammatical ways of locating TT relative to TU. The second subclaim, which says that in Sinitic the explicit plotting of the events on the time axis is administered by means of temporal adverbs or context, is only true if we add something like "in the absence of either of the two specific tense operators ge^3 and lei^4".

Notes

* Thanks are due to Lisa Cheng and Joanna Sio for help with the data and discussion. I also thank the *LIN*-reviewer and individuals from audiences in Utrecht, Leiden, Ghent and Paris for helpful questions and suggestions. The research reported here was conducted in the context of my "Vernieuwingsimpuls"-project on syntactic variation in southern China, co-funded by the Dutch Organization for Scientific Research NWO, Universiteit Leiden (main sponsors) and the International Institute for Asian Studies IIAS.

1. Or future events, for that matter. In this paper, I limit my attention to past events.

2. The terminology is Klein's (Klein 1994). For, the purposes of this paper, TU, TT and TSit are equivalent to Reichenbach's original S,R,E.

3. Zo^2 is compatible with statives with a duration phrase, which are telic.

4. Which makes the elements unlikely T1 elements themselves. Note that for Klein (1994), assertion is part the definition of finiteness.

5. Or they are complementizers accompanied by an operator in their Spec, just as Q-particles and negative elements are accompanied by operators in their Spec.

6. This explains why it is not compatible with telic sentences with zo^2, which denotes the completion of an event, resulting in a new state. With non-telic activities, zo^2 marks realization in the sense that it indicates that the event "has come into existence" (Sybesma 1997). Nothing is said about completion. As a consequence, lei^4 and zo^2 are compatible in sentences with non-telic activities.

References

Bianchi, V. (2002). 'On finiteness as logophoric anchoring'. Ms. Scuola Normale Superiore, Pisa.
Campbell, R. (1995). 'Inflectional domains and Comp features'. *Lingua* 96/2/3, 119–138.
Cheng, L. (1991). *On the typology of* wh-*questions*. Doctoral dissertation, MIT.

Cheung, S. H.-N. (1972). *Cantonese as spoken in Hong Kong*. The Chinese University of Hong Kong.

Enç, M. (1987). 'Anchoring conditions for Tense'. *Linguistic Inquiry* 18/4, 633–657.

Fung, R. S.-Y. (2000). *Final particles in Standard Cantonese: Semantic extension and pragmatic inference*. Doctoral dissertation, Ohio State University.

Guéron, J. and T. Hoekstra (1995). 'The temporal interpretation of predication'. In A. Cardinaletti and M. Guasti, eds., *Small clauses* [*Syntax and semantics* 28], 77–107. New York, Academic Press.

Hoekstra, T. (1992). 'ECP, tense and islands'. Ms. Universiteit Leiden. [To be included in T. Hoekstra, to app., *Arguments and structure. Studies on the architecture of the sentence*. Berlin, Mouton.]

Klein, W. (1994). *Time in language*. Routledge, London.

Matthewson, L. (2002). 'An underspecified Tense in St'át'imcets'. Paper presented at WECOL 2002.

Reichenbach, H. (1947). *Elements of symbolic logic*. University of California Press, Berkeley.

Stowell, T. (1996). 'The phrase structure of tense'. In J. Rooryck, and L. Zaring, eds., *Phrase structure and the lexicon*, 277–291. Kluwer, Dordrecht.

Sybesma, R. (1997). 'Why Chinese verb-*le* is a resultative predicate'. *Journal of East Asian Linguistics* 6/2, 215–261.

Sybesma, R. and G. Vanden Wyngaerd (1997). 'Realizing end points: the syntax and semantics of Dutch *ge* and Mandarin *le*'. In J. Coerts and H. de Hoop, eds., *Linguistics in the Netherlands 1997*, 207–218. John Benjamins, Amsterdam.

Tsai, W.-T. D. (1994). *On economizing the theoy of A-bar dependencies*. Doctoral dissertation, MIT.

Verkuyl, H. (1972). *On the compositional nature of aspect*. Foris, Dordrecht.

Pseudo coordination is not subordination

Mark de Vos
University of Leiden

1. Pseudo coordination

In English and many other languages, there is a subset of coordination structures which seem to be different to garden-variety coordination, namely
'subordinating' coordination, also described in traditional grammars as the
hendiadys construction. Henceforth, I will call this construction pseudo
coordination (PCO) and verbs like *sit* and *go* which enter into it PCO verbs.

(1) What has John sat and done all day?
     'What has John done with his time all day?'

(2) What has John gone and done all day?
     'What has John done with his time all day?'

These constructions are distinguished from garden-variety coordination by
several properties which have been well described in the literature (Wiklund
(1996), Jaeggli & Hyams (1993), Carden & Pesetsky (1977), Ross (1967) inter
alia). These include the fact that the first conjunct is restricted to limited
number of verbs, notably *come* and *go*.[1] Pseudo coordination also allows
systematic violations of the coordinate structure constraint (henceforth CSC)
(see (1) and (2)) and yields aspectual interpretations (notably durativity), as
well as 'surprise' (Carden & Pesetsky 1977) and pejorative readings. Finally,
both verbs must have the same morphological form. These are the focus of the
following section.

2. Pseudo coordination is not coordination

Several studies argue that PCO is different from garden-variety coordination.
Arguments supporting this view include the fact that extraction may occur from

the second conjunct, conjuncts may not be reordered and that semantic bleaching occurs concomitant with aspectual interpretations.

Extraction cannot occur from the second conjunct of an garden-variety coordination (3a) in the absence of ATB. It is nevertheless possible to extract from a PCO construction (3b,c).[2]

(3) a. *What has John painted a house and eaten?
     b. What has John gone and done now?
     c. What has John sat and done all day?

Garden-variety coordination, as in (4), allows one to reorder the conjuncts provided there is no consecutive ordering of events inferred from encyclopedic knowledge. This is not possible with PCO (5) and (6).

(4) a. John cut a mushroom and washed an apple
     b. John washed an apple and cut a mushroom

(5) a. John went and blushed a deep red
     b. *John blushed and went a deep red

(6) a. John sat and read a newspaper
     b. *John read and sat a newspaper

In garden-variety coordination, the full lexical meanings of both verbs are always accessible. However, in PCO constructions the first conjunct (*come, go, sit* etc) appears to be semantically bleached.

(7) a. Somebody went and read the constitution!
         'A person actually read the constitution'
     b. Somebody walked and read the constitution
         'A person physically walked and read the constitution at the same time'

(8) It went and rained again on Friday

In example (7a) the first conjunct (*went*) is bleached insofar as it does not require a deictic/movement interpretation as in example (7b). Furthermore, (7a) is felicitous even in contexts where no physical movement is required; for instance the reader may be bedridden, reading the constitution to pass the time. Even the expletive subject of weather verbs can occur in a PCO construction (8) where a deictic interpretation is impossible.

Sit seems to retain more of its lexical meaning than *go*, although there are still examples of bleaching.

(9) Big companies (Fortune 500) hire contractors to come in and do something or set the foundation. The employees <u>sit and age</u>[3]

(10) In Konitsa we finally had some sun during the day and we had a new moon (no moon at all) at night, which let all the stars <u>sit and shine</u> in the expansive heavens, surrounded by the mountains as the clouds came and went[4]

Example (9) concerns employees who are not physically sitting insofar as they are involved in managing a company (which involves many other actions than merely sitting). Also note that a contractor could potentially take months to complete a project; this time period is consistent with aging, but not with sitting. Clearly, *sit* has durative aspect in this example. Example (10) also exhibits semantic bleaching insofar as stars are inherently unable to 'sit' in the sky.

Garden-variety coordination typically conjoins elements of the same semantic sort.[5] PCO with *sit* and *go* differs from garden-variety coordination in that the former but not the latter requires that both verbs have the same morphological specification.[6] This is illustrated in (11) for PRES.3SG, by (12) for PAST and (13) for participle morphology.

(11) a.   John goes and throws a tantrum again
      b.   *John goes and throw a tantrum again
      c.   *John go and throws a tantrum again

(12) a.   John went and threw a tantrum again
      b.   *John went and throws a tantrum again
      c.   *John go and threw a tantrum again

(13) a.   John has gone and thrown a tantrum again
      b.   *John has gone and throws a tantrum again
      c.   *John has go and thrown a tantrum again

The fact that the 'sameness' condition applies to the morphology in PCO constructions marks them as being different to garden-variety coordination.[7]

Given these clear differences between PCO and coordination, I conclude, along with many others, including Wiklund (1996) and Carden & Pesetsky (1977), that PCO is not coordination of the garden variety. The following section will explore whether it can be analysed as subordination.

3.   It isn't subordination

PCO cannot be subordination of a monoclausal type since *sit* and *go* do not behave like auxiliaries. It also cannot be subordination of a biclausal type since the subject of the embedded clause cannot be licensed.

PCO verbs like *sit* and *go* do not behave like auxiliaries (Pollock 1994, Jaeggli & Hyams 1993, Carden & Pesetsky 1977). The operator *both* selects two separate events and can thus occur in garden-variety coordination (14a). It is blocked with *go* and *sit* (14b,c) (Carden & Pesetsky 1977).

(14) a.   John both ate and drank his fill
      b.   *John will both go and kiss Mary
      c.   *John will both sit and kiss Mary

However, *both* can modify coordinated modals and auxiliaries indicating that *go* and *sit* are neither modals nor auxiliaries.

(15)   John both can and will go to school

Another argument concerns verb raising. Modals and auxiliaries can raise across negation to T (16a) and can undergo Subject-auxiliary inversion (17a) (Pollock 1994). *Go* and *sit* can do neither.

(16)   a.   I will not speak to her
       b.   *I go not speak to her
       c.   *I sit not speak to her

(17)   a.   Will you speak to her?
       b.   *Go you speak to her?
       c.   *Sit you speak to her?

Sit and *go* do not appear to be auxiliaries or modals and thus cannot be explained by an analysis based on monoclausal subordination.

PCO also cannot be biclausal subordination as suggested by Wiklund (1996) since the subject position in the embedded clause cannot be filled by either PRO, pro, a trace of raising, nor an ATB trace given current theoretical assumptions. The central problem concerns the nature of the empty subject represented by **e** in (18).

(18)   *John$_i$* will go and **e**$_i$ take Mary on a date

By analogy with infinitivals one might suggest that the empty position is PRO.

(19)   *John$_i$* will go and **PRO**$_i$ take Mary on a date

However the fact that the embedded verb can also have person, number, tense and participle morphology (11,12,13) shows that it is *not* an infinitive and thus unable to license PRO; PRO must be ungoverned and tense is a potential governor.[8]

Another possibility is that the empty position is *pro*. However, English is not a pro-drop language and it would seem counterintuitive to postulate the existence of a category that never occurs independently in other contexts.

It is equally unlikely that the empty position is a trace left by movement. Raising occurs when a DP cannot get case in the lower clause. However, having demonstrated that the embedded verb is not an infinitive and thus perfectly able to assign nominative case, there is no rationale for a raising analysis. In addition, a true raising verb like *seem* is compatible with an expletive *there* in subject position. This is not true for *go* and *sit* (20b,c).

(20)   a.   There seems to be a fly in my soup
       b.   *There goes and drops a fly in my soup
       c.   *There sits and drops a fly in my soup

The final possibility is that the subject position of the embedded verb is a trace left by ATB extraction (21).

(21) $John_i$ will $t_{i(\text{ATB})}$ go and $t_{i(\text{ATB})}$ take Mary on a date

However, this would imply that PCO constructions involve garden-variety coordination, which I have already demonstrated to be false. Thus a paradox arises. I conclude, that there is no obvious empty category which could occur in the embedded clause. Consequently, PCO constructions cannot be instances of infinitival complementation (contra Wiklund (1996)).

4. Reduplicative coordination

At this point, we are in a quandary, having shown that PCO is neither coordination nor subordination. However, there is another construction that may shed some light on PCO. With this in mind, let us step back from PCO constructions of the *go, sit* type and consider reduplicative coordinative constructions of the *read and read* sort (henceforth ReCo).

(22) He begins reading about dinosaurs and tigers, and he <u>reads and reads</u> until the library closes[9]

There are several parallels between ReCo constructions and PCO ones. Both constructions share the same outward form, consisting of two or more verbs and a coordination marker. Furthermore, they also are subject to the sameness condition: both coordinated verbs must have the same morphological form.

(23) a. John reads and reads all day
      b. *John reads and read all day
      c. *John read and reads all day

ReCo constructions can be extracted from. Thus, just like PCO constructions, they constitute exceptions to the coordinate structure constraint.

(24) What did John read and read for three days without stopping

It might be suggested that (24) is merely ATB extraction. This is demonstrably untrue. The verb *to read up* is intransitive, any additional DP being introduced by a preposition. (25a) illustrates the reduplicative use of *read up*. (25b) shows that WH-extraction from such a construction is indeed possible. Note that (25b) cannot be ATB simply because there is no intermediate landing site for an extracted DP. (25c) illustrates what ATB would look like were it possible.

(25) a. John read up and read up on the case until he felt he was prepared for the trial
      b. What did John read up and read up on?
      c. *What did John read up on t_{ATB} and read up on t_{ATB}?

Both modification is also blocked in ReCo constructions, exactly like their *sit* and *go* counterparts (cf. (14)).

(26) a.   John both reads and writes books all day long
     b.   *John both reads and reads all day long

Concomitant with semantic bleaching we find aspectual readings associated with PCO constructions. They seem to denote durative, non-stative events.

(27) *Who did John go and resemble?   [States]

(28) Which board-game did John go and win?   [Achievements]

(29) Who did John go and drive back home safely?   [Accomplishments]

(30) Which board-game did John go and play for hours? [Activities]

The *sit* class are more restricted in what aspects they can combine with. They can combine with neither states nor achievements.

(31) *Who did John sit and resemble?   [States]

(32) *?Which board-game did John sit and win?   [Achievements]

(33) Who did John sit and drive back home safely?   [Accomplishments]

(34) Which board-game did John sit and play for hours? [Activities]

There does not seem to be a telic/atelic distinction. This is unsurprising since both accomplishments and achievements are telic, and both *go* and *sit* may combine with accomplishments.

(35) a.   John went and read a book in an hour
     b.   John went and read a book for an hour

(36) a.   John sat and read a book in an hour
     b.   John sat and read a book for an hour

ReCo constructions also have a durative aspectual reading. In fact, they may only combine with activities. Given that they can combine with neither achievements nor accomplishments, they are inherently atelic.

(37) *John resembled and resembled his father   [States]

(38) *John won and won the board-game   [Achievements]

(39) *John drove and drove Mary back home safely   [Accomplishments]

(40) John walked and walked for hours   [Activities]

It should be noted that ReCo constructions are not necessarily incompatible with telic predicates, merely that they always force an atelic or repetitive reading on them. This is especially clear with a verb like *drown* which has as its natural end point the death, by drowning, of the subject (41a).

(41) a.   John drowned [entails that…] John died
     b.   John drowned and drowned [*entails that…] John died

This is exemplified by the following example.

(42)   And he just <u>drowned and drowned</u> and I saw his head go under[10]

The only possible reading for (42) is that drowning is a durative event and that each 'drown' is actually a sub-stage of the larger drowning event. It is not even necessary that the subject eventually dies in this example, in contrast to normal usage of this verb. Thus for (42) it would be perfectly felicitous to continue the story in the following way.

(43)   ... but suddenly a lifeguard put an arm around him and lifted him to safety[11]

In the case of a predicate like *die*, a serial, iterative reading is more natural, especially in the following war-game, battlefield context where 'deaths' are quick, being determined by the result of a throw of dice. Note that given the nature of the game, death is punctual, not a gradual event. Thus, no internal stages of dying can be selected and contrasted by *and* to yield a durative reading. Only an iterative reading is available.[12]

(44)   Chaos Warriors <u>died, and died, and died</u>[13]

I have demonstrated that ReCo constructions exhibit more than a passing similarity to PCO constructions with *go* and *sit*. Assuming that these arguments are correct, ReCo constructions can shed light on PCO constructions. In particular, the aspectual possibilities of these constructions, when tabulated, indicate a gradual increase in restrictiveness with regard to which aspectual categories each can be combined with. This is potentially important because it allows us to characterize precisely the semantic contribution of each construction.

	STATES	ACHIEVE.	ACCOMPLISH.	ACTIVITIES
go	*	✓	✓	✓
sit	*	*	✓	✓
read & read	*	*	*	✓

5.   A proposal: What is ReCo?

The question then arises as to what exactly ReCo and PCO structures are. I propose that they are complex heads derived in the syntax itself i.e. not an item stored in the lexicon. There are at least three reasons why this must be the case. Firstly, the very productivity of the construction militates against it being stipulated in the lexicon. Secondly, ReCo/PCO constructions clearly have inflectional morphological marking. Since inflectional morphology is assumed not to occur within a terminal/word itself, the presence of such marking would militate against a lexical-compounding analysis. Finally, VV compounds seem to be a fairly systematic gap in the Germanic languages.[14] I would not want to propose that VERB+AND+VERB constructions are exempt.

The proposed structure looks like this.[15]

(45)

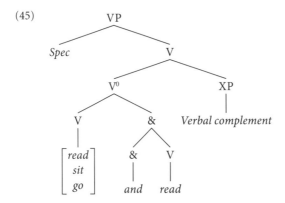

This structure can immediately account for a number of characteristics of ReCo constructions. Firstly, the extraction facts described in Sections 2 and 4 follow from the fact that in structure (45) traces of movement in the verbal complement are not contained by the coordination structure. Consequently, extraction of elements such as verbal arguments etc neither entails the crossing of a minimality barrier nor a violation of the CSC.

The fact that there is no subject in the second conjunct is a by-product of the fact that there is simply no subject position available within the complex predicate. The subject position (Spec VP) is projected by the complex predicate itself. Seen from this perspective, the problems associated with licensing an empty subject category (Section 3) simply evaporate: there is no PRO or similar empty category in the second conjunct because there is no clausal complementation relation between the two conjuncts.

Similarly, the differences in the behaviour between modals and the PCO constructions follow from this analysis (Section 3). Since both verbs are merged as part of a complex predicate within the VP, both of them pattern with lexical verbs vis a vis subject-auxiliary inversion and V-T raising. The fact that *both* modification is not tolerated with ReCo constructions is a result of the fact that *both* contrasts two entire events. In garden-variety coordination contexts where two IPs are coordinated, *both* modification can thus take place. However, in structure (45), there is only a single event: the entire complex predicate is located within the VP under a single verbal label.[16]

In summary, structure (45) accounts for a number of the ReCo/PCO facts previously discussed, and which are difficult to handle in other analyses.

Having proposed that ReCo/PCO constructions are complex-predicate heads, I will now discuss the internal structure of these heads. When considering an example like (22), there is only a single reading event extending over some time. Note that there is no implication that the reading event eventually culminated in the finishing of the book, in other words, it is imperfective. Whatever explanation we choose must account for the fact that there is only a single reading event and not two.

Pre-theoretically, it appears that ReCo/PCO *and* takes a single event, and divides it into two sub-stages. The function of *and* is that it marks a transition between the two sub-stages. Thus ReCo/PCo *and* is a two-place 'sameness' operator, each argument of which must be a sub-part of a larger event.[17] Informally, by 'sameness operator' I mean to imply that the 'meaning' of *and* is basically "given X, give me more of the same kind of it". In this respect, I take ReCo/PCO *and* to be identical in its lexical specification to the garden-variety coordinator, *and*. Semantically, both garden-variety and PCO *and* take 'same' categories. Syntactically, the sole difference between them is that garden-variety *and* projects an entire XP of its own, ReCo/PCO *and* projects only a head label. Thus, *and* can be defined as in (46a) and schematically represented as in (46b).

(46) a. *and*{Stage I_ε, Stage J_ε}, where I and J are stages of an event ε and where *and* marks a transition between I and J.

   b. *John read   and   read   all day long*
       stage1$_i$ OP$_{i/j}$ stage2$_j$

In this representation, *and* is an operator which requires that *i/j* are both bound by suitable sub-stages of an event. The effect of this is that *and* serves to introduce an additional layer of structure within a verbal event. Inherent in this structure is the notion that the event is non-stative and durative; stative events cannot be subdivided or have their internal event-structure modified.

However, providing internal structure to a simple event provides the grammar with a problem: how should such a complex event be interpreted?

(47) a. John read a book
   b. John read and read a book

The principle of Full Interpretation means that there can be no superfluous symbols at LF. Thus, (47b) must necessarily crash at LF unless the additional structure (namely, the operator and the additional verb) can be semantically licensed. I propose that the complex-predicate be placed in the scope of an operator such as *and*. The resulting meaning assigned to the complex event is loosely-speaking durative and non-stative. This follows very simply from the analysis of *and* as a substage-binding operator since any event which allows its internal substages to be modified must necessarily be durative and non-stative. This operation is illustrated schematically below.

(48) a. $and_{i\&j} \rightarrow$ read read   [Before binding]
   b. $and_{i\&j} \rightarrow$ read$_i$ read$_j$ [After binding]

Failure to merge such an operator results in the derivation crashing at LF as a result of a violation of Full Interpretation. This predicts that sentences such as (49a–c), which lack the 'sameness' operator are necessarily ungrammatical.

(49)   a.   *John read read a book all day
       b.   *John sits reads a book all day
       c.   *John goes reads a book all day

In other words, the analysis I am proposing is fully minimalist in the sense that the entire computation is driven by the requirements of the semantics interface.

6.   Conclusion

I have argued that PCO cannot be analysed either as coordination of the garden variety, or as subordination (contra Wiklund (1996) and Lødrup (2002)). The resulting impasse is resolved by considering ReCo constructions, which are argued to have many properties in common with PCO constructions, including the sameness condition, extractability and aspectual readings. ReCo constructions are utilized to explore the internal structure of *go* and *sit* PCO constructions. I suggest that an analysis based on merging complex predicates is the simplest explanation consistent with the facts. This approach has the distinct advantage over biclausal analyses insofar as these approaches require *and* to be lexically specified as is regarded as some manner of infinitival marker or complementizer. In contrast, the complex-predicate analysis proposed here does not need multiple lexical entries for *and*. The lexical entries of *and* vis a vis Reco, PCo and garden-variety coordination can be unified under the assumption that the same lexical item, namely *and*, either projects an XP or an X^0. This leads to a simplification of the representation of the lexicon.

Notes

1. In Mainland Scandinavian the class of verbs which can be first conjuncts is larger, but nevertheless a closed class.

2. It has been suggested by Cormack & Breheney (1994) that the unergativity of PCO verbs licenses violations of the coordinate structure constraint. However, the ungrammaticality of the following unergative and unaccusative examples in comparison with the well-formedness of the *sit* and *go* examples suggest that the argument structure of the first verbal conjunct does not explain the entire story.

(i)   a.   *What has John talked/resigned and done now?   [Unergatives]
      b.   *What has John arrived/fallen and done now?   [Unaccusatives]

3. http://discuss.fogcreek.com/joelonsoftware/default.asp?cmd=show&ixPost=60168

4. http://www.bikeabout.org/journal/notes 104.htm

5. Following Munn (1993) and Haspelmath (2004), I assume that the 'sameness' constraint on coordinated categories does not necessarily refer to categorial but to semantic information.

6. PCO with *try* is not subject to this restriction, and appears to differ to PCO with *sit* and *go* in a number of respects (see also Pullum (1990)). For this reason I shall not deal with it in this paper.

7. However, I do not want this phenomenon to mask the deeper semantic similarities which garden-variety *and* and PCO *and* share. I will discuss this more fully in Section 5.2.

8. A further argument against an analysis analogous to infinitivals is that there is a truth conditional distinction between infinitival *go* and PCO *go* (Jaeggli & Hyams 1993).

(i) a.   John goes and eats [entails that…] John eats
     b.   *John goes to eat [*entails that…] John eats

9. www.whitehouse.gov/news/releases/2003/05/20030520-17.html

10. http://www.abc.net.au/austory/transcripts/s418748.htm

11. In the story on the web-site where this example originated, the subject died.

12. It is worth noting that insofar as *drown and drown* does not necessarily imply the death of the subject, the full semantics of *drown* do not seem to be available to the syntax. This is a parallel with the semantic bleaching evident in *sit* and *go* constructions.

13. www.eldaronline.com/fluff/fiction astandunited.shtml

14. There are arguably some examples in Afrikaans eg. *laat spaander* 'get going'.

15. The complex-predicate analysis also captures the argument by a number of researchers that PCo constructions form complex heads (Pollock 1994, Postma 1995).

16. In approaches such as that of Travis (2000), the complex predicate would be dominated by an Event Phrase which would serve to identify the entire complex predicate as being part of a single event.

17. Van Geenhoven (2004) proposes that continuous aspect marking (in general, but also of the ReCo type) is a temporal pluractional operator.

References

Carden, G. & D. Pesetsky (1977). 'Double-Verb Constructions, Markedness and a Fake Coordination'. *Papers From the Thirteenth Regional Meeting: Chicago Linguistic Society* pp. 82–92.

Cormack, A. & R. Breheney (1994). 'Projections for functional categories'. *UCL working papers in linguistics* 6, pp. 35–62.

Haspelmath, M. (2004). 'Coordination'. To appear in T. Shopen (ed.) *Language typology and syntactic description*. 2nd ed. Cambridge University Press, Cambridge.

Jaeggli, O. & N. Hyams (1993). 'On the independence and interdependence of syntactic and morphological properties: English aspectual *come* and *go*'. *Natural Language and Linguistic Theory* 11, pp. 313–346.

Lødrup, H. (2002). 'The syntactic structures of Norwegian pseudocoordinations'. *Studia Linguistica* 56, pp. 121–143.

Munn, A. B. (1993). *Topics in the Syntax and Semantics of Coordinate Structures*. Ph.D. thesis, University of Maryland.

Pollock, J. (1994). 'Checking theory and bare verbs'. In Cinque, G. (ed.), *Paths towards Universal Grammar: Studies in honour of Richard S. Kayne*, Georgetown University Press, Washington D.C., pp. 293–310.

Postma, G. (1995). 'Zero semantics: The syntactic encoding of quantificational meaning'. In M. Den Dikken and K. Hengeveld (eds.), *Linguistics in the Netherlands*, John Benjamins, Amsterdam, vol. 12, pp. 175–190.

Pullum, J. (1990). 'Constraints on intransitive quasi-serial verb constructions in modern colloquial English'. In B. Joseph and A. Zwicky (eds.), *When Verbs Collide: Papers from the 1990 Ohio State Mini-Conference on Serial Verbs*, no. 39 in Ohio State University Working Papers in Linguistics, Ohio State University, Columbus, Ohio, pp. 218–239.

Ross, J. (1967). *Constraints on Variables in Syntax*. Ph.D. thesis, Massachusetts Institute of Technology.

Travis, L. (2000). 'Event structure in syntax'. In C. Tenny and J. Pustejovsky (eds.), *Events as Grammatical Objects*, CSLI Publications, Stanford, CA, pp. 145–185.

Van Geenhoven, V. (2004) 'Aspect, pluractionality and adverbial quantification'. Tp appear in A. Van Hout, H. De Swart, and H. Verkuyl (eds.), *Perspectives on Aspect*. Kluwer Academic Publishers, Netherlands.

Wiklund, A.-L. (1996). Pseudocoordination is subordination. *Working papers in Scandinavian syntax* 58, pp. 29–54.

Head-internal relative clauses in Dutch?

Mark de Vries
University of Groningen

1. Introduction

In Dutch, relative clauses are postnominal (as in English). Therefore, the existence of the two constructions illustrated in (1a/b) is remarkable:

(1) a. Welke *onverlaat* zoiets doet, krijgt straf.
which miscreant such.a.thing does gets punishment
'Whichever miscreant does such a thing will be punished.'

b. "In de ban van de ring", welk *boek van Tolkien* zeer populair is,
"in the spell of the ring" which book by Tolkien very popular is
is verfilmd.
has.been filmed
'"The lord of the rings", which book by Tolkien is very popular, has been filmed.'

There seems to be an internal head NP *onverlaat* in (1a), where the subject looks like a free relative. In (1b), which contains an appositive (= non-restrictive) relative, there is an additional internal head NP *boek van Tolkien* next to the antecedent "*In de ban van de ring*". Henceforth, I will refer to these constructions as the Head-Internal Free Relative (HIFR) and the Head-Internal Appositive Relative (HIAR), respectively. We will see that they are closely related.

As far as I know, head-internal relatives in Dutch have not been discussed before in the literature. Therefore, let us examine their properties here. I will show that the HIFR and HIAR neatly fit into the Dutch system of relativization. They cannot be directly related to the more exotic circumnominal and correlative head-internal constructions, which can be found in e.g. Quechua resp. Hindi.

Linguistics in the Netherlands 2004 21 (2004), 193–204.
ISSN 0929–7332 / E-ISSN 1569–9919 © Algemene Vereniging voor Taalwetenschap

2. Free relatives with an internal head

2.1 Introductory examples

Let me start by presenting some examples of HIFRs, which — as any relative clause — can be used at every argument position; see e.g. (2):

(2) a. Welke student ook maar spiekt bij het tentamen,   zal gestraft   worden.
         which student NPI   copies at the examination will punished be
         'Whichever student copies at the examination, will be punished.'
     b. Ik lees welk   boek me ook maar onder ogen komt.
         I read which book me NPI   under eyes comes
         'I read whichever book I get a look at.'
     c. Ik ga naar welk   museum ze me ook maar aanraadt.
         I go to   which museum she me NPI   recommends
         'I go to whichever museum she recommends (to me).'
     d. Hij eet taart bij welke gelegenheid zich ook maar voordoet.
         he eats cake at which occasion   SE   NPI   occurs
         'He eats cake at whichever occasion occurs.'

Observe that the internal role of the head NP is independent of the external role. For instance, in (2d) *welke gelegenheid* is a subject in the subordinate clause, but the whole relative construction is an adverbial prepositional object in the matrix.

There are four ways to build a restrictive relative construction, namely as a normal headed restrictive, as a semi-free relative, as a free relative, and as a head-internal free relative; this is illustrated in (3):

(3) a. de man die zoiets   doet   [RRC]
         the man who such.a.thing does
     b. hij/degene die zoiets   doet   [semi-FR]
         he/the one who such.a.thing does
     c. wie zoiets   doet   [FR]
         who such.a.thing does
     d. welke vent zoiets   doet   [HIFR]
         which fellow such.a.thing does

As is well-known, the first two types pattern alike, but free relatives behave differently in some respects. Below we will see that the HIFR is a special instance of a free relative. Notice that a semi-HIFR cannot be construed: *degene welke vent...* '*the-one which fellow...'. In order to explain it, we must know more about the syntax of free relatives and internal heads. First, however, it is useful to examine the meaning of (free) relatives.

2.2 Universal interpretation

An important difference between headed and free relatives lies in the semantics of the constructions. A free relative always has a definite or universal interpretation, but a headed relative can also be indefinite (see e.g. Jacobson 1995). Therefore, *wie* in *wie zoiets doet* (3c) refers to a specific person or a person in general, but not to an unidentified individual. In other words, the relative pronoun can be related to the determiners *the* and *all*, but not *a*. This can be tested in a presentative context, which normally requires an indefinite subject; see (4):

(4) a.   Er   verscheen een/*de/*elke man die   een zwarte cape droeg
          there appeared a/*the/*every man who a   black   cape wore
          in de deuropening.   [RRC]
          in the doorway
     b.   *Er verscheen wie een zwarte cape droeg in de deuropening.
          int. 'There appeared who a black cape wore in the doorway.'   [FR]

The explanation for the restricted interpretation of free relatives is that a semantic 'maximalization operation' takes place in some *wh*-constructions, including FRs; see Rullman (1995) and Grosu & Landman (1998). In informal terms, the idea is as follows. First note that a free relative is a nominalized clause, and functions as a full argument; therefore it is commonly analysed as [D CP], where D is usually abstract. The meaning of a restrictive relative is constructed by set intersection of the properties of the head and the predication. In a free relative the maximum of the individuals in this set is selected. The external determiner quantifies over this set maximum. If originally the set contains only one member, we obtain a definite interpretation. A larger set gives a universal reading, namely the combined members. An indefinite reading is impossible, since the individual members of the set are not accessible anymore after maximalization.

Grosu & Landman (1998:148) state the following generalization: "if the head [of a relative construction] is semantically CP-internal, no semantically independent CP-external material is allowed". The head of a free relative is semantically internal, since the antecedent is implied in the relative pronoun. As there is an external determiner, maximalization must take place. Namely, in constructions where there is maximalization, the one-to-one correspondence between the external determiner and the set-maximum mentioned ensures that the external material is not independent. On the other hand, if there is a semantically external head NP, as in normal headed restrictive or appositive relatives, there is no need for maximalization, according to Grosu & Landman's generalization.[1]

Let us consider how head-internal free relatives are interpreted. It turns out that their semantics is even more restricted than that of free relatives. The examples in (5) and (6) show that only a universal interpretation is available.[2]

(5) a. Welke bakker zo'n   grote winkel heeft, zal vast wel witbrood
         which bakery such-a big   store   has   will probably white-bread
         verkopen.   [univ]
         sell
         'Whichever bakery has such a big store probably sells white bread.'
     b. *Welke bakker hier op de hoek zit, zal vast wel witbrood verkopen.   [def]
         int. 'Which bakery is here at the corner, probably sells white bread.'

(6) a. Je   behoort geld   te geven aan welke bedelaar je   ook maar ziet. [univ]
         you ought   money to give to   which beggar you NPI   see
         'You ought to give money to whichever beggar you see.'
     b. *Ik gaf twee euro aan welke bedelaar ik vandaag bij de supermarkt zag. [def]
         int. 'I gave two euros to which beggar I saw today at the supermarket.'

I think the explanation is straightforward. Because of the internal head, maximalization is necessary. Furthermore, *welke* is a dependent relative pronoun,
and the phrase *welke NP* 'which NP' presupposes a group of NPs. As a consequence, the set-maximum will be established on the basis of more than one
member; hence the possibility of a definite reading disappears.

2.3 Pied piping

A further difference between headed and free relatives is related to pied piping.
In De Vries (2004) it was concluded that pied piping is generally impossible in
free relatives, contrary to the situation in headed relatives; cf. Bresnan &
Grimshaw (1978) and Smits (1991).[3] Some examples are given in (7/8):

(7) a. De man *met wie*   ik gesproken had, vertrok.   [RRC]
         the man with whom I spoken   had left
         'The man with whom I had spoken left.'
     b. **Met wie* ik gesproken had, vertrok.   [FR]
         int. 'With whom I had spoken, left.'

(8) a. Anna groette de man *met wiens broer*   ze gesproken had.   [RRC]
         Anna greeted the man with whose brother she spoken   had
         'Anna greeted the man with whose brother she had spoken.'
     b. *Anna groette *met wiens broer* ze gesproken had.   [FR]
         int. 'Anna greeted with whose brother she had spoken.'

A universal reading cannot save (7b/8b). (This reading can be facilitated by
adding *ook maar*.) Therefore it comes as no surprise that pied piping in HIFRs
is blocked as well; see (9/10):[4]

(9) a. Elke vijand *met wie*   je de degens kruist, zal proberen je te
         every enemy with whom you the swords cross   will try   you to
         vermoorden.   [RRC]
         kill
         'Every enemy with whom you cross the sword will try to kill you.'

      b.   *Met welke vijand* je ook maar de degens kruist, zal proberen je te
           vermoorden.   [HIFR]
           int. 'With whichever enemy you cross the sword, will try to kill you.'

(10)   a.   Anna groette elke   man *met wiens broer*   ze ooit gesproken had. [RRC]
           Anna greeted every man with whose brother she ever spoken   has
           'Anna used to greet every man with whose brother she had ever spoken.'
      b.   *Anna groette *met welke mans broer* ze ooit ook maar gesproken
           had.   [HIFR]
           int. 'Anna used to greet with whichever man's brother she had ever spoken.'

This leaves us with the following questions:

(11)   a.   *Why is pied piping impossible in free relatives, including HIFRs?*
      b.   *Why does the ban on pied piping not affect the internal head in HIFRs?*

Consider the syntactic structure of the left periphery of a free relative. As stated before, a free relative is a nominalized clause. This is represented by the structure $[_{DP}$ D CP]. Within the embedded clause a relative pronoun is fronted (*wh*-moved). According to Bianchi (1999), a relative pronoun is a special type of determiner, say D_{rel}. As any determiner, it is the head of a complete nominal group: $[_{DP\text{-}rel} D_{rel}$ NP]. Thus we have (12):

(12) $[_{DP}$ D $[_{CP} [_{DP\text{-}rel} D_{rel} [_{NP} N]]_i \ldots t_{i\ldots}]]$

In a free relative, the antecedent is included in the relative pronoun. For example, the free relative pronoun *wie* 'who' has a triple function; it stands for *the/any person who*. This can be established by combining the elements D, D_{rel} and N; see also De Vries (2002a, 2004). In (13), the syntactic relation between them (head movement) is indicated by arrows.

(13) $[_{DP}$ D $[_{CP} [_{DP\text{-}rel} D_{rel} [_{NP} N]]_i \ldots t_{i\ldots}]]$.
         ↑_____↓↑____|

From the structure in (12/13) it is immediately clear what the position of an internal head in a HIFR is; see (14):

(14) $[_{DP}$ D $[_{CP} [_{DP\text{-}rel}$ *welke* $[_{NP}$ *onverlaat*]]$_i \ldots t_{i\ldots}]] \ldots$
         ↑_____|

Here, too, D_{rel} *welke* must be related to the external D. This explains why the external DP takes over the φ-features (person, number, gender) of the internal DP. Furthermore, it explains why the external D cannot be spelled out independently from D_{rel}; see (15):

(15)   *{De(gene), deze, hij, elke} welke idioot zoiets hardop zegt, is gek!
       int. '{The (one), this, he, every} which(ever) idiot says such a thing aloud, is crazy.'

Finally, the ban on pied piping in free relatives can be explained. If there is pied piping, the fronted DP_{rel} would be embedded in a larger constituent XP (usually a PP). But then the relation between D and D_{rel} would have to cross an intervening head, which is a violation of a generally endorsed locality constraint; see (16).

(16) $*[_{DP} D [_{CP} [_{XP} X [_{DP\text{-}rel} D_{rel} NP]]_i \ldots t_{i\ldots}]]$

Notice that the internal head NP does not intervene between D and D_{rel}. This answers the question in (11b): as the head NP is inside DP_{rel}, it is automatically pied piped without causing any problem for external relations.

2.4 A brief comparison with circumnominal relatives and correlatives

From a cross-linguistic perspective we know that the position of a relative head NP varies with respect to the relative clause. For example, Dutch and English are head-initial, but Japanese and Turkish are head-final. Interestingly, there is also a head-internal (i.e. circumnominal) strategy $[_{RC\ldots}$ head…], e.g. in Quechua, Tibetan and Lakota. Circumnominal relatives are nominalized, and they occur at DP-positions. An example from Dagbani (a Gur language spoken in Ghana) is given in (17), taken from Lehmann (1984: 117).[5]

> (17)   A   mi   [o nə ti   saan-so   lǝgri] la
>   you know he SR give stranger-SPEC/LEV money PTL
>   'You know the stranger whom he gave the money.'

Although (17) contains an internal head, it is clearly different from the Dutch HIFR: there is no relative pronoun and the head NP is not fronted within the relative clause; furthermore, the interpretation in this example is definite, whereas a HIFR is always universal.

   Another candidate for comparison is the so-called correlative construction used in e.g. Hindi, Tamil and Kala Lagaw Ya (Mabuiag). A Hindi example is (18), taken from Mahajan (2000).[6]

> (18)   [jo a:dmi: si:ta:-ko pasand hɛ]   mujhe vo accʰa: nahĩ: lagta:
>   REL man   Sita-DAT love   be-PRES I=DAT DEM nice   not   seem-IMP
>   lit. 'Which man Sita loves, to me he seems not nice.'
>   'I don't like the man who Sita loves.'

In this case there is a relative pronoun that is fronted together with the internal head.[7] However, there are substantial differences with the HIFR construction, again. The interpretation of a correlative can be definite, as in (18). Furthermore, Keenan (1985: 164) stresses that a correlative clause is not nominalized, as there is never an external determiner, Case ending or affixed adposition. It does not occur in argument positions, but sentence-initially. The open spot in the matrix is occupied by a demonstrative or personal pronoun.

   An overview of some important properties of free relatives, HIFRs, correlative and circumnominal relatives is given in Table 1.

Table 1. Properties of free and head-internal relative constructions

	FR	HIFR	correlative	circumnominal
meaning	univ/def	universal	univ/def	univ/def/(indef)
subordinate clause nominalized	yes	yes	no	yes
position relative clause	DP-position	DP-position	sentence-initial	DP-position
resumptive pronoun in matrix	no	no	yes	no
relative pronoun	yes	yes	yes	no
preposing of head NP	yes	yes	yes	no
pied piping	no	no	yes?	d.n.a.

From the table it can be concluded that the HIFR in Dutch is a special type of a free relative, although it is superficially reminiscent of other head-internal constructions such as the correlative or circumnominal relative construction.

3. Appositive relatives with an additional internal head

3.1 Introductory examples

The second construction announced in the introduction is the HIAR. An example is given in (19).

(19) Ze zwaaide naar Joop, *welke stakkerd* zijn been had gebroken bij het skieën.
      she waved   at   Joop   which wretch   his leg   had broken   at the skiing
      'She waved at Joop, which wretch had broken his leg during skiing.'

The internal head NP is preceded by the real antecedent. One of the reasons that the HIAR sounds special is that anaphora by a full noun phrase is unusual; normally we use a pronoun. Therefore, the way of referring is to be compared to e.g. (20):

(20) *De inbreker* sloop   de donkere kamer binnen, maar *de oen*   was z'n
      the burglar sneaked the dark   room   into   but the blockhead had his
      zaklamp   vergeten.
      flashlight forgotten
      'The burglar sneaked into the dark room, but the blockhead had forgotten his flashlight.'

The sentence in (19) can be paraphrased similarly:

(21) Ze zwaaide naar *Joop. De stakkerd* had zijn been gebroken bij het skieën.
      'She waved at Joop. The wretch had broken his leg during skiing.'

In each case the second noun phrase (the epithet) represents a property of the first: the burglar is a blockhead, Joop is a wretch, etc.

Furthermore, a remarkable property of appositive relatives is that they can take antecedents of any category, contrary to restrictives. It turns out that this is the case for HIARs as well; see (22):

> (22) a. De aarde is bolvormig, *welk feit* reeds   lang bekend is.   [CP]
>   the earth is spherical   which fact already long known is
>   b. Ze vindt   Joop aardig, *welke eigenschap* ik hem bepaald   niet
>   she regards Joop nice   which property   I him certainly not
>   toe zou dichten.   [AP]
>   would ascribe
>   c. Joop zat in de tuin,   *op welke plek* hij graag vertoeft.   [PP]
>   Joop sat in the garden at which place he gladly stays

In short, next to the HIFR Dutch has the HIAR, which is a special variant of an appositive relative.

3.2 Differences with HIFRs and restrictive relatives

Although appositive relatives can have an additional internal head, (23) shows that it is completely impossible in restrictives:

> (23) a. *Ze zag een man *welke stakkerd* zijn been had gebroken.
>   int. 'She saw a man which wrech had broken his leg.'
>   b. *Ze las een boek *welke roman* door Reve was geschreven.
>   int. 'He read a book which novel was written by Reve.'

This will be explained in the next section.

There are also differences between the HIAR and the HIFR. Recall from Section 2.2 that HIFRs cannot have a definite interpretation. The HIAR in e.g. (19) above, however, is clearly definite. The reason is that there is no maximalization in appositive relative constructions, as there is a semantically and syntactically external head NP, i.e. the real antecedent (*Joop* in (19)). Secondly, Section 2.3 showed that there cannot be pied piping in HIFRs, but this restriction does not apply in HIARs; see (24):

> (24) a. "De avonden", *aan welk   boek van Reve* vaak gerefereerd wordt,
>   "the evenings" to   which book by Reve often referred   is
>   is   herdrukt.
>   is
>   has.been reprinted
>   b. De geoloog benadrukte dat de aarde bolvormig is, *over welk feit*
>   the geologist emphasized that the earth spherical is of   which fact
>   geen van de aanwezigen   recentelijk had nagedacht.
>   none of the persons.present recently   had thought

The reason is again the presence of an external antecedent. There is no implied antecedent, and therefore no syntactic relation $D_{rel} \rightarrow D$, as defined in Section 2.3. As a consequence, a pied piped preposition is harmless.

The question that remains to be answered is why an internal head is possible in appositive relatives as well as free relatives, but not in normal (headed) restrictive relatives. This is the subject of the next section.

3.3 Head raising and specifying coordination

According to the 'raising analysis' (developed by Vergnaud 1974, Kayne 1994, Bianchi 1999, De Vries 2002a), the structure of a restrictive relative is (25):

(25) $[D \ [_{CP} \ [_{DP\text{-rel}} \ NP \ D_{rel} \ t_{np}]_i \ ... \ t_{i...}]]$

The head NP is generated within the relative clause and consequently 'raised'. A relative pronoun is a determiner generated in combination with the head NP: a 'relative determiner' D_{rel}. Notice that the external determiner D takes scope over the restrictive relative clause. For instance, *all cats who like meat* must have the bracketing [all [cats who like meat]], not [[all cats] who like meat].[8] The latter possibility is correct for appositive relatives, though.

The raising analysis is supported by three types of evidence: theoretical (antisymmetry, no right-adjunction), cross-linguistic (it generalizes over different types of relative constructions, including circumnominal relatives and degree relatives), and empirical (connectivity effects between the head NP and the gap). An example of the last type is given in (26), where the local anaphor *zichzelf* is embedded in the head NP; it is bound by the subject of the relative clause *Joop*.

(26)   De [verhalen over   zichzelf$_k$]$_i$ die$_i$ Joop$_k$ gisteren   hoorde, waren
       the stories   about SE-SELF   that Joop yesterday heard   were
       pure leugens.   [RRC]
       mere lies
       'The stories that Joop heard about himself yesterday were mere lies.'

Since the relative pronoun *die* has another referent, it cannot replace *zichzelf* for the binding relation. Therefore, the head NP itself must be reconstructed into the position of the gap, where it is c-commanded by *Joop*.

Let us return to the issue of internal headedness. The structure in (25) straightforwardly explains why there cannot be an additional internal head in normal restrictive relatives: there is simply no room for it, because the only relevant NP position is already occupied by the actual antecedent.

In free relatives the head NP is empty. Therefore, it can in principle be filled, which gives the HIFR, as explained in Section 2 above. In appositive relatives the situation is different again. Importantly, the raising analysis is not supported for appositives: empirically, there are no attested connectivity effects (cf. Bianchi 1999); cross-linguistically, it seems that there are no true internally headed appositive relatives (cf. Lehmann 1984, Grosu & Landmann 1998). Thus, the antecedent of an appositive relative is external to it. Since the position of the gap in the relative clause represents a full argument (DP) position, there is room for an additional internal head, in principle; this gives the HIAR.

Now we predict the following with respect to connectivity effects. In restrictive relatives, reconstruction of the head NP is possible because of 'raising', as shown in (26) above. In normal appositive relatives, reconstruction is impossible because there is no raising of the overt antecedent. In a HIAR, however, the additional internal head can be reconstructed because it is pied piped with the *wh*-moved relative pronoun. This is shown by means of anaphor binding in (27):

(27) a. $^{?*}$Deze verhalen over zichzelf$_i$, die Joop$_i$ gisteren toevallig had gehoord, waren pure leugens.   [ARC]
          int. 'These stories about himself, which Joop happened to hear yesterday, were mere lies.'
      b. "De ochtenden", *welke roman over zichzelf*$_i$ Joop$_i$ aan het schrijven is, kan men niet als bijster origineel beschouwen.   [HIAR]
          '"The mornings", which novel about himself Joop is writing, can be regarded as none too original.'

In (27b) *zichzelf* is bound by the subordinate clause subject *Joop*.

In previous work (e.g. De Vries 2002a) I have argued that an appositive relative clause is in fact a complex apposition, coordinated to its antecedent. If this is correct, the HIAR has the structure in (28):

(28) [$_{CoP}$ [$_{DP}$ antecedent] &: [$_{DP}$ D [$_{CP}$ [D$_{rel}$ NP]$_{wh}$ … t$_{wh…}$]]]]

Here the head &: of the coordination phrase CoP symbolizes 'specifying coordination', a connection (often asyndetic) meaning "namely/or/that is to say"; cf. Koster's (2000) 'colon phrase'. For instance, DP$_{ant}$ could be "*De avonden*", D$_{rel}$ the relative pronoun *welk* and NP the additional internal head *boek van Reve*. (D is abstract.)

The reader will have noticed that the second conjunct in (28) equals the structure we assumed for the HIFR in Section 2.3. This is an important result. In general, an appositive relative is a (semi-)free relative in apposition to its antecedent. In particular, the HIAR is a HIFR in apposition to its antecedent. The differences (e.g. with respect to definiteness and pied piping) follow from the different context, as explained in Section 3.2.

4. Conclusion

Dutch has two related types of head-internal relative clauses: the head-internal free relative (HIFR) and the appositive relative construction with an additional internal head (HIAR). In both types the internal head NP is accompanied by the relative determiner *welk(e)*; together they are fronted (*wh*-moved) within the relative clause. I have shown that the HIAR can be seen as a HIFR in apposition to its antecedent; the differences follow from the different context. The HIFR and HIAR are not directly related to 'exotic' head-internal types of relatives, but they fit neatly within the Dutch system of relativization.

The raising analysis of relative clauses explains why restrictives cannot have an additional internal head NP: there is no NP position available. The appositive construction is arguably different from the restrictive in that the antecedent is externally generated; hence the argument position in the relative clause can be occupied in principle; this gives the HIAR. The HIAR is unusual because the internal antecedent serves as an epithet. In free relatives, there is also an open NP position that can be filled; this gives the HIFR. A special property of the HIFR is that its interpretation is always universal. I have related this to a semantic maximalization procedure. In other respects HIFRs behave like normal free relatives. I have shown that FRs and HIFRs do not allow for pied piping, contrary to headed restrictive and appositive relatives, including the HIAR.

Notes

1. More interesting cases addressed by Grosu & Landman are amount relatives and irrealis free relatives.

2. There is a subtle difference between a universal reading and a free choice reading (see Giannakidou 2003), which I will ignore for reasons of space. It seems that the presence of the free choice item *wh…ook maar* is preferred in HIFRs in an object position, whereas the universal reading for HIFRs in the subject position is somewhat easier to get. None of this is crucial for the argumentation here.

3. See De Vries (to appear, b) for a discussion of pied piping in headed relatives.

4. In left-dislocation constructions the situation is more complicated. This is discussed in De Vries (to appear, a).

5. Here, SR is subordinator, SPEC specific, LEV living, PTL particle.

6. REL is relative pronoun, DAT is dative, PRES is present tense, DEM is demonstrative pronoun, IMP is imperfect tense.

7. This is the most frequent pattern. See Srivastav (1991) and Mahajan (2000) for a more complete overview of the possibilities.

8. Notice that D+N do not form a constituent in restrictive relatives. (This is no different in a right-adjunction analysis.) Therefore the traditional term 'antecedent' is odd; see De Vries (2002b).

References

Bianchi, V. (1999) *Consequences of Antisymmetry: Headed Relative Clauses.* Mouton de Gruyter, Berlin.

Bresnan, J. & J. Grimshaw (1978) 'The Syntax of Free Relatives in English'. *Linguistic Inquiry* 9, 331–391.

Chomsky, N. (1977) 'On *Wh*-Movement'. In P. Culicover et al. (eds) *Formal Syntax.* Academic Press, New York.

Giannakidou, A. (2001) 'The Meaning of Free Choice.' *Linguistics and Philosophy* 24, 659–735.

Grosu, A. & Landman, F. (1998) 'Strange Relatives of the Third Kind'. *Natural Language Semantics* 6: 125–170.

Jacobson, P. (1995) 'On the quantificational force in English Free Relatives'. In E. Bach et al. (eds) *Quantification in Natural Languages.* Kluwer, Dordrecht, pp. 451–486.

Kayne, R. (1994) *The Antisymmetry of Syntax.* MIT Press, Cambridge, Mass.

Keenan, E. (1985) 'Relative Clauses'. In T. Shopen (ed.) *Language Typology and Syntactic Description. Volume II. Complex Constructions.* Cambridge University Press, Cambridge, pp. 141–170.

Koster, J. (2000) 'Extraposition as parallel construal.' Ms, University of Groningen.

Lehmann, C. (1984) *Der Relativsatz.* Gunter Narr, Tübingen.

Mahajan, A. (2000) 'Relative Asymmetries and Hindi Correlatives'. In A. Alexiadou et al. (eds) *The Syntax of Relative Clauses.* John Benjamins, Amsterdam, pp. 201–229.

Rullmann, H. (1995) *Maximality in the Semantics of Wh-Constructions.* PhD Dissertation, University of Massachusetts, Amherst.

Smits, R. (1991) 'On the division of labour between the grammar and the parser: Some evidence from matching phenomena.' In W. Abraham et al. (eds) *Issues in Germanic Syntax.* Mouton de Gruyter, Berlin, pp. 119–134.

Srivastav, V. (1991) 'The Syntax and Semantics of Correlatives'. *Natural Language and Linguistic Theory* 9, 637–686.

Vergnaud, J.-R. (1974) *French Relative Clauses.* PhD Dissertation, MIT.

Vries, M. de (2002a) *The Syntax of Relativization.* PhD Dissertation, University of Amsterdam. Published by LOT, Utrecht.

Vries, M. de (2002b) 'De constituent die niet bestaat. Over het antecedent van betrekkelijke bijzinnen'. In *In verband met Jan Luif.* Farewell CD-ROM in honour of Jan Luif, University of Amsterdam.

Vries, M. de (2004) 'Congruentie-effecten in vrije en uitbreidende relatieve zinnen'. *Nederlandse Taalkunde* 9, 29–47.

Vries, M. de (to appear, a) 'Hoofd-interne relatiefzinnen in het Nederlands. Over vrije relatieven, pied piping en links-dislokatie'. *Nederlandse Taalkunde.*

Vries, M. de (to appear, b) 'Possessive Relatives and (Heavy) Pied Piping'. *Journal of Comparative Germanic Linguistics.*

Cross-linguistic confusion of vowels produced and perceived by Chinese, Dutch and American speakers of English

Hongyan Wang and Vincent J. van Heuven
Jilin University / University of Leiden

1. Introduction

Foreign accent consists in a deviation from the generally accepted pronunciation norm of a language that is reminiscent of another language, i.e., the foreign speaker's native language. It is caused by established structures of language representation that have been shaped by the requirements of the native language (L1) that are confronted with speech data from the second language (L2). As a source of variability in speech, foreign accent can be detrimental to speech perception and may result in partial or complete misidentification when listeners are unable to recognize phonetic segments, words, or larger units.

Our research focusses on English as the target language and Dutch and Chinese as the source languages. We compare the intelligibility of Chinese-accented English, Dutch-accented English and native American English in an attempt to clarify how well these people understand each other and themselves when they are speaking English with their respective accents. As a part of a larger project, the present paper targets the intelligibility of English vowels. It may provide answers to questions such as: how well are English vowels identified by native American, Chinese and Dutch listeners? What is their confusion structure? Can we relate the confusions to specific interference patterns that reflect structural properties of the mother tongue of the non-native speaker and/or listener?

We hypothesize that foreign-accented English must be more difficult for English listeners as the source language deviates more from English, but native listeners still have strategies which non-native listeners lack for coping with all sorts of non-optimal speech, including foreign accents. Generally, then, native

Linguistics in the Netherlands 2004 21 (2004), 205–216.
ISSN 0929–7332 / E-ISSN 1569–9919 © Algemene Vereniging voor Taalwetenschap

English listeners will be at an advantage over foreigners when listening to non-native English. There may just be one exception to this rule: non-native listeners may understand their own accented English better than native English listeners do. Since the foreign listeners are acquainted with the interfering native language, they may be sensitive to cues in the source language that native English listeners fail to pick up (see Bent & Bradlow 2003, Wang & van Heuven 2003).

2. Method

For the present pilot experiment we recorded one male and one female speaker for each of three nationalities: Chinese, Dutch and American. All six speakers studied in the Netherlands at the time the recordings were made. Dutch and Chinese speakers had not studied English after secondary school. Speakers did not have, or had in the past, regular contact with English-speaking friends or relatives, nor had they ever lived in an English-speaking country. For a full description of the methods used in the pilot experiment see Wang & van Heuven (2003). For the present article we will just recapitulate the materials and proce-dures employed to assess the production and perception of the vowels.

A list of words containing 19 full vowels and diphthongs (so excluding schwa) in identical /hVd/ contexts was recorded: *heed, hid, hayed, head, had, who'd, hood, hoed, hawed, hod, hard, hud, heard, hide, hoyed, how'd, here'd, hoored, haired*. The /h_d/ consonant frame is fully productive in English, allowing al the vowels of English to appear in a word or short phrase.

Speakers were recorded on digital audio tape (DAT) in a sound-insulated recording booth through a Sennheiser MKH-416 microphone. Materials were downsampled (16 KHz, 16 bits), stored on computer disk, and then used to construct a listening experiment. The listening test contained the 19 /hVd/ items for all six speakers in random order across speakers, preceded by six practice items, yielding a total of 120 items.

Listeners were drafted from the same pool from which the speakers had been drawn. Twelve were Chinese, twelve Dutch, and twelve American. Across nationalities, subjects were roughly evenly divided over the sexes. Stimuli were presented over headphones. The listeners read standardized written instruc-tions, and listened to the practice items in order to get familiar with their task, the layout of the answer sheets, and with the time constraints of the stimulus presentation.

3.   Overall results

The overall results for vowel intelligibility are presented in Figure 1, broken down by nationality of the listeners and broken down further by nationality of the speakers.

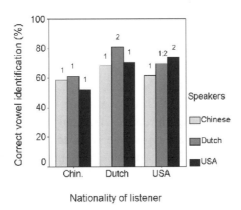

Figure 1. Percent correctly identified vowels broken down by listener group and by nationality of speaker.

Across speaker groups, the Chinese listeners have the lowest vowel identification scores (50–60% correct). Dutch listeners perform best (65–80% correct), and the American listeners are intermediate (60–70% correct). Across listener groups, Dutch speakers were most intelligible, closely followed by American speakers, while Chinese speakers were poorest.[1] Crucially, the results also show that American listeners identified vowels produced by American speakers better than Chinese and Dutch listeners. Similarly, Dutch listeners identified Dutch-accented vowels better than Chinese and American listeners. Chinese listeners, however, identified Dutch-accented English vowels better than Chinese-accented or native American tokens. This small advantage of Dutch-accented English for Chinese listeners may have been caused by the circumstance that our Chinese listeners had lived in the Netherlands for some six months, and therefore had had more exposure to Dutch-accented English than to L1 American English.[2]

For the purpose of the present paper we are not so much concerned with differences in overall intelligibility. Rather we will examine the extent to which errors in the production and perception of English vowels by the non-native speakers and listeners can be traced to properties of the L2 languages of these individuals.

4. Confusion structure

The experimental literature on foreign-language interference typically addresses one specific contrast at a time. For instance, there is a vast literature on the acquisition of the English /r~l/ contrast by speakers of Asian backgrounds (where the contrast is no part of the phonology). In the area of vowels much effort has been made to study the details of the acquision of such 'new' contrasts as English /e~æ/ by Germans, or to give just one final example of the English /iː~ɪ/ contrast by hispanic learners (Flege, 1995). However, experimental studies targeting the confusion structure in an entire vowel inventory in a cross-linguistic setting are far and few between.

Before we present and analyse the confusion structure in Chinese, Dutch and American tokens of English vowels, let us consider the vowel inventories in the three languages in an attempt to derive specific predictions as to where confusions may arize in Chinese and Dutch-accented varieties of English.

English vowel inventory. General American English (GA, as exemplified in the American English pronouncing dictionary by Kenyon & Knott 1944), has four degrees of vowel height (high, high-mid, low-mid and low) and three degrees of backness (front, central, back). Also, GA has a series of tense vowels with peripheral locations and a more centralized series of lax vowels. The phonetic relationship between the tense and lax vowels is difficult to capture within the 4×3 height-backness grid. In Figure 2 we have therefore superimposed (more or less) concentric rings on the grid, as proposed by Delattre (1971). In the outer ring we find the tense vowels; the more centralised lax vowels are located in the middle ring. The inner circle, finally, is taken up by /r/-coloured vowels.[3] GA has two diphthongs, /ai, au/, which start at an open position and glide towards a close position along the front and back side of the vowel space, respectively. The third diphthong is /ɔi/, which runs from back to front in the mid part of the space. The GA English set then contains six lax vowels, six tense vowels, five r-colored vowels, and three diphthongs (Table 1).[4]

The Dutch vowel system (Table 2) is in many respects similar to English. It also has tense and lax vowels, and distinguishes four degrees of height and three

Table 1. Structural representation of the General American vowel inventory.

	front		central		back	
	tense	lax	tense	lax	tense	lax
high	iː, ɪəʳ				uː, ʊəʳ	
hi-mid	eː, ɛəʳ	ɪ			oː, (ɔəʳ)	ʊ
lo-mid		ɛ	əːʳ	ʌ	ɔː, ɔi	ɔ
low	ai	æ			aː, au	

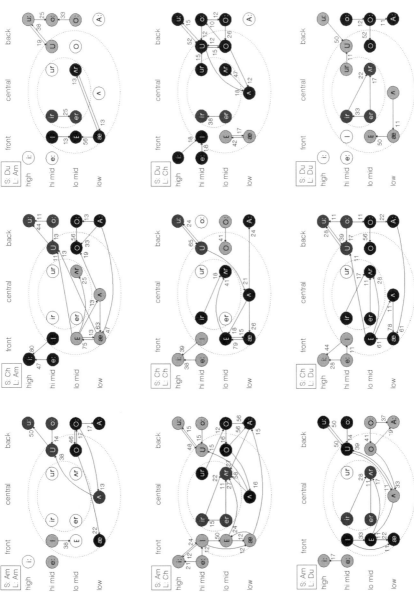

Figure 2. Vowel confusion graphs for nine combinations of speaker (S) and listener (L) language backgrounds.

Table 2. Structural representation of the Dutch vowel inventory.

| | front | | central | | back | |
	tense	lax	tense	lax	tense	lax
high	iː		yː		uː	
hi-mid	eː	ɪ	øː	ə	oː	
lo-mid	ɛi	ɛ	œy			ɔ
low			aː		ɑu	ɑ

degrees of backness. However, the central part of the vowel space is more densely filled as Dutch has (rounded) central high and hi-mid vowels. In the lax front vowels Dutch distinguishes two degrees of height for the /ɪ~ɛ/ contrast, where English has three: /ɪ~e~æ/. Dutch is underdifferentiated relative to English in the high back vowels, where English has the tense~lax opposition /uː~ʊ/ while Dutch only has /uː/. Confusions are expected in each of the vowels mentioned here. Dutch also has a number of vowels that are absent in the English system; such overdifferentiation is hardly ever a source of confusion.

Mandarin is basically a seven-vowel system. It has three high vowels /i, y, u/, three mid vowels /e, ɤ, o/ and one low vowel /a/.[5] It has front, (rounded) central and back vowels, but no length (i.e. no tense~lax) contrast. We predict problems when Chinese learners try to pronounce or recognize English vowels. Chinese has no /iː~ɪ/, no /uː~ʊ/, no /ɔ~ɔː~oː/, and no /e~æ/ contrasts. We expect, then, that Chinese L2 learners of English vowels will experience all the problems of Dutch learners of English, plus a number of additional difficulties caused by the absence of the tense~lax parameter in Chinese.

Table 3. Structural representation of the Mandarin vowel inventory.

	front	central	back
high	i	y	u
mid	e	ɤ	o
low		a	

Representation of vowel confusion patterns. Confusions in an identification task are customarily presented in a confusion matrix. Here the rows list the intended (stimulus) categories, while the columns represent the perceived categories. Correctly perceived stimuli appear in the cells along the main diagonal from top-left to bottom-right; errors are in the off-diagonal cells. As an illustration Table 4 presents the confusion matrix for the 19 English vowels as produced by Chinese speakers and identified by Dutch listeners.

Table 4 shows, first of all, that the three English diphthongs were never a

Table 4. Sample confusion matrix for 19 Am. English vowels produced by Chinese speakers and identified by Dutch listeners. Correct responses (in percent) are in bold.

		iː	ɪ	eː	ɛ	aː	æ	uː	ʊ	ɔː	ɔ	oː	ʌ	ɜː	ai	ɔi	au	ɪə	ʊə	ɛə
	iː	**94**	6																	
	ɪ	44	**50**										6							
	eː	28	11	**50**										6						6
	ɛ			44		6	6	11					6	28						
	aː				28	**61**					6		6							
	æ					61	**39**													
Stimulus vowels	uː							**61**	39											
	ʊ							28	**72**											
	ɔː				22				17	**56**						6				
	ɔ				6						**94**									
	oː								11	17	11	**50**				11				
	ʌ						78							22						
	ɜː													**100**						
	ai														**100**					
	ɔi														3	**97**				
	au																**100**			
	ɪə													17				**78**		6
	ʊə								6										**94**	
	ɛə													11					6	**83**

problem: /ai, ɔi, au/ are the least confused vowel types. In order to reduce the complexity of the analytic problem, we will not be concerned with the diphthongs in the remainder of this article.

The next step in the analysis would normally be the generation of a hierarchical cluster scheme (HCS), a tree structure that visualizes which vowels constitute highly confusable subsets. Alternatively, data reduction can be attempted by Multidimensional Scaling (MDS). We feel, however, that neither HCS not MDS do justice to what actually goes on in the data. Both techniques presuppose a symmetrical confusion matrix, that is, the likelihood of vowel *x* to be confused with vowel *y* must be equal to that of *y* being confused with *x*. As

Table 4 shows, this is hardly ever the case. For example, /æ/ is perceived as /ɛ/ in no less than 61% but the reverse confusion, /ɛ>æ/, occurs in less than 10%. Such perceptual asymmetries cannot be expressed in HCS or MDS; the /æ>ɛ/ and the /ɛ>æ/ confusions would average to a symmetrical 34%. Therefore, we have taken recourse to an more informal representation by means of confusion graphs.

In Figure 2, we present the complete confusion structure in the English vowels as produced by American, Chinese and Dutch speakers (S, arranged column-wise) and as perceived by listeners of the same language backgrounds (L, arranged in rows). Vowels are arranged according to the 4 (height) × 3 (backness) vowel quality grid, with a finer distinction between tense, lax and r-colored vowels by means of superposed 'concentric' rings as explained above. Confusion between any two vowels is indicated by an arrow from the intended to the non-intended vowel. The confusion percentage is indicated at the tip of the arrow. Arrows were drawn only for 'problematic' vowel pairs, defined as pairs that were confused in at least 10 percent of the responses. Subsets of vowels that have strong mutual confusions are identified in the graphs by gray shades.

Let us begin by looking at the confusion structure when American listeners identify vowels produced by fellow American speakers (S: Am, L: Am). The literature shows that even in such situations vowel identification is far from perfect, with scores ranging between 54 and 88 percent correct (Peterson & Barney 1952, Strange, Verbrugge, Shankweiler & Edman 1976, and references therein). Our results are no exception. Confusions typically occur among lax vowels: /ɪ>ɛ/ (lax mid cluster), /ʌ>ʊ/ and /ɔ>æ/. Also, there are two prominent tense~lax confusions: /ʊ>uː/ (high-back cluster), and /ɔː>ɔ/ (low-back cluster). Eight out of the total of 362 possible confusion pairs (19×18, including diphthongs) were problematic, i.e., confused in more than 10 percent of the cases. Accordingly, there are eight arrows in the confusion graph.

When the American vowels are identified by Chinese listeners (S: Am, L: Ch), there is much more confusion. All front vowels are confused in height in one or even two degrees, as well as along the tenseness dimension. There is confusion among all three high-back vowels, and in the low-back vowels. There is also considerable confusion among the central vowels. There are 23 problematic vowel pairs in all.

Dutch listeners to American-spoken vowels (S: Am, L: Du) have problems with the height distinction among the lax front vowels /ɪ~ɛ~æ/. They also predictably confuse /ʊ~uː/ (but symmetrically, unlike American listeners) and there is more confusion among the low-back vowels. There is also confusion among the central vowels, though not as much as with the Chinese listeners. There are 17 problem pairs.

When Americans listen to Chinese speakers (S: Ch, L: Am), there is confusion of height and tenseness in the high-front as well as in the high-back vowels. There is also heavy confusion in the lower front vowels /ɪ~ɛ~æ/ and in the low back vowels /ɔː~ɔ~ɑː/; there is even considerable confusion for /ɑː>æ/, so that the entire lower region proves massively confused. Fifteen vowel pairs are problematic.

When Chinese listeners respond to Chinese-accented vowels (S: Ch, L: Ch), the confusion pattern is very much the same as when listeners are American. It would seem, then, that the American listeners did not miss any subtle cues that Chinese speakers might have coded into their vowels. Sixteen vowel pairs are problematic.

Dutch listeners are less proficient in distinguishing among the Chinese-accented vowels (S: Ch, L: Du). By and large the same clusters of difficulty are found again: the high-front vowels /iː~ɪ~eː/, the high-back vowels /ʊ~uː/, the lower front vowels /ɛ~æ/, and the lower back vowels /ɔː~ɔ~ɑː/. The graph contains 19 problem pairs.

When Americans listen to Dutch speakers (S: Du, L: Am), confusion occurs in the lax front vowels /ɪ~ɛ~æ/ and the high-back pair /ʊ~uː/. These are the two English vowel contrasts that do not occur in Dutch. Unexpectedly, the three non-low tense back vowels are confused: /uː>oː/, /ɔː>oː/. There are eleven problematic vowel pairs.

Chinese listeners to Dutch-accented English (S: Du, L: Ch) have the same problems as the American listeners but add several more. Typically, there is widespread confusion among the central and back vowels (except /ɑː/).

When Dutch listeners are exposed to their own type of accent, a lot of the confusion disappears. Just three confusable clusters remain, predictably the /ɛ~æ/ and /ʊ~uː/ pairs, and the non-high back vowels /oː~ɔː~ɔ~ɑː/. The graph contains just ten problematic vowel pairs.

Table 5 summarizes the observations we made in the above on the incidence of problematic vowel pairs. The percentages are broken down for the nine combinations of speaker and listener language background.

Table 5 shows that, overall, native American listeners have fewer problems with the English vowels than L2 listeners. Dutch listeners are a good second, and Chinese listeners clearly have problems. More generally, the language background of the listener exerts a stronger influence on the number of

Table 5. Number of problematic vowel pairs (see text) broken down by nationality of speaker (down) and of listener (across)

Language background of speaker (down)	Language background of listener (across)			
	American	Chinese	Dutch	Total
American	8	23	17	48
Chinese	15	16	19	50
Dutch	11	21	10	42
Total number	34	60	46	

confused vowel pairs than the L1 of the speaker. The table also shows that listeners tend to identify those vowel tokens best that were produced by speakers of their own language background. In each column listeners who share the L1 of the speakers, have by far the smallest number of problematic vowel pairs. This, then, shows that knowledge of the phonemic codes of both target and source language is important in non-native communication.

5.   Conclusion and discussion

Our first hypothesis was that English will be more difficult to understand as the foreign speaker's native language is more unlike English. We predict, then, that Chinese-accented English vowels will be more difficult to identify for native English listeners than, for instance, Dutch-accented vowels. Conversely, English vowels produced by native English speakers should then be more intelligible to Dutch listeners than to Chinese listeners. Both predictions were clearly borne out by the experimental results. Although these results can indeed be seen as experimental support for our typological distance hypothesis, it should be pointed out that cultural and educational differences between the People's Republic of China (with little exposure to English) and the Netherlands (with an abundance of English) will also have contributed to the difference in intelligibility.

The confusion structure in the foreign-accented Englishes can partly be accounted for by a contrastive analysis of the vowel inventories of the target and source languages involved. For Dutch-accented English, we predicted problems with the non-high lax front vowels /ɪ~e~æ/ and with the /uː~ʊ/ contrast. The results show that these were, indeed, the most frequent confusion types, not only when L1 English listeners identified Dutch-accented vowels, but also when Dutch L2 listeners identified native English vowel tokens. Moreover, our contrastive analysis predicted that Chinese-accented English would have all the problems of Dutch English but would additionally suffer from massive tense~lax vowel confusion, both in production and in perception. The experimental results show that this prediction is correct.

On the other hand, we found a number of problematic vowel contrasts that are not easily predicted from a contrastive analysis, e.g. the /uː > oː/ and /ɔː > oː/ confusions for Dutch speakers identified by American listeners. We did not encounter any cases where predicted problems did not arise. Our results, then, provide partial support for the transfer hypothesis in foreign language learning, which claims that L2 learners will not distinguish between contrasts in the target language that do not occur in their native tongue. At the same time, a weaker version of the transfer hypothesis seems called for in that, although it makes no false predictions, it predicts only a subset of the L2 vowel learning problems.

Notes

1. For an more elaborate presentation of these (and other) results and accompanying statistical analyses, see Wang & van Heuven (2003).

2. A larger-scale study is in preparation involving 20 Chinese, 20 Dutch and 20 American speakers of English. Optimal selections of recorded materials were submitted to identification tests with groups of 20 listeners. Within each speaker group the most typical (i.e. median) male and female speakers have now been selected on basis of vowel and consonant identification scores within their own language community, who will be representative for the populations of Chinese and Dutch L2 speakers of English and of L1 American speakers of English.

3. In non-rhotic varieties of English (such as Southern British English, but also American varieties spoken in the New England area) postvocalic /r/ is not pronounced but merges with the vowel into a so-called murmur diphthong or centring diphthong. In GA, which is a rhotic variety, the vowels are also realised as centring diphthongs (ending in a schwa-like vowel) but the coda /r/ is pronounced.

4. The r-colored vowels come in two types. The first type can always be analyzed as an allophonic variant of a tense non-low vowel with a phonetically lowered and centralized onset and an schwa-like offglide due to the presence of coda /r/. The normal realization, of course, applies in all other contexts. So, besides the normal variant of /iː, eː, uː, oː/ as in *steaming* /stiːmɪŋ/, *dating* /deːtɪŋ/, *tooling* /tuːlɪŋ/, *polling* /poːlɪŋ/, there are four allophones in complementary distribution with the former when followed by /r/ within the morpheme: *steering* /stiːr+ɪŋ/ > [stɪərɪŋ], *daring* /deːr+ɪŋ/ > [dɛərɪŋ], *touring* /tuːr+ɪŋ/ > [tʊərɪŋ] and *pooring* /poːr+ɪŋ/ > [pɔərɪŋ, pɔːrɪŋ]. Since [ɔə] generally monophthongizes to long [ɔː], only the latter vowel was elicited in our materials, yielding a vowel set of 19 rather than 20. The second set comprise /ɚ, aː/. The former, /ɚ/, exclusively occurs before tautomorphemic /r/; there is no other tense vowel in the inventory from which it can be derived as a centralized version due to r-coloring. Neither can it be analysed as an r-colored allophone of lax /ʌ/ given the existence of words such as *hurry* /hʌrɪ/, *worry* /wʌrɪ/, where /ʌr/ does not surface as [ɚ(r)]. The latter, /aː/, must be set up as a separate phoneme as it also surfaces in contexts where it is not followed by /r/, in no English present or past variety, e.g. *father* /faːðər/. However, occurrences of /aː/ not followed by (underlying) /r/ are extremely rare in GA.

5. The /ɚ/ is strongly r-colored and cannot be followed by a coda consonant. All other vowels can be followed by a coda nasal /m, n, ŋ/.

References

Bent, T., and A. R. Bradlow (2003). The interlanguage speech intelligibility benefit. *Journal of the Acoustical Society of America*, 114, 1600–1610.

Delattre, P. (1971). *Comparing the phonetic features of English, German, French and Spanish.* Julius Gross Verlag, Heidelberg.

Flege, J. E. (1995): 'Second language speech learning: Theory, findings and problems'. In W. Strange (ed.) *Speech perception and linguistic experience: Issues in cross-language research.* Timonium, MD: York Press, 233–277.

Kenyon J., and T. Knott (1944). *A pronouncing dictionary of American English.* Merriam, Springfield.

Peterson. G. E. and H. L. Barney (1952). Control methods used in a study of the vowels. *Journal of the Acoustical Society of America*, 24, 175–184.

Strange, W., R. R. Verbrugge, D. P. Shankweiler and T. R. Edman (1976). Consonant environment specifies vowel identification. *Journal of the Acoustical Society of America*, 60, 213–224.

Wang, H. and V. J. van Heuven (2003). Mutual intelligibility of Chinese, Dutch ad American speakers of English. In L. Cornips, P. Fikkert (eds.) *Linguistics in the Netherlands 2003*, John Benjamins, Amsterdam, 213–224.

On segmental complexity

Affricates and patterns of segmental modification in consonant inventories[*]

Jeroen van de Weijer and Frans Hinskens

University of Leiden / Meertens Institute and Free University Amsterdam

1. Introduction

Affricates occur in over two thirds of the world's languages. They are therefore a common type of segment; as a matter of fact, cross-linguistically they are by far the most common type of complex segments. It is also common for languages to have some type of segmental modification, such as labialization (and other types of secondary articulation), aspiration (and other phonation types) or prenasalization. This paper investigates whether there is a relation between segmental complexity in affricates and in segments with segmental modification. Evidence for such a relation could consist of languages allowing for *both* affricates *and* other types of segmental modification, or languages ruling out both. In the former case, the branching structure that is present in both would be generally permitted, in the latter case it would be generally ruled out. This would amount to a more abstract, structural interpretation of Clements' (2003) notion of "feature economy".

However, it could also be possible — off hand — that languages compensate a lack of affricates by allowing for modified segments. This would argue for a trade-off relationship between complex segments (affricates and perhaps prenasalized stops) and segments with segmental modification. — i.e. between segments with "contouring" complexity and segments with "compounding" complexity.

In Section 2, we describe earlier feature-geometrical approaches to affrication and several types of segmental modification. In Section 3, we investigate the occurrence of both in Maddieson (1984), a large, typologically balanced sample of languages and a statistical investigation of these findings. We will see

ISSN 0929–7332 / E-ISSN 1569–9919 © Algemene Vereniging voor Taalwetenschap

that there is usually no trade-off relationship between complex segments and segments with segmental modification. Unlike what might be expected, there is no relation between prenasalized and affricated segments, although both are described as "contour" segments in Sagey (1986).

Section 4 is a brief conclusion. It sums up the findings and places them in an overall framework which links empirical questions to a formal proposal.

2. Affrication and other types of segmental complexity

Traditionally, affricates have been described as complex segments, and, more in particular, as segments which combine features characteristic of stops with features characteristic of fricatives. The following partial representation of affricates is based on Sagey (1986).

(1)   *Affricates as contour segments* (Sagey 1986)

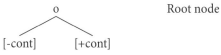

It is a matter of some debate where exactly the feature [cont] is located; in the model presented by Clements & Hume (1995), the structure of affricates is as represented in (2):

(2)   *Branching at the Oral Cavity node* (Clements & Hume 1995)

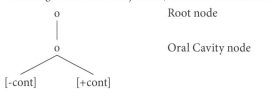

We will abstract away from differences such as these.

Representations such as those in (1) and (2) have come under attack in the past few years. For instance, in Hinskens & van de Weijer (2003a), we show on the basis of the large and typologically balanced sample of languages in Maddieson (1984) that affricates behave like stops with respect to the types of segmental modification (henceforth MOD) they take. Other work has also shown that affricates primarily behave like stops in phonological processes and might therefore be represented as such (e.g. Kehrein 2002, Lin, to appear and references cited there).

On the other hand, affricates behave like fricatives with respect to the place of articulation they take: (coronal) affricates typically occur at the same places of articulation as (coronal) fricatives in segmental inventories (van de Weijer 1996).

The present paper is related to this debate, by examining whether the branching relation in (1) falls under the scope of the same constraint that has been argued to be relevant for the type of segmental complexity present in, for instance, secondary articulation. This would represent an extension of Clements' idea of "feature economy" (Clements 2003, following Martinet 1955 and others), one aspect of which is made explicit in (3):

(3) *Prediction 1: Mutual Attraction* (Clements 2003)
A sound S will have a higher than expected frequency in languages that have another sound T bearing one of its features, and vice versa.

Clements (2003) rephrases his Prediction 1 as "if a feature is used once in a system, it will tend to be used again". This paper essentially extends this prediction to a structural (as opposed to featural) level by examining whether languages tend to make use of segmental branching in a range of segments, rather than in just one segment or category of segments. We will rephrase this idea as the hypothesis in (4):

(4) *Hypothesis*
If segmental branching is permitted for a certain segment (or class of segments) in a given language, then it will be permitted at a higher than chance frequency for other segments (or classes of segments) in that language.

If confirmed, then languages allow both affricates and complex segments and if disconfirmed, then there may well be a general tendency for affricates and complex segments to be in a trade-off relationship.

Let us, with this idea in mind, examine what other types of segmental complexity might exist, in order to test this hypothesis. We do not claim that the types of complexity examined here necessarily represent an exhaustive list. For instance, in some theoretical frameworks nasal consonants are also represented as involving some type of branching. In this paper, we will limit our investigation to segment types which involve some articulatory and/or acoustic complexity.

A first obvious candidate is secondary articulation. In Clements & Hume (1995: 287), secondary articulation is represented as follows:

(5) *Secondary articulation* (Clements & Hume 1995)

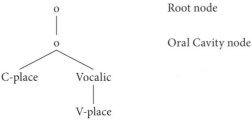

It is seen that both affricates and segments with secondary articulation involve segmental branching. The same goes for segments with distinctive laryngeal modification, such as aspirated stops (see (6) below).

(6)   *Aspirated stops*

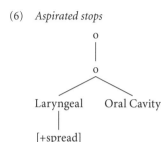

The question is whether affricates and modified segments involve the same relation or whether they are fundamentally different and independent.

One observation to make is that in secondary articulation (and phonatory complexity) there is a "compounding" kind of complexity, in which two nodes (here the C- and V-place nodes) are present (whereas non-complex consonants or vowels only have one). Affricates (and prenasalized stops, see below), on the other hand, have a "contouring" relation of "+" and "−" values of the same feature. If compounding and contouring complexity are not independent, structural constraints may be expected to take both types in their scope.

An issue arises concerning the representation of secondary articulation as in (5). Kehrein (2002) argues that properties such as labialization and palatalization but also aspiration, etc. are not properly described as Root-internal properties. In other words, they do not involve segmental complexity, but rather they should be represented as prosodic properties, i.e. linked to nodes such as Onset, Nucleus, or Coda. Examples of representations that illustrate this idea, taking laryngeal features as the relevant secondary property, are given below (Kehrein 2002:69).[1]

(7)   *The prosodic approach* (after Kehrein 2002)

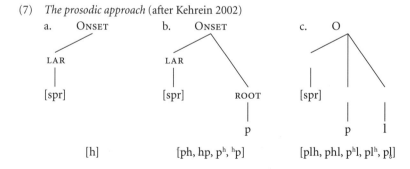

In individual languages, phonological representations like these are interpreted by the phonetics as one of the realizations given beneath each feature tree; hence, these realizations cannot contrast *phonologically*. For instance, in this proposal, a contrast between pre- and postaspiration is not possible phonemically.

This proposal is very interesting because it makes a large number of very specific predictions, such as the following:

(8)   –   contrasts like /ph/ vs. /hp/, /pʰ/ vs. /ʰp/ (etc.) are not possible underlyingly, unlike /p/ vs. /pʰ/, etc.

   –   there can be no conflicting laryngeal specifications within onsets (e.g. */tʰnˀ/, in which /t/ would be aspirated and /n/ would be glottalized)

   –   assimilation (and neutralization, etc.) of voice (or other laryngeal features) always concern entire prosodic constituents, not individual segments

So far, this proposal has held out well against possible counterevidence. In his thesis, Kehrein looks at a number of possible counterexamples and shows how they can be re-analysed.

Our investigation is to some extent independent of this question, although it assumes, in line with earlier work (Hinskens & van de Weijer 2003a), that there is a close connection between natural class (e.g. velars, or voiceless stops) and segmental modification, maybe even a specific modification type (e.g. labialization, or aspiration, respectively). We prefer to express this by assuming a direct, segmental (not prosodic) relation between both. The difference between Kehrein's and our view can be illustrated with the following two representations of an onset with an aspirated voiceless stop:

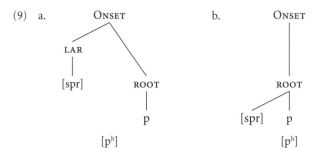

In (9a), Kehrein's representation of an aspirated stop is repeated. This does not directly express the relation between aspiration and the natural class on which aspiration typically occurs, i.e. that of voiceless stops, while this relation is more directly captured in the more traditional representation of (9b), where both are under the same root node. On the other hand, the fact that aspiration typically occurs in Onsets is more directly captured by (9a). The fact that voiceless stops are preferably in the onset, i.e. a matter of phonotactics or more generally markedness, may reconcile both positions.

The question whether constraints exist that take segment-internal branching in general in its scope could be investigated for a range of other segments which have been described as complex, e.g. prenasalized stops (10) or segments which have a laryngeal MOD type, such as aspirated stops (see (6) above):[2]

(10)   *Prenasalized stops*

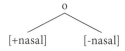

In this paper we examine these types of complexity from a cross-linguistic perspective. Are there languages that ban all types of complexity illustrated so far? This would argue for a maximally general constraint on segmental complexity. Alternatively, if languages ban, say, affricates, do they allow other types of complex segments to compensate, and if so, are these preferably of the secondary articulation (5), laryngeal (6), or the nasal (10) type? We investigate these questions in the next section.

3.   Cross-linguistic patterning of affrication and segmental modification

In earlier work (Hinskens & van de Weijer 2003a,b; van de Weijer & Hinskens 2003) we surveyed MOD in the languages of the world, basing ourselves on the data offered in Maddieson (1984). 166 out of the 317 languages in Maddieson's survey have one or several instances of MOD. In all, these 166 languages have 283 instances of MOD. In 55 out of these 283 cases, MOD is completely redundant, in the sense that all segments at issue lack MOD-less counterparts (Hinskens & van de Weijer 2003b).

In (11) we present the types of modification that occur in the languages in the sample. For each single type of modification, we add an abbreviation as well as the diacritic.

(11)   a.   *secondary articulation (supralaryngeal/oral)*
       labialization   LAB C^w
       palatalization   PAL C^j
       velarization   VEL $\mathcal{C}$
       pharyngealization   PHA $C^ʕ$
    b.   *phonation types (laryngeal)*
       aspiration   ASP C^h
       preaspiration   PRA ^hC
       breathy voice   BRV $\underset{..}{C}$
       with breathy release   BRR $C^ɦ$
       laryngealization   LAR $\underset{~}{C}$
       ejectivity   EJE C'
    c.   *nasality*
       prenasalization   PRN ^NC

For the present investigation, we included information on affrication for each of the 317 languages in the sample. It turned out that 219 languages (=69%) in the sample had one or more affricates in their segmental inventory. Some language families are particularly rich in affricates (e.g. the Amerindian languages) or particularly poor (e.g. the Australian ones).

In Table 1, we present the main findings for the quantitative patterning of affrication and MOD in the sample.

Table 1. The quantitative patterning of affrication and segmental modification; n of languages

		Affricates?		total
		yes	no	
MOD?	yes	136	30	166
	no	83	68	151
total		219	98	317

The overwhelming majority of languages in the sample ($n=136$) has both affricates and MOD (e.g. Armenian, with both affrication and ejectivity, Sedang with both affrication and prenasalization, and Tlingit, with both affrication and labialization). The second-largest group ($n=83$) is formed by the type of languages that have affricates but lack MOD (e.g. Suena, a New Guinea language, and Andamese, an Indo-Pacific language). There are languages that appear to lack any kind of segmental complexity; of the 98 languages that have no affricates, 68 lack MOD. Kanakuru lacks both affricates and any other type of segmental modification, while Nambakaengo has no affricates but does have labialization and palatalization.

A statistical way of answering the question whether affrication and segmental modification are structurally related or not requires a test of the mutual independence of affrication and MOD. The outcomes of the chi square test ($\chi^2=26.92$ df$=1$ $p<.001$) show that in our sample both are far from independent. On the contrary, there is a highly significant relationship between the two properties.[3] It turns out that languages with affricates in most cases also have MOD and, at the same time, languages without affricates in most cases also lack MOD. So it would appear that the presence or absence of primary complexity goes hand in hand with the presence or absence of secondary complexity, respectively. Thus, there is no evidence for the idea that there is a trade off-relationship between complex segments such as affricates and segments with MOD. On the overall level, our hypothesis in (4) is confirmed by the languages in the sample.

On closer inspection of the figures in Table 1, the situation turns out to be somewhat less straightforward, however. Whereas languages with MOD in most cases also have affricates, most of the languages without MOD nevertheless have affricates. Hence, we face a problem of interpretation: as there is obviously no perfect reciprocity, what is predictable by what?

One way of tackling the problem is a purely quantitative one, i.e. comparing the proportions. While $136/219 = 62.10\%$ of the languages with affricates also have MOD, $68/98 = 69.39\%$ of the languages without affricates also lack MOD. For the complementary dimension, the proportions differ considerably: whereas $136/166 = 81.93\%$ of the languages with MOD have affricates, $83/151 = 54.97\%$ of the languages without MOD nevertheless have affricates. In the dimension 'presence versus absence of MOD', the difference in percentage points is hence considerably larger than in the dimension 'presence versus absence of affricates'. Therefore one might decide that the MOD dimension outweighs the affricate dimension. Cross-linguistically, MOD is thus the better predictor of affrication than the other way around.

Note that our segmental modifications involve a number of properties: both laryngeal, supralaryngeal or oral and nasal properties are lumped together. It might be the case that one of these is an even better predictor of affrication than (some of the) others. To investigate this, we split up the MOD types into laryngeal ones, supralaryngeal ones and nasal ones, and cross-classified them with affrication.

Table 2. The quantitative patterning of affrication and segmental modification, broken down for category; n of instances of MOD

		Affricates?		total
		yes	no	
	Laryngeal	162	22	184
MOD	Oral	67	12	79
	Nasal	10	9	19
	total	239	43	283

In Table 2, we present the raw figures concerning patterning of affrication and segmental modification, broken down for category. Note that in this table, we deal with numbers of instances of segmental modification, rather than numbers of languages, as in Table 1. Still, both tables refer to the same data.[4]

This pattern of distribution is highly significant ($\chi^2 = 16,75$ df$=2$ $p<.001$). Obviously, the relationship between MOD category and the presence or absence of affricates is, that the overwhelming majority if languages with MOD also have affricates, with the exception of nasal modification.

Let us look at prenasalization and affrication in some more detail. Unlike other types of segmental complexity, such as aspiration and labialization, which we referred to as "compounding" types of complexity, both prenasalization and affrication were described in terms of "contouring" of a binary distinctive feature in Sagey (1986).

(12) *Affricates and prenasalized stops* (Sagey 1986)

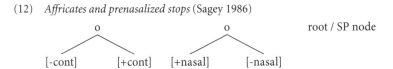

We must note that, just like in the case of affricates, some doubt the status of prenasalized stops as single segments. Downing (to appear), for instance, argues on the basis of a variety of evidence that prenasalized stops in Bantu are more properly described as coda-onset *sequences* of segments, although she explicitly remains uncommitted on the status of prenasalized stops in other language families (see also Herbert 1986).

If the representations in (12) are correct — contrary to Downing's proposal —, i.e. if prenasalized stops are single segments and if prenasalization and affrication are indeed of the same nature, we might expect to find that languages would tend to have both, or ban both. However, as was shown in Table 2 above, of the 19 languages that have prenasalization in our sample (Maddieson 1984), 10 also have affricates, 9 do not.[5] To the extent that this finding can be generalized, we conclude that there is no reason to believe that the incidence of affrication and prenasalization is in any way correlated.

To conclude this section, MOD and affrication are mutually dependent for laryngeal and oral modification, but they are independent for nasal modification (i.e. prenasalization). For MOD of the laryngeal and oral categories, our hypothesis is confirmed, while for MOD of the nasal category it is disconfirmed.

4. Discussion and conclusion

In this study we have seen that affricates on the one hand and oral and laryngeal modification on the other are positively correlated. In our analyses, we have treated segmental modification and affrication as if they were mutually unrelated. This is, of course, an artifact of our strictly synchronic view. It is a well-known fact, that the affricates of modern German, for instance, have developed out of aspirated stops, i.e. out of modified simplex segments. Similarly, palatalization on coronals may well give rise to affricates and have done so in many languages (e.g. in Muinane, as discussed in Hinskens & van de Weijer 2003: 1074). It may not always be simple to keep the diachrony and synchrony apart in cases like these. Ladefoged & Maddieson (1995: 368) expressed the role MOD can play in diachrony as: "Today's secondary articulations may be the primary articulations of the future". This results from the process which Clements (1991) calls 'feature promotion'.

Taking this caveat into consideration, we have looked at four different types of segmental complexity involved in affricates, prenasalized stops, secondary articulation and laryngeal modification, i.e. phonation types. *All* these types of complexity have come under attack in recent years: affricates are "really" stops (Hinskens & van de Weijer 2003a, among much other work), prenasalized stops are "really" clusters (Downing to appear, among other work), and secondary articulation and laryngeal complexity "really" involve prosodic rather than segmental properties (Kehrein 2002). Note that these re-analyses of these types of complexity are directed in different ways: elimination of affrication as a phonological property, clustering and prosodification. It would therefore not be expected that these types of complexity are correlated in any way in segmental inventories. In this paper, we hope to have shown that — although a number of issues should clearly still be resolved — there *are* interesting relations between these types of complexity. These relations can be illustrated by way of the diagram in (13):

(13)

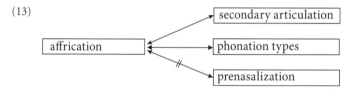

To capture the correspondences expressed in (13), we propose a simple OT constraint that militates against segmental branching in general (cf. also van de Weijer & Hinskens 2003):

(14) *Complex(segment)
      No segment-internal branching

For languages that permit both affricates and the various types of segmental modifications, the constraint in (14) is low-ranked in the grammar. For languages that rule out both, the constraint is high-ranked. Languages that permit affricates and rule out segmental modifications, or vice versa, are defined as the focus of investigation: they will have to show whether the constraint in (14) can be maintained in its pure form, or whether, ultimately, it must be reformulated as a family of constraints.

In future work, we will look more closely at the relations between supra-laryngeal MOD types and laryngeal MOD types, and between each of these and prenasalization, i.e. the relations between the types of complexity on the right-hand side in (13). It might also be possible to investigate other types of complexity, e.g. that in doubly-articulated stops or in diphthongs.

Notes

* This paper was presented at the TINdag 2003 in Utrecht. We thank the audience, and in particular Norval Smith, for questions and suggestions. We also thank Laura Downing, Wolfgang Kehrein, Marc van Oostendorp and an anonymous reviewer for comments on an earlier version of this paper. The usual disclaimers apply.

1. Note that Kehrein (2002:65) maintains that his Laryngeal node "consists of" the three laryngeal features, [spread], [voice] and [constricted glottis], although in (7) these features (in this case [spread glottis]) are attached to this node.

2. In this proposal, we might investigate whether voiced stops are also represented as "complex", especially in a theory in which voiceless stops are unmarked and voiced stops have a feature [voice].

3. The chi square test compares the actual mutual distribution of the values of two variables (*in casu* the presence or absence of affrication and the presence or absence of MOD) to chance, i.e. to the independence of the two variables, which is the zero hypothesis. In the zero hypothesis scenario, the values in the cells in the table perfectly reflect the proportion of the row and column totals to the grand total. As the discrepancy between the actual distribution and chance increases, the effect of chance (p) decreases and the dependence between the two variables becomes more probable.

4. The total number of instances of MOD investigated in Hinskens & van de Weijer (2003a) was 281, while in Hinskens & van de Weijer (2003b) it was 280. The different numbers are due to a) an original inaccuracy and b) the fact that in three languages MOD occurs merely on affricates and affricates (which were the object of a separate hypothesis) were excluded from the analyses reported in those contributions.

5. The relatively small number of languages with prenasalization does not necessarily lead us to expect them to show an essentially different pattern of distribution with respect to the co-occurrence with affricates than the oral and laryngeal MOD types. Moreover, the chi square test calibrates for large differences in absolute numbers.

References

Clements, G.N. (1991) Place of articulation in consonants and vowels: a unified theory. *Working Papers of the Cornell Phonetics Laboratory* 5, 77–123.

Clements, G.N. (2003) Feature economy as an organizational principle of sound systems. Paper presented at the First Old World Conference in Phonology, Leiden, January 2003. Ms, University of Paris 3, CNRS.

Clements, G.N. & E.V. Hume (1995) The internal organization of speech sounds. In J.A. Goldsmith (ed.) *The Handbook of Phonological Theory*, 245–306. Basil Blackwell, Oxford.

Downing, L. (to appear) On the ambiguous segmental status of nasals in homorganic NC sequences. In M. van Oostendorp & J.M. van de Weijer (eds.) *The Internal Organization of Phonological Segments*. Mouton de Gruyter, Berlin.

Herbert, R.K. (1986) *Language Universals, Markedness Theory, and Natural Phonetic Processes*. Trends in Linguistics, 25. Mouton de Gruyter, Berlin (revised Doctoral dissertation, Ohio State University, 1977).

Hinskens, F. & J.M. van de Weijer (2003a) Patterns of segmental modification in consonant inventories: A cross-linguistic study. *Linguistics* 41, 1041–1084.

Hinskens, F. & J.M. van de Weijer (2003b) Patterns of segmental modification in consonant inventories: Contrastive vs. redundant systems and phonology vs. phonetics. In P. Fikkert & L. Cornips (eds.) *Linguistics in the Netherlands 2003*, 71–81. John Benjamins, Amsterdam and Philadelphia.

Kehrein, W. (2002) *Phonological Representation and Phonetic Phasing: Affricates and Laryngeals*. Niemeyer, Tübingen.

Lin, Y.-H. (to appear) Piro affricates: Phonological edge effects and phonetic anti-edge effects? In M. van Oostendorp & J.M. van de Weijer (eds.) *The Internal Organization of Phonological Segments*. Mouton de Gruyter, Berlin.

Maddieson, I. (1984) *Patterns of Sounds*. Cambridge University Press, Cambridge.

Martinet, A. (1955) *Économie des changements phonétiques*. Francke, Paris.

Sagey, E.C. (1986) The Representation of Features and Relations in Non-Linear Phonology. Doctoral dissertation, MIT, Cambridge, Massachusetts.

Weijer, J.M. van de (1996) *Segmental Structure and Complex Segments*. Niemeyer, Tübingen (revised Doctoral dissertation, Leiden University, 1994).

Weijer, J.M. van de & F. Hinskens (2003) Patterns of segmental modification in consonant inventories: Contrastive vs. redundant systems. In B. Palek, O. Fujimora & S. Haraguchi (eds.) *Proceedings of LP2002* (Web version). Printed version to be published by Charles University Press, Prague and Meikai University Press, Uruyasu.

Access to on-line full-text subscriptions

John Benjamins Publishing Company's journals are available in on-line full-text format to regular subscribers as of each volume starting from the year 2000. Some of our journals have additional (non-print) information available through this medium that is referred to in the articles.

Registration with *ingentaJournals* is included in your regular subscription. If you do not subscribe, we offer a pay-per-view service per article.

Full text is provided in PDF. In order to read these documents you will need Adobe Acrobat Reader which is freely available from
http://www.adobe.com/products/acrobat/readermain.html

How to register

www.ingenta.com/isis/register/ChooseRegistration/ingenta

To register, *Ingenta* will ask for your subscription or client number. This number appears on your invoice and on the address label on your printed copy.

Institutional subscribers can take advantage of Direct Access allowing your users to log in from a registered location without having to register username and password each time.

Subscriptions through your agent: If your agent provides Benjamins with your address data, you can register as described above with your Benjamins client number. When your registration has been processed, you can access *Ingenta* directly or via your agent's gateway.

Private subscribers have access to the on-line service and will be provided with an individual username and password by *Ingenta* when registering with their client number.

Ingenta offers a full range of electronic journal services such as direct links to your subscribed journals and new-publication alerts.

Further information is available on

www.ingenta.com and
www.benjamins.com/jbp/journals/e_instruct.html